# Forbid Them Not

# Involving Children in Sunday Worship

### Based on the Common Lectionary, Year C

# Forbid Them Not

# Carolyn C. Brown

Abingdon Press
*Nashville*

FORBID THEM NOT:
INVOLVING CHILDREN IN SUNDAY WORSHIP
Based on the Common Lectionary, Year C

This book is printed on acid-free paper.

**Library of Congress Cataloging-in-Publication Data**

Brown, Carolyn C. (Carolyn Carter), 1947–
    Forbid them not: involving children in Sunday worship/
Carolyn C. Brown.
    p.   cm.
Includes index.
    **ISBN 0-687-13254-1** (alk. paper)
    1. Children in public worship. 2. Common lectionary. 3. Worship
(Religious education) I. Title.
BV26.2.B76   1991
264'.0083—dc20                                              90-45012

MANUFACTURED IN THE UNITED STATES OF AMERICA

# CONTENTS

# WHAT IS IN THIS BOOK, AND HOW CAN I USE IT?

There seem to be two opposing camps when it comes to children's participation in congregational worship. On one side are those who say that worship is really for adults—that children should be taught to behave until they appreciate what is going on, or that they (and their parents) should be relieved by the provision of a "children's church" or other activities during the worship hour. On the other side are those who say that the congregation's worship should be reworked entirely to make it appealing to children. Proponents of this side claim that once adults loosen up and begin worshiping as children worship, they will not miss the staid old adult-oriented forms.

This book carves out a middle ground based on the convictions that

• children do belong in the sanctuary, worshiping with God's people;

• worship planners are responsible for creating worship experiences that are meaningful to all who come to the sanctuary, including children, youths, and adults (this does not require that all worshipers find all parts of worship equally meaningful, but that each has some appreciation for the whole, and special appreciation for certain parts within the whole);

• children can worship meaningfully, using traditional forms, *if* they are learning the meaning of those forms, and *if* the forms include content that reflects *their* lives and concerns as well as those of adults.

This book is written for worship leaders who share these views and want to be responsive to the elementary-school-aged children in worship, but who are uncertain about how to do this effectively and do not have large amounts of time to develop their skills in this area. It is written for those whose consciousness has been raised by the books that advocate the inclusion of children in congregational worship, but who are at a loss for "what to do this Sunday." This book offers specific suggestions for prayers, litanies, sermon illustrations, and ways to present Scripture that include children without offending adults. Although it is based on the texts of the Common Lectionary, those who do not follow the lectionary can use the index on page 201 to locate suggestions related to any Scripture passages.

This book can be used by the pastor who plans worship alone, by a staff team, by a liturgical team that includes both clergy and laity, or by a worship committee. It is a reference to be used with commentaries and liturgical resources in preparing a service for each Sunday. As you gain confidence and insight into what is meaningful for the children in your congregation; the ideas in this book should become springboards to other ideas and to home-grown prayers, litanies, and so forth.

Materials for each Sunday include:

**From a Child's Point of View,** a commentary on each of the readings for the day. The main ideas of each passage are expressed in children's terms and connected to children's concerns.

**Watch Words** offers vocabulary helps, warning against the use of words that are beyond the understanding of elementary children or that are easily misunderstood by them, and suggesting words that speak clearly to worshipers of all ages.

**Let the Children Sing** suggests several hymns (chosen from church hymnals) related to the Scripture themes, and which children can sing— at least in part. The assumption here is not that every hymn sung in worship ought to be child-accessible, but that one or two each week could be. These hymns have been chosen because they have concrete language, themes to which children respond, or tunes that are easily sung. Some have been included because of the repetition of a word, phrase, or chorus which even a nonreader can sing each time it appears (e.g., the "Alleluias" in "Jesus Christ Is Risen Today").

**The Liturgical Child** outlines a variety of ways to use the passages in worship to bring them alive for children (and for adults). Specific directions for dramatic readings, litanies, and congregational readings are given for some passages. Children's prayer concerns related to the theme or time of year are listed for inclusion in the congregation's prayers. In addition, possibilities for relating other parts of the worship service to the day's theme for the children are raised. No worship planner will use every idea offered for each week, but can select several that fit the worship experience as it is planned for the congregation.

**Sermon Resources** are offered in the belief that children do listen to at least parts of sermons and can learn from those parts. These resources are offered to be included in the "real" sermon rather than in a segregated children's sermon. The assumption is that if we communicate to children that the sermon is for them too, they will learn to listen to more and more of it as their attention span for verbal messages grows. This section includes potential sermon illustrations and stories that will catch the attention of children and will speak to adults also, based on their childhood experiences. Too, you will find occasional sermon-related assignments for children to do during the sermon.

Finally, for each week there is a one-page **Worship Worksheet**—a sheet of games, puzzles, or questions related to the day's passages. Just as children often work on projects (even their homework) while they watch TV, they are often more apt to listen to the sermon if they have something to do with their hands while they listen.

The purchase of this book gives you permission to reproduce these Worship Worksheets for your children each week. Look carefully at the worksheet before reproducing it. Some, especially those for Propers in which the readings do not share one central theme, offer two half-page activities related to separate themes. Choose the activity that goes with your worship theme and enlarge it to full-page size on a copy machine. Then reproduce that page for the children.

Worship Worksheets can be distributed by ushers as children enter the sanctuary, left in a designated place for the children (or parents) to pick up, or they can be put into Worship Kits.

A Worship Kit is a large paper envelope or sealable plastic bag which contains the Sunday bulletin, the Worship Worksheet, a small pencil, and bookmarks for marking the hymns and readings for the morning. The bookmarks can be strips of poster board decorated with appropriate stickers. To emphasize the church year, poster board of liturgically correct colors can be used. An older children's class, a group of teenagers, or an adult may be willing to prepare such bookmarks as a contribution to the congregation's worship life. Children can be asked to leave the bookmarks and pencils in the envelopes and place the envelopes on their seats to be picked up for use the next week.

Note: In some congregations the Worship Worksheets may be difficult to reproduce. Worship leaders in such congregations may focus their efforts on other suggestions.

# ADVENT FROM A CHILD'S POINT OF VIEW

The church year officially begins with a very adult season—Advent. During Advent we await and get ready for One who has already come—a rather strange thing to do, from a child's point of view.

As adults we can speak of God's kingdom which came in Christ and is yet to come in its fullness. We can celebrate the coming of the Child in the manger and ask how fully we welcome Jesus and his message into our hearts today. But those who study child development tell us that until the age of eight or nine, children have great difficulty in comprehending time. So to talk about a king who came, who is coming, and who will come is talking nonsense.

It is tempting to avoid such difficulties and have the children simply count down the days until Christmas, make decorations, and prepare gifts. But this passes over the real meaning of the season, some of which can be presented to children.

Children can hear the stories of people who waited for Jesus. They can celebrate Ruth, the outsider who was an ancestor of Jesus. They can hear John's insistence that all people work together to make the world a more loving place while they wait for Jesus. They can bask in the prophetic promises that God will always love and care for them—will even come to live with them. Each of the lections for the season has a message children can appreciate when it is appropriately presented to them.

In addition, the candles, evergreens, flowers, and special music of Advent can speak to children in the language of feelings and senses. These things will speak more clearly if we shape them with the children's presence in mind.

We can include the children actively in lighting an Advent wreath during worship. In more formal churches, members of an older children's class can take turns being acolytes (complete with robes) to light the candles, while a teenager or adult reads an appropriate Scripture or meditation. Families can also light the Advent wreath, the entire family coming forward to light the candles and make the statement. (If you use families, be sure to include single-parent families and families of all shapes and sizes.) We can further increase the significance of the Advent wreath by helping families create wreaths to light in their homes. (Many religious bookstores provide orders of family worship for lighting the Advent wreath.)

We can help the children recall the story of biblical waiting and preparation by moving crèche pieces around the sanctuary toward the manger. The pieces can be moved before worship each week, and their movement mentioned in the sermon or Scriptures of the day. Or the pieces can be moved during worship—perhaps as part of a children's sermon.

We can decorate trees with Chrismons. If the congregation already has a Chrismon tree, we can help children learn the meaning of the symbols. We can use the ornaments to make points in sermons, or we can make one ornament the center of attention each week in worship. We can even hang some simple child-made Chrismons on the tree.

We can include the children in the special music of the season. Young instrumentalists can play a carol as the prelude. A children's class can become a one-Sunday choir—even if you do not usually have a children's choir. In a day when religious carols are not taught in many schools, we in the church need to make an extra effort to pass on our musical heritage. The quoting or exploring of verses of carols within the sermon, or the carefully planned introductions to hymns can make congregational singing prime teaching opportunities.

Think about each of the Advent traditions of your church. Which are child-accessible? How could they be more so? The answers to these questions can more often lead to honing what is already being done, than to adding new programming to an already hectic season.

# FIRST SUNDAY OF ADVENT

## From a Child's Point of View

*Old Testament: Jeremiah 33:14-16.* The child's cry, "But, it's not fair!" reminds us that justice and fairness are big concerns for children. They yearn for teachers, parents, and playmates who are fair. They want just rules for the groups in which they participate and the games they play. They protest vehemently when they sense injustice—especially when it affects them. Therefore Jeremiah's Advent promise—that when God's kingdom comes fully, there will be justice for everyone and a leader who deals with people fairly—is good news for children.

*Psalm 25:1-10.* This passage is a personal prayer, asking God that I be treated well by others, that God teach me how to live, and that God not remember all my sins and shortcomings. It is a prayer for people of all ages.

*Epistle: I Thessalonians 3:9-13.* In this loving message to friends in the church at Thessalonica, Paul prays that God will help them love one another and the people beyond their church as much as Paul and God love them. To love others that much is a good Advent challenge for children.

*Gospel: Luke 21:25-36.* This apocalyptic passage is filled with images that are not easy for children to understand, and an idea (that we should watch and be prepared) that is hard for children to grasp. It is probably best to read the passage for the older worshipers and present the idea for the children during the sermon.

One interpretation of this passage that speaks to children is that some frightening, horrible things happen in human experience, but that God is still in control and will be there for us even after "the worst." Given this, we are called to avoid both (1) worrying too much about the awful things and (2) ignoring the awful things by partying and being self-centered. Instead, we are to remember that God is in control, and we are to live accordingly.

Warning: Do not underestimate the "horrible things" children worry about. At an early age they see television's graphic pictures of war, famine, natural disasters, and the potential for nuclear annihilation. Many see the devastation of divorce in their own families or in those of their friends. More children than we wish have been mugged by older kids and know the fear of participating in the drug culture. Children need to know that God will see them through even these "horrible things." They also need to hear that such things are the products of our imperfect age and that when God's kingdom comes in its fullness, those things will end.

## Watch Words

Avoid *tribulation, affliction,* and other big words that describe suffering. They are obsolete. Instead, use specific, concrete words to describe wars, natural disasters, and personal tragedies.

Be careful about using *righteousness.* If children have heard the word at all, it has probably been used with a negative connotation, such as *self-righteous.* Speak about living by God's rules, or take time to explore what righteousness means today.

Children use the word *fair* before they use *justice*. Using the words interchangeably will help make the connection between them.

## Let the Children Sing

The simple words and tune of "Lift up Your Head, Ye Mighty Gates" make it accessible to children. Point out before the hymn is sung that we are singing about two kinds of doors—the doors of a city being opened to receive a king and the doors of our hearts being opened to receive God.

## The Liturgical Child

1. In the congregation's prayers, pray for fair teachers, coaches, community leaders, and government officials. Also, ask for God's wisdom to see unjust situations at home, at school, on the job, and in the community, and for God's courage to do what we can to change them. Ask the choir to sing "Lead Me, Lord, in Thy Righteousness" (a paraphrase of Psalm 25:4-5) as a choral call to this prayer.

2. Psalm 25 is best understood and claimed when it is read in its original responsive form from a translation such as *Today's English Version*, the Good News Bible. So invite the congregation (or half the congregation) to read verses 1-7, with the understanding that they are "I." A worship leader (or the other half of the congregation) then can assume the priest's part and read verses 8-10 to assure the worshipers that God wants the same things for them.

3. One effective use of the Epistle passage would be to recite verses 12 and 13 from the Good News Bible as the charge and benediction with which worship concludes.

## Sermon Resources

1. Challenge children to draw a picture of an unjust or unfair situation *and* a picture of the same people, in the same situation, acting justly or fairly. Invite them to share the pictures with you as they leave the sanctuary.

2. Invite the congregation to follow along in their hymnals as you work through the verses of "Lift up Your Heads, Ye Mighty Gates," interpreting them as instructions for ways to celebrate Advent this year.

Color each space with a dot in it to fill in the missing word.

Today we begin the season of _____ .

This a season for justice.

Draw a picture of people doing something unjust or unfair.

Now change your picture to make it fair.

# SECOND SUNDAY OF ADVENT

## From a Child's Point of View

*Old Testament: Malachi 3:1-4.* Malachi spoke harshly to people who expected God to endorse whatever they were doing. He warned of the coming of a messenger who would bring "strong soap" and "refiner's fire." Today's soap (except some shampoo) seldom burns, and few children have experience with refiner's fires. But children do know that hurting is sometimes part of healing and that discipline leads to strength. Medicine that stings, painful therapy for a broken bone, and sport disciplines teach them this. Still, Malachi's idea that God may come as a demanding coach or teacher, rather than as a supportive, somewhat indulgent parent, may be new to children. So explain that Malachi's message means that to be fully God's people, they must be disciplined and obedient to God. Point out specific disciplines such as attending worship and church school, obeying God's rules, practicing peacemaking, and seeking justice every day. Challenge the children to choose an Advent discipline.

*Psalm 126.* It takes more explanation than worship time allows for children to understand the details of what is going on with this psalmist. But they can glean from hearing the psalm that hope comes from knowing that God always loves and cares for us.

*Gospel: Luke 3:1-6.* Child-development experts have found that children cannot interpret symbolic imagery until late childhood or even early adolescence. This means that calls to fill in the valleys, bring the hills low, and make crooked paths straight can sound like calls to massive construction projects. Even children who sense that these calls are not to be taken literally need help to convert them into sensible calls to repentance. One way to help is to provide parallel examples from everyday life (e.g., straighten out your life, live by God's rules, treat others more kindly).

*Epistle: Philippians 1:3-11.* While John the Baptist speaks harshly to people who need to repent, Paul writes to encourage people who are repenting. Paul gives repentance a good name and feel. He indicates that all Christians are always repenting, and he offers those who repent his love and support in their efforts. Use this passage to help children understand repentance as a positive, lifelong activity for Christians, as individuals and as congregations.

## Watch Words

They key word is *repent*. Be sure the children understand the difference between being sorry about something and repenting. We can be sorry about failing a spelling test because we did not study. But when we repent, we make time to study so we can pass the test next week. It is easy to be sorry we cannot get along with a difficult person at school or at work. But when we repent, we work to improve our relationship with that person.

## Let the Children Sing

A good choice is "Lord, I Want to Be a Christian."

"Open My eyes, That I May See" and "Take My Life and Let It Be Consecrated" have some difficult vocabulary. But their references to "using our bodies to repent" make them understandable to children.

## The Liturgical Child

1. Bring these Scriptures to life with very dramatic readings. Let Malachi and John the Baptist thunder in your best street-corner-preacher style. Shake your fist and point your finger for emphasis. Read the psalm in a reflective mood, stressing the hope-filled words. When reading Paul's letter, imagine yourself in prison, writing to friends you love and miss. Let that love show in your voice.

2. To give a personal twist to Paul's message, suggest that worshipers listen as if Paul were speaking to them individually and/or to the congregation.

3. Challenge children (and adults) to write about or draw a picture of some repenting they want to do during Advent. Invite them to place their paper in the offering plate as an Advent commitment to God. Instruct ushers to respect the privacy of those notes and pictures.

4. Lead corporate prayer, with pauses for individual prayer about repenting:

Lord, we hear John and Malachi call us to repent, but we think they must be talking to someone else. We do not often stop to think about the repenting we need to do. Help us to look honestly at ourselves.

We know we need to repent in our families. It is strange but true that we often treat members of our families with less care than we give strangers. We expect others in our family to accept us when we feel cross and tired, but we are not so ready to put up with them when they are fussy. Help us see the changes we need to make in our families. (Pause)

And we know we are not always kind and loving at school or at work. We want things done our way. We become angry when our work or our ideas are criticized or when we get bad grades. There are people we need to forgive, but we do not. Help us make some changes, God. (Pause)

Lord, we are all members of groups. We are Scouts, Jaycees, Women's Leaguers, Virginians, and Americans (adapt to fit your congregation). We enjoy these groups, but we know we are to work in them for your peace and justice. Sometimes it is easier to go along with the others than to stand up for your ways. Help us change the groups to which we belong. (Pause)

God, be with us during Advent as we repent. Help us see the changes we need to make, and give us the courage and power to make them; for we pray in Jesus' name. Amen.

## Sermon Resource

The movie *Karate Kid*, which many children and parents have seen, provides a current example of Malachi's "strong soap" or "refiner's fire." After agreeing to teach him karate, the old master puts the boy to work—washing and polishing cars, then sanding and painting a long wooden fence. After a while the boy objects that this is not what he came to do. The wise teacher then demonstrates that the work has strengthened his muscles and made certain crucial moves second nature. If you have not seen this fine movie/video, do so now as sermon preparation—and for a treat!

REPENT means to change our ways.
John the Baptist said, "REPENT! God's Kingdom
    is coming!"
Write REPENT in the box below every time you hear
    it, say it, or sing it in worship today.

You may have to repent many times to find your
    way through this maze to Christmas Joy.

# THIRD SUNDAY OF ADVENT

## From a Child's Point of View

"God is at work in and through history, reconciling all the world to himself." In children's words, God has a plan that we all will become friends with one another and with God. God is working on this plan every day. God has the power to make this plan work, and God wants us to help.

*Old Testament: Zephaniah 3:14-20.* To fully understand the word pictures in this poem, the hearer must have detailed knowledge of Old Testament history. Most children do not. However, if they are told that when the prophet spoke of Jerusalem and Zion, he also was speaking of all God's people (even us today), and if they are challenged to listen to the passage as if it were addressed to each of them as one of God's people (which it is), then they can grasp the prophet's message that God's plan has a good ending for them and that God has the power to make this plan a reality.

*Psalm: Isaiah 12:2-6.* This song of praise was included in today's lections as a response to the messages of Zephaniah, John the Baptist, and Paul. It is full of short, simple phrases praising the strong, active God who saves us.

*Gospel: Luke 3:7-18.* When reading this passage with the other lections for the day, do not place the emphasis on John's call to repentance, but on his expectation of One who is coming from God; One so great that John is not worthy to tie his shoelaces; One who will baptize us with the Holy Spirit; and, yes, One who will judge us.

John's sense of expectation might be compared to the way an eight-year-old would feel if Michael Jordan were coming to coach her basketball team, or if she were going to study with a New York ballet company. Joy, excitement, fear of higher standards, and hope for what she could become as she works with some of the best instructors in the world, would be all rolled up together. Expectantly, she would practice harder to be ready. With this as a frame of reference, children can sense John's excitement that God is coming to live among us; they can understand John's insistence that we get ready by working harder to live up to God's standards.

*Epistle: Philippians 4:4-9.* Paul restates John's message to encourage his friends at Philippi. Paul's list (vs. 8) is abstract. Children will need help in identifying which kinds of interests and activities fall in each category (e.g., a backyard club may not be pure and noble if it cuts people out and encourages ridicule). The vocabulary in the New International Version of the Bible is the clearest for children.

## Watch Words

*Avoid* theological generalities like *salvation* and *reconciliation.* Instead, talk about specifics. Praise God for specific saving events in the life of your congregation and community. Cite local examples of people who have become friends with one another and with God.

## Let the Children Sing

"Rejoice, the Lord Is King" is a good choice because the chorus can be sung even by nonreading children.

"Now Thank We All Our God" is a praise hymn frequently suggested in church school materials. Its familiarity and concrete language make it another good choice.

## The Liturgical Child

1. Plan for two people to read the Gospel—one to read the words of John the Baptist and the other to read the narrative. One reader could stand in the lectern, the other in the pulpit. Or a dramatic "John," perhaps in costume, could memorize his lines, come through a side door, speak from the front of the sanctuary, and leave. In preparation for either approach, practice with "John" answering the questioners in verses 10-14 in a way that would encourage the questioners to prepare for the wonderful One who is coming, rather than berate them.

2. Read Zephaniah 3:14-20 (GNB) responsively to get the happy feel of these promises. Assign half the congregation to read #1 and the other half to read #2. Read "All" in unison.

> All: Sing and shout for joy, people of Israel! Rejoice with all your heart, Jerusalem!
> #1: The LORD has stopped your punishment;
> #2: he has removed all your enemies.
> #1: The LORD, the king of Israel, is with you;
> #2: there is no reason now to be afraid.
> All: The time is coming when they will say to Jerusalem,
> #1: "Do not be afraid, city of Zion!
> #2: Do not let your hands hang limp!
> All: The LORD your God is with you; his power gives you victory.
> #1: The LORD will take delight in you.
> #2: and in his love he will give you new life.
> #1: He will sing and be joyful over you,
> #2: as joyful as people at a festival."
> All: The LORD says,
> #1: "I have ended the threat of doom
> #2: and taken away your disgrace.
> All: The time is coming!
> #1: I will punish your oppressors;
> #2: I will rescue all the lame
> #1: and bring the exiles home.
> #2: I will turn their shame to honor, and all the world will praise them.
> All: The time is coming!
> #1: I will bring your scattered people home;
> #2: I will make you famous throughout the world and make you prosperous once again."
> All: The LORD has spoken.

3. Present (reciting if possible) the Philippians text as a personal charge to worshipers just before the benediction.

## Sermon Resources

1. Spin a tale in which children in your town prepare for the arrival of Michael Jordan, who is to coach their basketball team.

2. If you focus on the questions to John about what preparations to make, challenge the children (and other worshipers) to imagine what John would say to them during this Advent season, if they were to ask, "What should I do, John?" To prime their thinking, re-create John's encounter to include people of today. Try a few safely obvious ones, such as:

The sports professionals asked, "What shall we do?" and John replied, "Be content with reasonable salaries. Play fair."

But also tackle students, businessmen, Christmas gift buyers, and so on.

3. If you have a Chrismon tree in your sanctuary, point out and describe the significance of ornaments that relate to today's theme. Consider some of the following:

- Cross Over the World—God has a wonderful plan for the whole world. God's plan will be successful.
- Jerusalem Cross—God's plan began with Jesus in Jerusalem and spread to the four corners of the earth.
- Crowns—Jesus is King!

Draw a picture of God's work in each box.

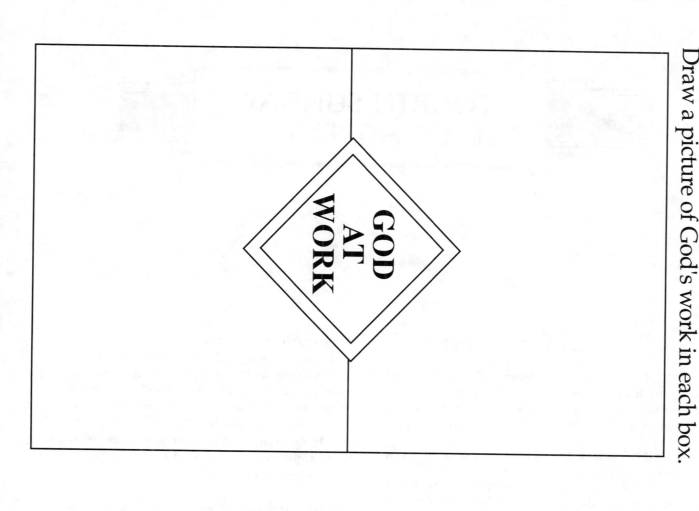

GOD
AT
WORK

Paul said to practice things that are:

true    noble    right

praiseworthy

admirable    pure

excellent

Write each word in Paul's suggestion on a line below. Match a letter in the word to a letter in PRACTICE. Add one "practice" suggestion of your own.

P _____
R _____
A _____
*EXCELLENT*
T _____
I _____
C _____
E _____

*Third Sunday of Advent* / © 1991 by Abingdon Press.

# FOURTH SUNDAY OF ADVENT

## From a Child's Point of View

Today's Scriptures celebrate God's choice of small, insignificant people and places, for the big, exciting tasks. For children who often feel small, insignificant, and overlooked, this offers hope.

*Old Testament: Micah 5:2-5a.* Micah announces that God's promised leader will not come from a big, famous city, but from Bethlehem, the littlest town in one of the smallest tribes in the Jewish nation. That's like being born in a small town in the smallest state or province in the country. Comparing Bethlehem to an insignificant town in your area gives it reality.

*Psalm 80:1-7.* To understand this prayer, hearers need to know about the winged figures on the Ark of the Covenant; recognize the names of the tribes of Israel; and understand the situation during the Babylonian exile. This one is definitely for adult Bible students.

*Gospel: Luke 1:39-55.* Mary praises God for choosing her, a poor nobody, to be the mother of the Messiah. Although adults may wish she had been a bit more humble, children can identify with her excitement: "From now on people will call me happy, because of the great things the Mighty God has done for me" (48b-49 GNB). Any child who has ever been chosen last for a ball game or a spelling bee can appreciate being chosen first, over much more likely candidates.

Older children can hear Mary celebrate God's preference for the poor and overlooked. For children who do experience poverty and oppression in their daily lives, this is welcome news.

For children who know they are among "the proud," "the mighty," and "the rich," it is as disconcerting as it is for their parents. But this message can remind them not to look down on those who wear poorer clothes, have less money, are less gifted, or are less "anything" than they are. It can remind all children that being the biggest, the best, or the most is not God's main goal for their lives.

*Epistle: Hebrews 10:5-10.* The technical discussion of atonement theology is beyond children. The one phrase in this passage that can speak to them is Christ's statement, "Here I am, O God, to do your will." It echoes Mary's annunciation response: "I am the Lord's servant. Let it happen to me as you have said" (Luke 1:38 GNB). It calls each of us, no matter what our age, to do whatever God wants us to do. Children, although aware of the loving actions God would have them take (e.g., when a younger sibling wants help or a classmate is teasing unkindly), often choose easier, more self-serving courses. This passage reminds them that, like Jesus, they are to be God's obedient servants.

## Watch Words

Fortunately, we have yet to invent a complicated word for God's tendency to work through the insignificant rather than the powerful. So vocabulary holds few traps today.

If you use the term *Magnificat* for Mary's song, explain its Latin origin.

## Let the Children Sing

"O Little Town of Bethlehem," although it focuses on tiny Bethlehem, is not a carol children understand or generally choose to sing.

"Away in a Manger" or "Once in David's Royal City" will stress the humbleness of Jesus' birth in children's language.

"My Soul Gives Glory to My God," based on Mary's song of praise, is a new hymn with simple words and a familiar tune.

## The Liturgical Child

1. Invite two women to read the Gospel. One (perhaps an older woman) might read the narration in verses 39-46a, and the other (perhaps a teenager) might read Mary's song in 46b-55. Practice with "Mary" to prepare a strong, dramatic reading full of feeling. The Good News Bible provides the clearest translation of Mary's song for children.

2. Create a litany prayer of petition and intercession. The congregation responds to the leader's prayers with Jesus' statement, "Here I am, O God, to do your will." Among the prayers, include petitions about expected visits with friends and relatives and requests for lovingkindness during the excitement of the days between now and Christmas.

## Sermon Resources

1. Remember some of the insignificant people God chose, such as Miriam, who advised a princess on the care of her brother; David, the youngest brother who became king; Esther, the pretty teenager who saved her people from a ruthless oppressor; and the scruffy bunch Jesus chose as his friends and disciples.

2. Tell the stories of the insignificant people God uses today, such as Samantha Smith, the Maine schoolgirl who wrote a letter to Mikhail Gorbachev urging peace. When Gorbachev invited Samantha to visit the Soviet Union, she became a goodwill ambassador between the United States and the Soviet Union. The Soviets printed a stamp with her picture on it. Such stories challenge children (and all of us unimportant people) to be God's servants where we are.

3. If there is a Chrismon tree in your sanctuary, point out and describe the significance of ornaments related to today's theme:

- Stars—Consider building a sermon around the stars on the tree, particularly if Christmas Eve is on the fourth Sunday of Advent or falls early in the week. You may have a five-pointed nativity star, the six-pointed star of David, and Creation Stars (these may have seven points, or lots of toothpick rays). Check a Chrismons book for descriptions of other star designs.
- Rose Centered on a Star—The rose is a symbol for both Mary and Jesus. Centered on a star, the rose reminds us that Mary's decision to do God's will made the star of Bethlehem possible.
- The Shepherd's Cross—This may be the one way to present the message of Psalm 80 to children—that the Messiah will lead us as a shepherd leads and cares for the sheep.

# JESUS SAID...

In the space below each letter, write the letter that comes before it in the alphabet. One has been done for you.

I F S F   J   B N,   P   H P E,

H _____   _____,   _____,   _____ _____,

U P   E P   Z P V S   X J M M."

_____ _____   _____ _____   _____ _____ _____ _____   _____ _____ _____ _____."

*Hebrews 10:7*

Answer: Here I am, O God, to do your will.

Do you have your Christmas gifts ready? What will you give God for Christmas?

Draw or write about your gift for God in the package below.

To: God
From:

# CHRISTMAS EVE/DAY (FIRST PROPER)

## From a Child's Point of View

*Old Testament: Isaiah 9:2-7.* This prophetic poem, with all its imagery, is a passage children can feel, rather than understand. It is best "felt" during a candlelight worship service. The one thing children need to know before hearing the poem is that the ruler it describes is Jesus. Although this is obvious to adults, it is not immediately clear to children.

The text makes more intellectual sense to children when the birth announcement in verses 6-7 is read and explored *before* they hear verses 2-5, which describe our response to that birth.

*Psalm: Psalm 96.* This psalm is a collection of short statements praising God. Most are easily understood by children, and those that are not are quickly followed by some that are. Again, the Good News Bible offers a clear translation in vocabulary children can understand.

*Gospel: Luke 2:1-20.* The story is simple, powerful, and easy to follow. But do remember that even older children are still trying to put the details of this story, which they hear only one month a year, into coherent order. Few children understand why taxes made a trip necessary. Older children appreciate the hardship of the journey if the approximately sixty miles are compared to a similar distance in your area. Younger children are likely to define a manger as "a bed for baby Jesus" unless they are told of its other use as a feed trough for animals. With that background, children are able to make sense of the angels' clue that the shepherds would know they had found the right baby when they found a baby in a manger. A manger was not a normal place to find a baby. "Glory to God in the highest," although commonly used in carols and on Christmas cards, requires explanation if it is to be more than "what the angels say at Christmas."

*Epistle: Titus 2:11-14.* Let's face it—on Christmas Eve or Christmas Day, few children will tune in to this theological reflection on the events of Luke's story and Isaiah's poem-prophecy. This passage is for adults.

## Watch Words

Wrap Jesus in *soft cloths*, not *swaddling clothes*. Avoid *incarnation* and *salvation*. Instead, describe what God did in this very specific situation and how that affected the people in the story and us today.

## Let the Children Sing

"Silent Night" is probably the most familiar carol. It is sung by children (and many adults) with emphasis on the feelings of the music, rather than with appreciation for the meaning of the words.

"There's a Star in the Sky" is less familiar but has simple words and a singable tune.

"Away in a Manger" is well known, but is viewed by many older children as a baby's song. So if you sing it, invite people of all ages to sing together, rather than ask the children to sing it while the adults listen. Older children generally feel exploited by such requests.

## The Liturgical Child

1. Begin Christmas Eve worship in a darkened, quiet sanctuary. Read the Isaiah passage as candles around the sanctuary are lighted by one or several acolytes. Then invite the congregation to sing a Christmas praise song.

2. Although it cannot be proved, I think the angel choirs must have sung something like Psalm 96 when Jesus was born. It is easy to imagine groups of angels singing the short praise statements back and forth through the sky. So invite your congregation to join the angel choirs by reading the psalm responsively. Worship leaders and people could alternate, or the right side and left side of the congregation could alternate.

| Group 1 | Group 2 |
| --- | --- |
| verse 1a | verse 1b |
| 2a | 2b |
| 3a | 3b |
| 4 | 5 |
| 6a | 6b |
| 7a | 7b |
| 8a | 8b |
| 9 | 10 |
| 11-12a | 12b-13a |
| 13b | 13c |

Or a Sunday school class (perhaps fourth- through sixth-graders) could prepare in advance to read the psalm responsively during the service.

3. Although there have been other pageants during the season, consider staging a simple pageant of Luke's account during the reading.

Ask a couple with a baby to be Mary, Joseph, and Jesus. Find another family with several children to be the shepherds. A third group can be angels—or the angels can be left to the imagination. A manger is the only prop needed. The actors, wearing simple costumes, walk through the story as it is read from Luke. One forty-five minute rehearsal before the service is adequate preparation when adults and children are working in teams.

Note: For families new in town, this can be a very special Christmas Eve experience in their new church.

This pageant could take the place of the sermon at a family service. Or the acts of the story could be interspersed with carols and prayers in a lessons-and-carols format as the outline of the entire service. At the end of the service, invite the congregation to get a closer look as they file quietly out of the sanctuary, or send the actors on their way in accord with the story.

## Sermon Resources

1. Children are not ready to listen to sermons on Christmas Eve or Christmas Day. For them, a lively presentation of the Scriptures for the day and a chance to sing and pray in a setting that involves all their senses are most effective.

2. There is no Worship Worksheet for Christmas Eve or Christmas Day. Worship on this day should be so full of feeling and so story-dominated that paper and pencils would deter rather than help children enter worship.

# FIRST SUNDAY AFTER CHRISTMAS

## From a Child's Point of View

All of us, both children and adults, are always growing. To the delight of children, today's readings ask adults to follow the example of two growing children, rather than ask that children follow the example of adults.

*Old Testament: I Samuel 2:18-20, 26.* This story offers two important messages for children. First, Samuel wore "the sacred linen apron." That is, he had an important job at the Temple. He wasn't just watching the grown-ups work. (What mission and worship work do the children of your congregation do?) Second, while Samuel was growing up, he was respected by people of all ages and by God. Remind the children that their gifts and ideas also are appreciated and respected *now*.

Warning: Even though Samuel was not living with his parents, they continued to love and care for him. They were proud of his special place at the Temple. God did not ask Samuel's parents to abandon Samuel, nor will God ask the children's parents to give them away. It is easy for children to miss this truth.

Avoid the alternative reading (Ecclus. 3:3-7, 14-17) which includes thorny teachings about honoring parents.

*Psalm 111.* This is an alphabet poem. The first line begins with the Hebrew letter Aleph. The New Jerusalem Bible happily translates this line with an "A" word—"Alleluia!" The lines that follow are short praise statements beginning with sequential letters of the Hebrew alphabet. Some of the lines make sense to children; others require background information. But children respond more to the format than to the content. They too can write alphabet poems stating their praises of God.

*Epistle: Colossians 3:12-17.* These verses can be viewed as Paul's guidelines for growing up as a Christian. Paul informs us that how we do our growing-up work is important. Whether we are learning to ride a bicycle, struggling to learn math at school, or trying to cope with a neighborhood bully, we are to be compassionate, kind, humble, gentle, and so forth. If we do this, we will grow in wisdom and favor with God and with people— just as Samuel and Jesus did.

*Gospel: Luke 2:41-52.* This story about Jesus at age twelve echoes that of young Samuel. Again, the child is respected in the congregation. In this story, Jesus' questions and ideas are taken seriously. So adults are called to listen to children and talk with them about our faith, and children are called to learn all they can about God and to ask all their questions—even the ones that may sound odd.

## Watch Words

Speak simply of the everyday business of growing up.

## Let the Children Sing

"O Come, All Ye Faithful" and "Joy to the World!" are appropriate for the Sunday after Christmas and are known by most children. The words to "O Come, All Ye Faithful" are easier for children to understand.

"O Sing a Song of Bethlehem" traces Jesus' growing up with simple words and a singable tune.

## The Liturgical Child

1. Provide silent prayer time for worshipers to thank God for growth they can see in themselves.

2. Pray your way through Paul's instructions in Colossians:

> Lord, you have called us your people. You have loved us and chosen us for your own. In return, you have asked us to be compassionate, kind, gentle, and patient. None of that comes easy for us. We try to ignore people who need our help. Hear our confessions about our lack of compassion. (Pause)
>
> We leave unsaid the kind words friends need to hear and avoid doing gentle deeds that would make others happy. Hear our confessions about our failures to be kind and gentle. (Pause)
>
> And we all want to do what we want to do when we want to do it. Having patience with those who are slower than we are or who want to do things another way is not easy. Hear our prayers for patience. (Pause)
>
> Lord, You have asked us to tolerate others. Hear our prayers about the people we need to tolerate at home, at school, and at work. (Pause)
>
> You have asked us to forgive one another. Hear our prayers about people we are trying to forgive. (Pause)

> Be with us. Give us your peace and love to guide us; for we pray in Jesus' name. Amen.

3. Invite the congregation to respond by saying "Alleluia" or "Praise the Lord" after each line of Psalm 111 as it is read.

4. Turn Paul's instructions in Colossians into a pre-benediction charge by pausing after each phrase for the congregation to respond, "With God's help, we will try."

## Sermon Resources

1. Celebrate growing up with lots of everyday examples—going to school for the first time, getting a driver's license, learning to be a good husband or wife, learning how to live alone after a spouse leaves or dies. Share with children and remind older worshipers that we are never "grown-up" but are always facing new tasks that call us to grow even more. Remember that Jesus also grew up just as we do—being a big brother, learning new games from friends, and accepting new responsibilities.

2. Stress the importance of asking questions and talking together about God to keep us growing as God's people. This is a chance to push Christian education for all ages.

3. As children leave the sanctuary, be ready to read alphabet poems about growth and to comment on the children's illustrations on their Worship Worksheets.

Write an **alphabet psalm** for God about growing up. For each letter below, write a short prayer that begins with that letter. Some have been started for you.

**A**lleluia! God I am growing up!

**B**e with me when _____

**C** _____

**D** _____

**E** _____

**F**orgive me for _____

**G** _____

**H**urrah for growing up like Jesus!

Draw a picture of Jesus for each verse of "O Sing A Song of Bethlehem."

| | |
|---|---|
| 1. | 2. |
| 3. | 4. |

*First Sunday After Christmas* / © *1991 by Abingdon Press.*

# NEW YEAR'S EVE/DAY

## From a Child's Point of View

*Old Testament: Isaiah 49:1-10.* This text, in which "I" seems to be either the nation and/or an individual who will save the nation, is all but impossible for children to understand as it is read. But they can appreciate the message that God's people are to be "a light to the nations." Fifth- and sixth-graders, who are keenly aware of such world concerns as hunger and homelessness, are especially responsive to Isaiah's call. But do remember that even these older children have trouble with symbolic language, so you will need to offer specific examples of what it means to be a "light to the nations."

*Psalm 90:1-12.* The brevity of life mourned by the psalmist is not real to children, for whom the time between Christmas and Easter is immense, and the finality of death is only beginning to become clear to them. But children do need to bask in the greatness of God, who was there before the world was created, who sees a thousand years as an evening, and who will live long after we die. Knowledge that such a powerful God is in charge provides great security.

*Epistle: Ephesians 3:1-10.* Paul announces that his mission to the Gentiles is part of God's secret plan for both Jews and non-Jews to recognize themselves as members of God's one big family. Children are called to join Paul in helping the people they study and play with recognize that they also are brothers and sisters in God's family.
Note: The compound/complex sentences in this text are hard for children to follow. You will need to put Paul's announcement into simpler statements.

*Gospel: Luke 14:16-24.* Of today's texts, this is the most child-accessible. The basic message of this parable is that each of us is responsible. The choices we make matter. Each guest chose to do something other than attend the feast. Each of us must decide whether to join Scouts or the soccer team; whether to do our homework or watch TV; whether to sit with one friend or another on the bus or at lunch, and so on. Just as none of the guests chose something "bad," not all of our choices are either "good" or "bad." Just as those who decided not to go to the feast never tasted the food, so we must live with the consequences of our decisions. Making New Year's resolutions primes us all to think about the choices we make.

## Watch Words

Do not use *light to the nations* without offering specific examples of children and adults who are "lights" today.

Define or describe words such as *immortal* and *eternal* when using them. Children usually encounter these words only at church.

## Let the Children Sing

If you sing "O God, Our Help in Ages Past," point out the comparison to Psalm 90. The abstract language of this hymn makes it hard for children to sing with understanding.

Only after exploring its meaning, sing "Immortal, Invisible, God Only Wise" to celebrate God.

"Father, Lead Me Day by Day" is a children's hymn about making choices. It is a good choice for worshipers of all ages.

"Let There Be Peace on Earth" provides the opportunity to sing in simple language about building God's family on earth.

## The Liturgical Child

1. Pray for wisdom to make difficult choices, courage to make frightening choices, and kindness to make loving choices.

2. To create a responsive intercessory prayer, plan prayer requests about places where God's light is needed in families, at school, and in our world. The congregational response to each request: "Lord, make us a light to the nations."

Include requests for light needed by bored children on vacation from school, for light needed when Christmas toys are broken, and so forth. Pray for the kindness to be more interested in what others received and did for Christmas than in telling what you received and did.

3. For the Gospel reading, invite the children to sit with you at the front of the sanctuary (perhaps on the chancel steps). Greet them by name with friendly comments as they are seated. Explain that Jesus liked to sit and talk with his friends like this. Point out that today's Gospel lesson is a story Jesus told his friends while they were sitting around eating dinner together. Open a Bible in your lap, perhaps the big pulpit Bible, and read the parable from it. Then send the children back to their seats.

## Sermon Resources

1. Focus on God's greatness (new years come and go, but God stays the same). Introduce words and symbols which remind us that God is more than we can imagine (e.g., Alpha, Omega, and the "O" words: *omnipotent*—all powerful; *omniscient*—all knowing; *omnipresent*—everywhere at once).

Ask the people to open their hymnals and explore with you all the big words and ideas about God in one or two verses of "Immortal, Invisible, God Only Wise."

Open such a sermon by challenging worshipers to remember their last year's New Year's resolutions or what they did on Christmas one year ago. Then compare our human understanding of the length of a year with God's understanding of it.

2. Challenge worshipers to accept being a light to the nations as a New Year's resolution. Outline some specific ways people of different ages can keep that resolution. Describe some of the mission work of your congregation and denomination in terms of the light it brings to dark places and lives. Note ways worshipers can add their lights to these efforts. Encourage people of all ages to write letters to officials, shedding light on causes they think God supports.

Finally, invite worshipers to write or draw on a slip of paper one specific resolution related to being a light to the nations and place the papers in the offering plate as resolutions before God. Promise privacy and instruct the ushers to respect the privacy of these resolutions.

# Have you made any New Year's resolutions?

Listen to what we hear, say, sing, and pray to get ideas about New Year's resolutions God would like you to make. Write or draw one resolution below.

This year I will. . .

Cross out every fourth letter to find God's promise to people who make New Year's resolutions.

Start Here

I W I K L
I M I W
T H I M E
R O U A X L
Y A E T
S M Y B A M

Promise: I will be with you always.

" _ _ _ _ _ _ _ _ "

(Matthew 28:20)

# EPIPHANY

Note: In 1992 and 1998, when the day of Epiphany falls very close to Sunday, use the Epiphany lessons rather than those for the Second Sunday of Christmas.

## From a Child's Point of View

*Gospel: Matthew 2:1-12.* The details of this story are often missed in children's Christmas pageants, when wise men simply follow the star to the manger. The encounter with Herod is skipped. When the story of the wise men is the focus of the day, it is possible to mine from the story two themes that are important to children.

First, God went to some trouble (by providing the star) to announce Jesus' birth to people of another race and country. In other words, God loves all people everywhere. Jesus came to all people. Thus, as Jesus' followers, we are to be one family with all people everywhere. We are to exclude no one from God's church or from our family. Although this inclusiveness is to be extended to people in our own school and community, Matthew's account of the wise men focuses on God's insistence on racial, national, and cultural inclusiveness.

Elementary children get heavy doses of national and cultural pride in school, Scouts, and similar activities. This is a chance to balance that pride with deep appreciation for other nations and cultures. It is also an opportunity to explore the value of nations working together and of cultures sharing their ways of doing things.

Second, this is a story of palace intrigue in which God and several foreigners outwit an evil ruler. The wise men learn from Herod where to find Jesus, but do not give Herod the information he needs to kill the child. God is at work on the side of the powerless. This is one of the success stories in the struggle of the powerless. Invite children to celebrate the story.

*Epistle: Ephesians 3:1-12.* (Yes, this was the New Year's Eve/Day Epistle lection, too.) Paul's announcement of God's "secret plan" reminds us that all people are members of God's family. Therefore, the wise men, like the Gentiles, are not "foreigners" but "kin." Today most children have contact at school or in their communities with children of other nationalities, races, and cultures. Older children are aware of people in other countries who dress, eat, speak, and act differently from the way we do. Paul's secret is that all these people are part of God's family. We must, therefore, respect them and treat them lovingly.

Note: The compound/complex sentences in this text are hard for children to follow. You will need to put Paul's announcement into simpler statements.

*Psalm 72:1-14.* This is both a prayer for, and a description of, a ruler who is everything Herod is not. This king is God's ideal—fair, caring, and kind. Christians have interpreted the passage as a description of the king that Jesus would be. But it also can be instructive for team captains, class officers, Scout patrol leaders, and other young leaders.

*Old Testament: Isaiah 60:1-6.* This Old Testament prophecy is read today to point to the arrival of the wise men. The connection is too obscure for most children.

31

## Watch Words

Our tendency to use the terms *wise men, magi,* and *kings* interchangeably can confuse children. Stick with one of the terms (the Bible uses "wise men"), or explain your use of others.

Do not assume that the children recognize the word *Epiphany* and understand its significance.

## Let the Children Sing

"We Three Kings of Orient Are" is an obvious choice, but it includes abstract vocabulary that needs detailed explanation before children can sing all the verses with understanding.

"Come, Christians, Join to Sing" praises Christ the King with a repeated chorus of "Alleluia, Amen!"—in which even nonreaders can join (a specific invitation helps!).

"Jesus Loves the Little Children" is a familiar children's song celebrating the worldwide family of God. Perhaps a young children's class could sing it for the congregation, or the entire congregation could sing it as a hymn or in response to a point within the sermon.

## The Liturgical Child

1. Light the Christ candle in your Advent wreath once more today. Then use it to light any other candles in your worship center. Explain the significance of the candles as they are lit. For example, many congregations light two candles on the table to recall Jesus' "twin" statements that he is the light of the world and that we also are called to be the light of the world.

2. Psalm 72 is a combination of the good wishes (or prayers) and cheers of a crowd celebrating their good king. So have four readers read the psalm with enthusiasm:

| | |
|---|---|
| Reader 1: Verse 1 | Reader 1: Verse 9 |
| Reader 2: Verse 2 | Reader 2: Verse 10a |
| Reader 3: Verse 3 | Reader 3: Verse 10b |
| Reader 4: Verse 4 | Reader 4: Verse 11 |
| Reader 1: Verse 5 | Reader 1: Verse 12a |
| Reader 2: Verse 6 | Reader 2: Verse 12b |
| Reader 3: Verse 7 | Reader 3: Verse 13 |
| Reader 4: Verse 8 | Reader 4: Verse 14 |

After delivering a sermon on leadership, repeat this reading as a prayer for specific leaders in the world today.

3. Use the characteristics of a good king found in Psalm 72:1-4; 12-14 as the basis of a prayer for leaders of the world today—name presidents, governors, and local leaders. Be sure to include leaders of countries other than your own.

4. Include prayers and music from different cultures and branches of Christianity in today's worship to celebrate the worldwide family of God. Perhaps a choir can prepare a hymn from another culture as an anthem. Create a display of hats from around the world in your worship center. (An older children's class might be enlisted to gather such hats.)

5. Pray for people of different nations and cultures. Using weather as a format, note the different kinds of weather in which Christians are gathering to worship on this day; then move to deeper concerns for the worldwide family of God.

For example, in a northern-hemisphere congregation, we might say, "It is hard to remember that for some Christians, today is the middle of summer. We remember our brothers and sisters in South Africa who gather in hot buildings and summer clothes to worship you and to find ways for black and white Christians to live together as your children."

## Sermon Resources

1. Many children and adults would like to be "king." Compare three kings in this story: grasping, jealous Herod; the three worshiping kings; and King Jesus, who would be a serving, sacrificing king. Illustrate with stories about leaders of all ages.

2. Build a sermon around the three strange gifts the wise men brought. Consider using the verses of "We Three Kings of Orient Are" as an outline. Ask worshipers to follow along in open hymnbooks. Some religious bookstores sell samples of frankincense and myrrh, which you could display in your worship center.

Artists have drawn many very different pictures of the 3 wise men.

In some they come on camels.
In others they ride horses.

In some they wear crowns like kings.
In others they dress like teachers.
In still others they wear clothes from 3 different countries.

Draw YOUR picture of the 3 wise men.

Herod was a jealous, mean leader. The wise men worshiped a baby who would be a great leader. Jesus died for us all.

## What kind of leader are you?

Draw a picture of yourself being a leader or write a prayer telling God about the kind of leader you want to be.

# FIRST SUNDAY AFTER EPIPHANY/BAPTISM OF THE LORD

## From a Child's Point of View

Many themes relate to Jesus' baptism. Central to today's readings is the idea that in his baptism Jesus allied himself with those who are "dirty" because of their sense of sin or because they have been labeled "unworthy" by others.

*Gospel: Luke 3:15-17, 21-22.* This story, the heart of today's worship, appears simple at first glance but includes details that are confusing to children. John's promise of a baptism with the Holy Spirit and fire requires an understanding of the Pentecost events and of symbolism. The judgment message in verse 17 is set in unfamiliar harvest images, and the baptism scene gains significance only when examined in light of the other passages for the day. So the best course is to read the passage without trying to explain all the details. Children will begin to appreciate the significance of Jesus' baptism as they explore the other passages.

*Old Testament: Isaiah 61:1-4.* In the King James Version and Revised Standard Version of the Bible, these verses are so full of unfamiliar words and abstract images that children are quickly lost. But the short simple phrases of The Good News Bible are easy for children to understand. Verse 1, especially, makes sense and appeals to the idealism of fifth- and sixth-graders. To help children understand the passage in the context of today's theme, before reading the passage, tell them that Jesus chose these verses to introduce himself and his ministry. They were like mottos or business cards for Jesus.

*Acts 8:14-17.* For the purpose of today's theme, focus not so much on the apostles' giving of the Holy Spirit (a complicated issue for many adults today) as on the fact that people considered "dirty" by all Jews of that day were welcome because they had chosen to be baptized. Peter and John knew that anyone who loved Jesus enough to be baptized was now part of their family—the family of God. Children will recognize their responsibility to follow the example of Peter and John.

*Psalm 29.* Psalm 29 celebrates the power of God felt in a thunderstorm. The psalm traces the path of a storm as it comes in from the sea, crosses the mountains, and moves into the desert. Children will not appreciate the connection for which this passage is read today (i.e., the connection between the water, wind, and fire of baptism and that of a thunderstorm). However, they will respond to the psalmist's invitation to the fearful child in each of us—not to fear the power of the storm but to let it remind us of God's great strength.

## Watch Words

Avoid the harvest imagery (*winnowing shovel, threshing grain, burning chaff*). Today's nonagricultural children understand harvesting as gathering the good products, rather than as separating the good from the bad.

Reread your tradition's baptism ritual from a child's point of view. What jargon needs definition in children's language? What promises or statements need to be put into children's words?

Incorporate your learnings into today's liturgy and sermon.

## Let the Children Sing

Hymns about Jesus' baptism are filled with symbolic language that makes little sense to children. Choose general praise hymns. "Fairest Lord Jesus" or "I Sing the Almighty Power of God" may be sung in the spirit of praise found in Psalm 29.

## The Liturgical Child

1. To emphasize the sense of the thunderstorm in Psalm 29, invite the congregation to accompany the reading of the psalm by following a "hand-choir" director. The director stands near the reader and shows the congregation what to do:

| verses 1-2 | hands folded in lap |
|---|---|
| verses 3-4 | pat lap in strong, slow cadence |
| verses 5-6 | beat the pew sets or pewbacks a little faster |
| verses 7-9 | clap hands still faster |
| verses 10-11 | fold hands in laps again |

The reader will need to read with a strong voice to be heard and to emphasize the strength of God's voice in the storm. If you cannot imagine your congregation doing this, ask a children's class to serve as a hand choir to accompany the reader. This group and the reader should practice together.

2. Continue the Epiphany prayer discipline of praying for those who are "foreigners," "outsiders," or "dirty." Pray for the courage to be kind to those others tease, to be a friend to those others ignore, and to care for those with special needs.

3. If baptisms are part of today's worship, take time to link them to Jesus' baptism. Point out that just as God said to Jesus, "You are my son," we say to those we baptize, "You are part of our family, the family of God." If you plan a children's sermon, have it just before the baptism. If your tradition includes promises to be made by the congregation, help the children put the promises into their own words and discuss what it means for them to make these promises to the children who are to be baptized. Help them identify ways they can treat these children as part of the "family."

If infants or children are baptized, deal with practical possibilities, such as not running over them in the hall after Sunday school, taking special care of them at school or church, putting up with them even when they are acting like babies. Invite the children to stay up front where they can see the baptisms better.

4. Turn Isaiah 61:1-3a into a charge to the congregation by changing each of the tasks from a statement to a command (e.g., Take good news to the poor! Heal the brokenhearted!)

Move to the benediction in a paraphrase of verse 3b: You will be like trees the Lord himself has planted. You will do what is right, and God will be praised for what you have done.

## Sermon Resources

1. Begin with stories of dirty people—Scouts coming home after a rainy camp-out; sweaty athletes getting into a car with others who are dressed for a party; someone who has "dirty" breath after eating lots of onion or garlic; street people who are looked down on because they are dirty, and so on. Use these stories to introduce baptism as a ritual that makes dirty people acceptable. Explore how Jesus took the side of "dirty" people everywhere when he was baptized and claimed the job of Isaiah's messenger.

2. Match each of the tasks of Isaiah's servant with an outreach ministry of your congregation. Include projects in which the children participated. Point out that we take on the work of God's servant when we do these tasks.

*Luke 3:21-22*

After all the people had been baptized, Jesus also was baptized. While he was praying, heaven was opened, and the Holy Spirit came down upon him in bodily form like a dove. And a voice came from heaven, "You are my own dear Son. I am pleased with you."

THIS IS MY SON

Before printing presses were invented, books were copied by hand. Some Christians spent their whole lives making copies of the Bible. Often they decorated their work with beautiful drawings.

Add your drawings to this page of today's scripture.

# Isaiah 61:1-2

The Sovereign Lord has filled me
　with his spirit.
He has chosen me and sent me
To bring good news to the poor,
To heal the broken-hearted,
To announce release to captives
　and freedom to those in prison.
He has sent me to proclaim that
　the time has come when the
　Lord will save his people and
　defeat their enemies.
He has sent me to comfort
　all who mourn.

# SECOND SUNDAY AFTER EPIPHANY

## From a Child's Point of View

Today's readings speak of the way God's great power is shown to us—an important subject for children. Children need the security of knowing that God is the strongest power in the universe (Ps. 36). They also need to know that God uses this enormous power to care for us (John 2), to work in history on our behalf (Isa. 62), and to give each of us our own powers to use and enjoy (I Cor. 12). Because the language and images in these passages are often beyond children, worship leaders will need to concentrate on the theme, rather than on the passages.

*Old Testament: Isaiah 62:1-5.* The message is that God can and will eventually save us from our political and social messes. The specific example is that God will rescue the people of Jerusalem from captivity and reestablish the Jewish nation. To get from the specific example to the general message requires more explanation of Jewish history and Old Testament marriage images than time or the children will allow. This passage is for adult Bible students.

*Psalm 36:5-10.* The psalmist praises God by citing attributes such as faithfulness, righteousness, and justice—words that are too abstract for children. References to drinking from the river of God's goodness, finding protection in the shadow of God's wings, and seeing the light of God do not speak clearly to children. Still, if the psalm is read with a sense of happy confidence and joy, the children will feel, rather than understand, these praises.

*Epistle: I Corinthians 12:1-11.* Verses 4-11 of this passage may be the easiest of today's lections for the children to understand. God has the power to give each of us special gifts or powers. Although each gift or power is different, all are of great value. Paul makes his point clearly in verses 4-7. Unfortunately for children, the examples that follow are difficult to translate from their first-century setting. Rather than explain each example, help the children identify the gifts/powers from God that they see in themselves and in others in the congregation. In citing these gifts, be sure to include "gifts of the spirit," such as patience in dealing with others, as well as talents such as musical ability.

*Gospel: John 2:1-11.* The writer of John explains who Jesus is by presenting a series of meaning-filled signs that Jesus performed. The first sign of God's power and love is that, through Jesus, God keeps a party going by providing extra high-quality refreshments. John's message is that God has the power to give us more than just what we need; God surprises us with unnecessary abundance. To children, this says that God wants all of them to have more than just enough to get by or to meet their needs. God's plan is that everyone should have all the wonderful, good things of life.

Children are often puzzled by Jesus' conversation with his mother. John includes that conversation to make the point that Jesus acted as he did because he chose to live by God's plan—not because his mother or anyone else told him what to do. Likewise, children today are called to live by God's plan because they choose to do so—not because their parents, teachers, or anyone else tells them to do so.

## Watch Words

Watch out for the big power words such as *omnipotence, omniscience,* and *omnipresence.*

Rather than speaking of God's *vindication* of Jerusalem (Isa. 62) or of other oppressed groups, tell specifically what God did or promised.

Instead of *faithfulness* or *steadfastness* (Ps. 36), speak of *loyalty.* God is loyal to us, even when we are not loyal to God.

## Let the Children Sing

"I Sing the Almighty Power of God" is first choice.

This is a Sunday for several praise hymns, such as "Now Thank We All Our God," "For the Beauty of the Earth," and "All People That on Earth Do Dwell."

## The Liturgical Child

1. Read the psalm responsively, between either leader and people or two halves of the congregation. When introducing the psalm, point out that when we read it, we join the poet in telling God how great we think God is. Challenge worshipers to show how they feel by the way they say the words:

Lord, your constant love reaches the heavens;
  *Your faithfulness extends to the skies.*
Your righteousness is towering like the mountains;
  *Your justice is like the depths of the sea.*
Men and animals are in your care.
  *How precious, O God, is your constant love!*
We find protection under the shadow of your wings.
  *We feast on the abundant food you provide;*
You let us drink from the river of your goodness.
  *You are the source of all life,*
And because of your light, we see the light.
(All) Continue to love those who know you
  and to do good to those who are righteous.
                    (Based on GNB)

2. Today's Worship Worksheet challenges the children to create a rebus of the hymn "I Sing the Almighty Power of God." To give the children time to work on the rebus, plan to sing the hymn after the sermon. As you begin the sermon, challenge the children to work on the rebus while they listen, so they will be ready to sing the hymn with their own "picture words."

## Sermon Resources

1. To start the people thinking about power and the powerful people and groups in our world today, name political leaders and sports figures. If your children are caught up in Super Bowl frenzy, talk about the power claims in the chant "We're Number One!"

2. Name and discuss the power brokers of the cartoon world—Superman or Batman, Spider Woman, Masters of the Universe, and all the Transformers. For children who know themselves to be very unpowerful because of their size and age, such figures often become talismen against all the powers they fear. Children need to hear that God is even more powerful and dependable than any of those heroes and heroines. There is no evil power that God cannot conquer.

3. Compare "grabbing" power with "giving" power. Use the descriptions of God's power in today's lections as examples of giving power. Challenge worshipers to choose giving power by citing examples:

Albert Schweitzer was already becoming a famous concert organist. (This does not sound exciting today, but in his day, an organist was like a rock star.) But he chose to become a missionary doctor. He gave up riches and fame to spend the rest of his life taking care of people deep in the jungles of Africa.

Millard Fuller had made a million dollars by the time he was thirty years old. He had cars, houses, and a fancy boat. But he was not happy. Then he decided to change his goal. His new goal was to build a million homes for people who had no decent place to live. He founded Habitat for Humanity. Now thousands of people all around the world are working with him to build hundreds of homes every year. He says he is happier now in his small house and building houses for others than he ever was in his fancy house.

Cite examples of people in your congregation who put their giving power to work. Remember to include examples of children who sing in the choir, participate in mission projects, or whatever else your children do.

# In your hymnbook find
# I Sing the Almighty Power of God.

Draw pictures in the boxes of the things God made. If you sing this hymn today, use your picture words.

I sing the almighty power of God,

that made the [ mountains ] rise,

that spread the [ flowing seas ] abroad,

and built the [ lofty skies ] .

I sing the wisdom that ordained

the [ sun ] to rule the day,

the [ moon ] shines full at God's command

and all the [ stars ] obey.

*Second Sunday After Epiphany* / © 1991 by *Abingdon Press.*

# THIRD SUNDAY AFTER EPIPHANY

## From a Child's Point of View

*Old Testament: Nehemiah 8:1-4a, 5-6, 8-10.* Before children can understand all the excitement and tears in this story, they must know what the Law is. For this passage, the Law is five books of the Bible that include (1) the *stories of what God had done for people*, from Adam and Eve to Noah, to Abraham, to Moses and the people he led out of slavery in Egypt; and (2) *what God expected of people* (including the Ten Commandments). Children also must know that none of these people had heard the Law read for many years. (You might compare the situation to what would happen if the Gospels were read in your congregation for the first time in many years.)

With this background, children follow the story easily and generally are impressed by how long the crowd listened and by their tearful response. The key idea is that the stories and rules in the Law were very important to those people. We are challenged to see the importance of the Law (and the rest of the Bible) for our lives, too.

*Psalm 19:7-14.* No matter which translation you select, these verses are filled with big words that are synonyms for the Law. Older children are helped by hearing these words introduced as synonyms for the Law or the Bible, and by being reminded that Hebrew poets rhyme ideas, rather than sounds. So these verses are a repetitious list of wonderful things about the Bible.

*Epistle: I Corinthians 12:12-30.* This passage requires symbolic thinking beyond the ability of younger children, but this is a good opportunity to challenge older children to begin such thinking. The challenge is most effectively presented by working on both sides of Paul's symbol before trying to connect them.

Most children quickly understand the interdependence of the parts of a physical body. With some guidance, they can recognize that people within the congregation doing different kinds of work need one another and their differing gifts. The similarity between these two truths, however, will be a hard connection to make. It requires that children see themselves as parts of Christ's body. This vision often begins when an older adult thanks an errand-running child for "being my feet." Once children can see themselves as Grandma's feet, they can understand that they also can be Christ's feet. Many everyday examples of being Christ's hands, eyes, and so on will clarify this possibility. As this vision becomes clear, children will finally understand Paul's symbolic connection and, thus, his point. This is a job to chip away at over several years—not to complete in one sermon.

*Gospel: Luke 4:14-21.* In this passage Jesus introduces the goals for his life and ministry. His goals are ones children can understand, especially if they are given some help with difficult words. Children can be challenged to see Jesus' goals as goals for their congregation and to accept some or all of them as goals for their own lives.

## Watch Words

Define *Law*, and be careful about the synonyms you use. "Anointed me to" means "chose me to."

40

To "proclaim liberty to the captives" means "to free prisoners." To "proclaim the acceptable year of the Lord" is to promise that God (through me) is acting to save you now!

## Let the Children Sing

*About the Law (Bible):* "Wonderful Words of Life" has an easy chorus and repeats the title in each verse, making it an easy song for even non-readers.

"Tell Me the Stories of Jesus" does not celebrate the whole of the Bible, but only the stories about Jesus. It is one of the few hymns about the Bible that children can sing with understanding.

*About Jesus' Commitment, and Ours:* "Be Thou My Vision" is a hymn of commitment that many children love. Because it has some difficult words, use this hymn only if it is familiar. Try "Lord, Speak to Me That I May Speak."

## The Liturgical Child

1. Ask six older children, or six readers of a variety of ages, to present the following reading of Psalm 19: 7-14 (GNB). (This reading preserves the sense of parallel or rhyming ideas about God's Law.) In the sanctuary, practice reading loudly and clearly, with happy, proud voices.

| | |
|---|---|
| Reader One: | The law of the Lord is perfect; it gives new strength. |
| Reader Two: | The commands of the Lord are trustworthy, giving wisdom to those who lack it. |
| Reader Three: | The laws of the Lord are right, and those who obey them are happy. |
| Reader Four: | The commands of the Lord are just and give understanding to the mind. |
| Reader Five: | Reverence for the Lord is good; it will continue forever. |
| Reader Six: | The judgments of the Lord are just; they are always fair. |
| Reader One: | They are more desirable than the finest gold; |
| Reader Two: | they are sweeter than the purest honey. |
| Reader Three: | They give knowledge to me, your servant; |
| Reader Four: | I am rewarded for obeying them. |
| Reader One: | No one can see his own errors; |
| Reader Two: | deliver me, Lord, from hidden faults! |
| Reader Three: | Keep me safe, also, from willful sins; |
| Reader Four: | don't let them rule over me. |
| Reader Five: | Then I shall be perfect |
| Reader Six: | and free from the evil of sin. |
| All: | May my words and my thoughts be acceptable to you, O Lord, my refuge and my redeemer! |

2. To emphasize what Jesus read from Isaiah, begin reading the narrative in Luke from the Bible at the lectern. Then, from a large scroll, read the Isaiah passage in verses 18 and 19. If possible, step out of the lectern to read this passage. Then lay the scroll aside, step back to the center of the lectern, and continue Luke's narrative.

3. At the end of the service, change the pronouns in the Isaiah passage from first person to second person to charge the congregation: "The Spirit of the Lord is upon *you*, because God has chosen *you*." In the benediction, remind worshipers that just as Jesus sent out his disciples with the promise that he would be with them always, so he also sends us out with the same promise.

4. If you focus on the Law, pray for the church school classes and teachers. If you focus on work and goals, pray for the specific gifts and ministries of your congregation.

## Sermon Resources

1. If you focus on the Law, challenge all listeners to participate in the congregation's study classes; also offer other specific suggestions for reading the Bible.

*Pockets*, a monthly magazine published by The Upper Room, offers daily Bible readings with prayer suggestions (as well as stories and games) for elementary children. Give a copy to each child to introduce them and their families to this fine resource. Order from: *Pockets*, 1908 Grand Ave., P.O. Box 189, Nashville, TN 37202-9929.

2. If you link the New Testament lessons, write a paraphrase of Paul's message, using groups in your congregation. For example, the choir cannot

say to the church school teachers, "We do not need you." Nor can the youth group say to the women's circle, "God has no use for you anymore."

## Worship Worksheet

Depending on the Scriptures you choose, use the worksheet as it is, or enlarge the appropriate half to a full page.

Unscramble each group of letters to find the psalmist's prayer.

——— my ———  ——— and ———

——— my ——— be ———

——— to you, O ——— .

Psalm 19:14

I heard this psalm today when ——— .

Answer: May my words and my thoughts be acceptable to you, O Lord.

Draw pictures of ways your church works on Jesus' goals.

PROCLAIM GOOD NEWS TO THE POOR

FREE PRISONERS

TELL PEOPLE GOD SAVES THEM

*Third Sunday After Epiphany* / © 1991 by Abingdon Press.

# FOURTH SUNDAY AFTER EPIPHANY

## From a Child's Point of View

*Old Testament: Jeremiah 1:4-10.* God knew Jeremiah before he was born and had a plan for him. God assured Jeremiah that he was capable of following the plan, and God promised to be with him all the way. Although it is possible for children to hear Jeremiah's story as if it were a special case involving someone very unlike themselves, with direction, they can hear in it the truth about themselves. That is, God also knew them before they were born, God has a plan for each of their lives, God has given them everything they need to follow those plans, and God will be with them each step of the way. Each person is important to God. As one poster puts it, "God don't make no junk." (This is a great text for encouraging Christian self-esteem!) The fact that Jeremiah was young when God called him challenges children to begin doing God's work *now* instead of waiting until they grow up.

*Psalm 71:1-6.* This is the prayer of an old poet who knows from experience that God does indeed care for those who do God's work. Now in a tight corner, the poet calls on God for help (vss. 1-3) and remembers that God has helped in the past (vss. 4-6). Once children understand this, they will "catch" a few of the short phrases as the text is read, but probably will not follow the passage as a whole.

*Epistle: I Corinthians 13:1-13.* The most relevant message here for children is that the way to grow up is not to grow smarter, more skillful, or more articulate, but to grow more loving. Few children, however, will hear this message from

the text on their own. You will need to point it out to them, and then work through verses 4-7, which explore grown-up love. Consult several translations to gather the adjectives that will most clearly describe love to these particular children. To help younger children understand these verses, paraphrase them: "A loving person is . . . ," rather than "Love is . . . ."

*Gospel: Luke 4:21-30.* The message of this passage—God comes not only to us and to our friends, but also to some people we think are not worthy of God's attention—is one children need to hear and can respond to. But they (and many adults) will have difficulty pulling the message from the text. It helps to review or reread the beginning of the story in verses 16-20. Even so, most people will hear Jesus' point in the sermon, rather than in the lesson reading. Though youths and adults will benefit from explanations of Jesus' Old Testament examples, few children will follow them. Count on getting the children's attention when you summarize the message and explore its meaning for today. Identify some of the people in your community to whom God and Jesus come: the homeless, troublemakers at school, kids who are slow academically, "wimps," people with handicaps, people of other races, and so on.

## Watch Words

Try *friendship* or *a loving friend*, rather than *love*, for the sake of boys for whom love is a sweet, sissy term used by mothers and in sexual relationships.

In Jeremiah 1 and Psalm 71, the Good News Bible speaks of *before I was born*, rather than *from the womb,* which bypasses the giggles of children who know what a womb is and speaks clearly to those who do not.

## Let the Children Sing

Try "I Sing a Song of the Saints of God," a singable new hymn that is becoming a favorite.

Children can begin learning "God of Grace and God of Glory," a more traditional hymn of commitment, by joining in on "grant us wisdom, grant us courage."

"Lord, I Want to Be a Christian," with its verses about being more loving, joins the commitment theme in Jeremiah's call with the "love chapter."

## The Liturgical Child

1. Assign two readers or two halves of the congregation to read the psalm. Name one reader "Help Me, God" (vss. 1-3) and the other "I Can Trust God" (vss. 4-6), to reflect the message of these two sections of the psalm.

2. Use I Corinthians 13:4-7 as an outline for a prayer of confession. A leader prays each line, leaving a time of silence for individual confessions (e.g., "Love is patient and kind . . ." [Pause] "Love is not jealous or conceited or proud . . ." [Pause], etc.). Or the leader and congregation can read a responsive confession:

Love is patient and kind;

Lord, it is hard to be patient when there is so much we need to do and want to do. When other people slow us down, it is easy to forget to be kind.

Love is not jealous or conceited or proud;

But we are, God. We look at some people and think we are better than they are. We look at others and feel jealous of what they have and can do. Forgive us.

Love is not ill-mannered or selfish or irritable;

But we often blurt out rude, hurting names and accusations, almost before we know what we are saying. Help us learn to think before we speak.

Love does not keep a record of wrongs;

But we remember even those wrongs we have really tried to forgive. We remember them and bring them up when we are angry or when we want our own way. We use them to hurt even the people we love. Help us to forgive and forget.

Love is not happy with evil; love is happy with truth;

But it is hard not to take secret delight when people get what they had coming to them. Teach us compassion, God.

Love never gives up; and its faith, hope, and patience never fail.

But we give up easily. We give up on other people. We give up on ourselves. We give up on making a difference. We lose hope that anything will ever be any different. Forgive us, for we pray in Jesus' name. Amen.

*Assurance of Pardon:* Hear this about God's great love! God is patient and kind. God does not keep a record of our wrongs. God does not remember our failings at loving, but is happy about every one of our successes. God never gives up on us because God's love is forever!

3. For the charge and benediction, paraphrase God's call to Jeremiah as a call to each worshiper: "I chose you before I gave you life. . . . Do not be afraid, but go to the people to whom I send you. . . . I will protect you and give you the words you need."

## Sermon Resources

1. To explore Luke's lesson, tell a story in which Jesus comes to visit a playground, skating rink, or other place where children gather in your area. In your story, have all the children recognize Jesus and try to get his attention so he will talk and play with them and their friends. Describe some of the groups vying for Jesus' attention and their tactics. Then describe Jesus choosing to reach out to some children who are usually overlooked or looked down on. Tailor the story to fit your community.

2. To explore Paul's message about being a Christian grown-up, create a parable in which four "children" try to be grown-ups in different ways: One tries to act like a grown-up by wearing make-up, insisting on staying up late, even drinking or smoking; another tries to act grown up by bossing everyone around (pretending to know

everything); a third tries to make it with grown-ups by doing everything they want (becoming teacher's pet); and a fourth person tries to love and take care of other people. Challenge your hearers to decide which one was grown up, according to Paul's definition.

3. At the beginning of the sermon, mention the "opposites" activity on the Worship Worksheet and challenge the children to listen for opposites in the sermon. At the end of the sermon, or as children leave the sanctuary, hear and respond to some of their opposites.

# "I chose you before I gave you life."

Draw a picture of yourself doing something God chose to make you able to do.

Day and **night** are opposites.
**Pretty** and **ugly** are opposites.
**Good** and **bad** are opposites.

In the first column are words Paul used to tell us about love.

In the second column, write a word that means the opposite of each of Paul's words.

Love is . . .
patient
kind
_____
_____
_____

Love is not . . .
conceited
boastful
selfish
jealous
irritable
arrogant
_____

**Some words to try:** humble, generous, pleasant, friendly, helpful, gentle, giving, content.

Listen for love words in our worship.

Write a prayer about the way God made you.

*Fourth Sunday after Epiphany* / © 1991 by Abingdon Press.

# FIFTH SUNDAY AFTER EPIPHANY

## From a Child's Point of View

Today's texts include three accounts in which a person encounters the greatness of God, feels unable to face God, and then feels called by God. All three stories say to children, who are aware of their vulnerability and insignificance, that the God of the Universe cares about them and needs their help.

*Old Testament: Isaiah 6:1-8 (9-13).* This poetic description of the power of God is tough to present to literal-minded children. They tend to see it as a photographic peek at God. One approach is simply to read the passage, letting the children respond to the power scene literally. Such a scene makes Isaiah's response very understandable.

Another approach is to compare the passage to a poetic line, such as "my love is like a red, red rose"; then, to help older children analyze the seraphim, who had two wings to cover their eyes (because they were afraid to see God's great power and purity), two wings to cover their bodies (because they were afraid for God to see how unpure they were), and two wings to fly about to do God's will. With some direction, these older children can begin to understand the seraphim as pictures of the way we feel when we sense God's great power and holiness and do God's will.

Children will need help to interpret the burning coal as cleansing, rather than as punishment or torture. The examples of washing dishes in steamy hot water or burning a stick in a campfire before putting a hot dog on it may help children understand the cleansing function of the coal.

*Psalm 138.* This psalm, which praises God, is simple enough to understand, but it does not speak of things that are particularly important to children. It is a good psalm to read, but not one to explore in any depth.

*Epistle: I Corinthians 15:1-11.* This passage offers two key ideas to children. First, while Isaiah felt God's power and presence in the Temple, Paul encountered it in the life, death, and resurrection of Jesus. Though Paul did not meet Jesus while he lived on the earth, Paul knew Jesus' story and, based on that story, believed that God loves us, cares for us, and forgives us more than we can imagine. Paul knew Jesus in the same way children today know Jesus.

Second, God called Paul to discipleship, even though he had been a leader in killing Christians. As he wrote this passage, years after his Damascus road experience, Paul was still surprised that God called him instead of punishing him. To children, this says that if God could want Paul as a disciple after what Paul had done, God must surely want us as disciples, no matter what we have done or how little we think we have to offer.

*Gospel: Luke 5:1-11.* To understand Peter's response in this story, children need to know that he was responding to more than the marvelous catch of fish. Luke tells us that Peter had heard Jesus teach and had watched Jesus in action for a while before this event took place. So on this day, Peter sensed God's presence in all he had seen of Jesus—his loving healing, his demanding teachings, his control of nature. Peter realized, even before Jesus told him, that being Jesus' friend and disciple would not be safe and comfortable, but demanding and life changing. Children are

48

challenged to realize that for them to be Jesus' disciples (as Peter was) also will be exciting, demanding, and life changing.

## Watch Words

Take this opportunity to help children define the word *holy*—used only in religion and profanity today, and one of those words defined by words that are even less definable. *Holy* describes the separateness and perfection of God. Some child-sized words that describe *holiness* include *pure, awesome, respected, perfect,* and *unique* (as in a class by itself). If the Revised Standard Version or King James Version of the Bible are used often in your congregation, discuss what it means to "fear" God because God is *holy*. Remember—one sign of God's holiness that is important in today's text is that God does not flaunt (is not "stuck up" about) being *holy* when dealing with us, who are so *unholy*.

## Let the Children Sing

*Hymns of Praise and Adoration:* "Holy! Holy! Holy!" reflects Isaiah's vision and is first choice. With a little coaching, even nonreaders can sing the repeated "Holy! Holy! Holy!" If possible, describe the seraphim before singing this hymn and alert the children to their presence in the hymn. Also consider "For the Beauty of the Earth," "Now Thank We All Our God," or "How Great Thou Art" (if it is familiar to the children).

*Hymns of Commitment or Discipleship:* "Jesus Calls Us," a hymn based on Jesus' call to the fishing disciples, includes some difficult vocabulary. But children can pick up the short, simple phrases at the beginning and end of the verses.

## The Liturgical Child

1. In the major prayer of the day, invite people to pray following the stories from the readings. Use the outline below as introductory prayers for silent or spoken bidding prayers, or as the first lines of leader-stated prayers.

Holy, holy, holy, God! Your power and greatness are more than we can imagine. But like Isaiah and Paul and Peter, we do sense your presence in many ways. Hear each of us as we give thanks for the ways we meet you.

When we think of you, God, we are embarrassed about ourselves. Like Isaiah, we remember our unclean words. Like Paul, we remember our sins. Like Peter, we know how unholy we are. Hear each of us as we confess our sins and unworthiness.

We are grateful that you did not punish Isaiah or Paul or Peter, but called them to serve you. So we offer ourselves to do your will. Hear our prayers about the work we are doing in your name and the work you want us to do.

2. *Charge and Benediction:* When God asked, "Whom shall I send?" Isaiah replied, "Here am I. Send me." When Peter said, "I am unworthy," Jesus replied, "Follow me and you will catch men." And when God stopped Paul on his way to kill Christians, it was to send him to tell the Good News to foreigners. They went and did God's work.

Today, I charge you, in Jesus' name, to go into your schools, neighborhoods, and workplaces, to love people as God has loved you and to tell the Good News. As you go, remember God's promises that you will know what to say and do and that God will be with you always.

## Sermon Resources

1. Challenge the children to listen carefully to the Isaiah reading and then draw a picture of what Isaiah saw. Describe the seraphim in the beginning of the sermon to give the children input. Be ready to respond to their drawings as the children leave the church.

2. Talk about how we feel God's presence and power. Isaiah felt it in the Temple. Paul felt it in Jesus' death and resurrection. Peter felt it in Jesus' teachings and power over nature. Invite the children to draw pictures of the places and ways they sense God's presence and power. Respond to the drawings as the children leave the sanctuary.

3. Compare the flow from adoration to confession, to commitment, in each of today's three stories, to the flow of your morning worship service. Direct worshipers to the parts of worship in your printed order of worship, challenging them to see in every Sunday's worship the possibility of experiences like those of Isaiah, Paul, and Peter.

Use the decoder to find out what Isaiah said to God.

" 8 5 18 5    1 13 9 .

__ __ __ __ __ .

19 5 14 4    13 5 .

__ __ __ __ __ __ .

Isaiah 6:8

Decoder:
A=1  G=7   M=13  S=19  Y=25
B=2  H=8   N=14  T=20  Z=26
C=3  I=9   O=15  U=21
D=4  J=10  P=16  V=22
E=5  K=11  Q=17  W=23
F=6  L=12  R=18  X=24

Answer: Here am I. Send me.

Draw a picture or write a prayer about what God is sending you to do this week.

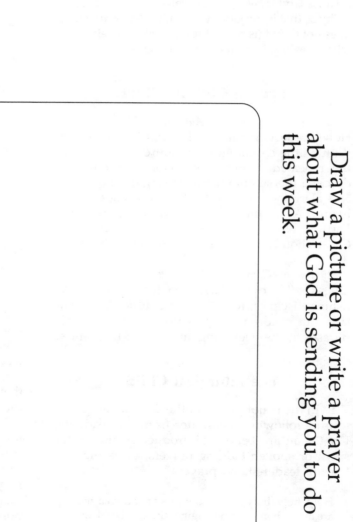

*Fifth Sunday after Epiphany / © 1991 by Abingdon Press.*

# SIXTH SUNDAY AFTER EPIPHANY

## From a Child's Point of View

*Old Testament: Jeremiah 17:5-10 and Psalm 1.* These passages give us one simple message: It is better, and even more rewarding, to be good than it is to be bad. Adults immediately sense problems with this simplification. But studies of the moral development of children indicate that the passages are on target for them. Young children accept rules as the unquestionable mandate of the always-correct all-powerful adults. Children make their earliest moral decisions—to obey or to disobey the rules—to avoid punishment. Growing beyond that, they obey in order to gain reward and pleasure. As older children realize that rules are not irrefutable but can be negotiated, they begin to obey in order to gain the respect and rewards of the group—to be thought of as a "good" boy or girl. Therefore, the clear delineation of the behavior of and rewards for "the good" and "the bad" in these passages speaks to children where they are in their development and forcefully challenges them to act like God's *good* people, thus reaping rewards and/or gaining the prestige of being known as one of God's people.

Second, although their mental development keeps them from fully appreciating the images in these passages, children can respond to the question, "Would you rather be a big leafy pear tree beside a cool river, or a dry leafless bush in a desert?" and accept the two examples as appropriate signs (like national flags) for the "good" people and the "bad" people.

*Gospel: Luke 6:17-26.* Verses 20-26 parallel the two Old Testament readings but add this insight: Sometimes it does not look as if it is better to be good than to be bad. The promise in these verses is that though this may seem to be true at the moment, eventually God will see that the good prosper. So children are challenged to put up with being called names or laughed at for doing what they know is right on the playground, in the classroom, or even with brothers and sisters at home.

Note: Working with these passages on the children's level provides the opportunity to challenge adults to cut through all the complications of modern ethical decision-making in order to remember that we are called simply to be God's good people.

*Epistle: I Corinthians 15:12-20.* This is the first of three consecutive readings in I Corinthians 15 related to the resurrection. Each reading offers a slightly different message for children. None of the readings is closely connected to the other readings of the day.

Although the complex sentences and involved logic of this passage are hard for children to follow, the message—that Christ has risen and that we will rise—is simple. Children will be less interested in Paul's insistence that Christ's resurrection and ours are linked than in the truth that God's love and care go beyond death. God did not allow death to be the end of Jesus, and God will not let death be the end of us. We can trust God to love us and care for us *always*—even beyond death.

## Watch Words

Choose words that emphasize the value of being among the good, rather than heaping judgment and curses upon the bad.

51

Avoid obsolete words such as *scoffers* and *mockers* to describe the wicked. The Good News Bible offers some good alternatives in Psalm 1.

*Resurrection* is a long word and a difficult concept. Devote the sermon to defining the word, using it again and again. Or talk instead about how God cares for us even after we die and does not let death be the end of us.

## Let the Children Sing

Sing "God of Grace and God of Glory" to celebrate being God's good people and ask for help to serve God well. Encourage younger children to join in on the line "Grant us wisdom, grant us courage" in each verse.

"I Sing a Song of the Saints of God" also celebrates God's good people and calls us to commit ourselves to be among the good people.

Both "The Lord's My Shepherd, I'll Not Want," which will be recognized by most children as Psalm 23 set to music, and "God Will Take Care of You," which repeats the simple phrase of its title, celebrating God's love, which continues even beyond death.

## The Liturgical Child

1. At the front of the sanctuary, place a lush, leafy, flowering plant and a dead branch stuck in a flower pot of sand. The person who provides flowers might enjoy the challenge of creating this display.

2. Have Jeremiah's sayings, Psalm 1, and the blessings and woes in Luke read by a pair (or three pair) of readers, standing in opposite lecterns or on opposite sides of the chancel (to emphasize the difference between the good and the bad people). Consider asking some fifth- or sixth-graders to prepare these readings.

| | |
|---|---|
| Jeremiah 17: | Reader 1: verses 5-6 |
| | Reader 2: verses 7-8 |
| | Readers 1 and 2 (in unison) |
| | or Reader 3: verses 9-10 |
| Psalm 1: | Reader 1: verses 1-3 |

| | |
|---|---|
| | Reader 2: verses 4-5 |
| | Reader 1: verse 6*a* |
| | Reader 2: verse 6*b* |
| Luke 6: | Reader 1: verses 20-23 |
| | Reader 2: verses 24-26 |

To highlight the similarity in these passages, read them continuously rather than interspacing them with songs and prayers.

## Sermon Resources

1. The key issue in the three related texts is that we all have choices to make and that God wants us to make good, loving choices. Tell stories about children who make choices about doing or not doing what they have been told to do, about families that decide how to work and play together, and about people of all ages who make decisions about helping or not helping others (e.g., deciding who to sit with in the lunchroom or on the bus, how to reach out to a child who is cut out by the others, etc.).

2. To explore I Corinthians 15:12-20, tell stories of people who seemed to be beyond God's help or care, but found they were not. Tell of the Hebrew slaves trapped between the Egyptian army and the sea; of Noah in the ark, floating on the destroying flood; of people today who have found hope in the face of death and new life in hopeless situations. Be sure to include the story of Jesus' arrest, trial, torture, and death, followed by resurrection.

Three of our lections call us to take a stand with God's good people. The fourth is a statement of faith about the resurrection. Therefore the Worship Worksheet focuses on creeds, one way we take a stand in worship. Consider using the Apostles' Creed this week. Be sure to note the location in your hymnbook of any creed you use, so that children and their parents can find it easily.

One way to worship God is to say a creed.

**Creed** means . . .
I believe.
I think.
This is what I know.

Look in your bulletin for a creed or affirmation of faith (a fancy way to say creed). If the creed is in your hymnbook, look it up.

Now you are ready to say "I believe" with everyone in your church.

Be proud. Stand tall.
Say the words clearly.

The **Apostles' Creed** has been said by Christians for hundreds of years. Find it in your hymnbook. (Hint: Look in the Table of Contents.)

Hidden below are 7 things we say that we believe when we say the Apostles' Creed. Can you find all of them?

```
J E S U S C H R I S T Q
X V A B Q C T E N P T Q
L E O L H P T S B X T Q
Z R A G O D Q U B C T Q
K L K N L P D R M H T Q
G A T H Y B N R Q U T Q
Z S S B G R S E P R T Q
S T B R H M N C K C T Q
B I A C O C B T T H T Q
F N Z X S G L I M N T Q
R G S T T V W O Z B T Q
C L D F G H J N K Q T Q
X I R Q K N M R T S T Q
P F O R G I V E N E S S
D E D C R I O E P Z T Q
```

# SEVENTH SUNDAY AFTER EPIPHANY

## From a Child's Point of View

*Old Testament: Genesis 45:3-11, 15.* Children with brothers or sisters are fascinated by the story of Joseph and his brothers. Few have considered selling their siblings (but most can enjoy day-dreaming about life without them). Although many children believe their siblings are mean and obnoxious, few would expect them to go to the lengths that Joseph's brothers did. One message for children, especially those whose parents are pressuring them to get along better with brothers and sisters, is simply that sibling rivalry is real. It is comforting to know that at least one biblical family was meaner than we are.

Thus reassured, children can hear the amazing fact that Joseph actually forgave his brothers and saved their lives. Joseph could forgive them because he was sure that God loved him and had a plan for his life. He knew that no problem—not even being sold by his brothers—could stop God's love or get in the way of God's plan. In psychological terms, Joseph had such good self-esteem that he could endure vicious attacks by friends and family as passing setbacks, rather than as the final word on his worth.

The challenge to preachers is not to bully children into following Joseph's example, but to instill in them such a sense of God's love that they will be able to see the frustrating events and people of their lives in the way Joseph saw such things in his life.

*Psalm 37:1-11.* This is a psalm Joseph could have sung. It is a psalm for those days when everything is going wrong and it seems that everyone is out to get you. Because each short statement in the psalm makes sense on its own, children can hear and respond to one phrase, or to the whole psalm. If your children recognize Yahweh as a name for God, read the strong translation in The New Jerusalem Bible.

*Gospel: Luke 6:27-38.* If verses 37-39 are read first, the opening verses of this passage make more sense. If you do not judge or condemn and are ready to forgive, you limit the number of people you consider your enemies. That is what Joseph did. He refused to judge his brothers. As one poster summarizes it, "The best way to get rid of an enemy is to make a friend." The challenge to children is to identify ways to think about and then treat their "enemies" as friends.

*Epistle: I Corinthians 15:35-38, 42-50.* This passage might be titled, "What will happen when I die?" For children, the question is, "What happened to Grandpa (or another loved person or pet) when she or he died?" Because few children understand the reality of their own death, their concern is more for the loved person or pet they have lost than for their own future.

Paul's picture of a seed and the plant that grows from it stretches children's mental abilities, but it can make sense to them—especially if parallel examples of things that grow and change in predictable ways are cited. The bottom line is that after death, we will be as different as a plant is different from a seed, but we will maintain our uniqueness, just as one kind of plant always grows from the same kind of seed. For children, this means that Grandpa is OK. God is still taking care of Grandpa, and Grandpa is experiencing a wonderful new kind of life. The interpretation also leaves room for us to miss (grieve for) those we love who have died.

## Watch Words

There are few word traps in Joseph's story.

Beware of comparing *mortal* to *immortal* and *physical* bodies to *spiritual* bodies. Ghosts, fairies, and other magical creatures in children's literature and television inhabit a confusingly separate, yet present territory for children. Therefore, it is easier to communicate Paul's point through the seed images than through these adjectives.

## Let the Children Sing

*Sing of Trusting God's Care and Plan:* "God Will Take Care of You" has a chorus children may know from church school. "The King of Love My Shepherd Is" is a good choice *if* the children know Psalm 23 well. Explain *balm* before singing "There Is a Balm in Gilead." Nonreading children often hear "There is a *bomb* in Gilead."

## The Liturgical Child

1. Introduce Psalm 37 as an alphabet psalm (an acrostic) for the days when everything is going wrong. Prepared readers (possibly older children) then flip up the appropriate Hebrew letter card before reading one stanza each.

| | | |
|---|---|---|
| Aleph | (א) | — verses 1-2 |
| Beth | (ב) | — verses 3-4 |
| Gimel | (ג) | — verses 5-6 |
| Daleth | (ד) | — verse 7 |
| He | (ה) | — verses 8-9 |
| Waw | (ו) | — verses 10-11 |

2. The vocabulary with which Jesus' question is posed in Luke 6 is different in various translations. Choose the one that will make most sense to your children.

3. Pray about family relationships today. Offer worshipers a chance to pray silently for each member of their family—especially brothers and sisters. Or pray about the changes that happen in our lives as we are born, grow up, and die. Provide opportunities to pray for people at different stages of life and for those facing changes as they grow.

## Sermon Resources

1. Today's texts assume that worshipers know the whole story of Joseph. Since many children (and adults) do not know the complete story, devote sermon time to telling the story of Joseph, placing emphasis on Joseph's self-understanding. Then use the related texts to explore the story's significance.

Try telling the story in sections. Conclude each section by saying a Refrain or inviting the congregation to do so. Consider the outline below:

Tell about the "braggy" boy who was sold into slavery. As he trudges off in slave chains, he thinks of his brothers and says,

(Refrain) I know God loves me and has a plan for me. It was not you who sent me here, but God.

Tell about Joseph the dream-explaining friend, who was forgotten in prison. As he sits alone, he thinks of the released friend and says,

(Refrain) I know God loves me and has a plan for me. It was not you who sent me here, but God.

Tell about Joseph the good slave, who was framed by his owner's wife and sent to prison. As the prison doors close, he thinks of his owners and says,

(Refrain) I know God loves me and has a plan for me. It was not you who sent me here, but God.

Tell about Joseph the powerful brother, who welcomed and cared for the brothers who had sold him. Paralleling today's text, he tells his brothers,

(Refrain) I know God loves me and has a plan for me. It was not you who sent me here, but God.

2. Joseph's dreams and special clothes made his brothers angry. Some of the things that cause sibling fights today are (1) messing with each other's room or possessions; (2) embarrassing each other in front of friends; (3) sensing that another child is getting better treatment from parents (older children see the younger ones as pampered pets, while younger children complain that the older ones get to do all the "good stuff" they are not allowed to do); (4) squabbling over goodies, from cookies to gifts to clothes. Tell stories about such situations to bring Joseph's situation home today.

3. To illustrate Paul's image, bring a seed and a plant (perhaps an acorn from an oak tree in the churchyard) and a picture of yourself as a baby, to compare to yourself as an adult.

Draw a picture of your family or write the name of each person in your family.

Talk to God in prayer about each person in your family.

The hymn "There Is a Balm in Gilead" promises that one day God will heal all our frustrations. Write a verse or draw a picture about one of your frustrations.

Idea: The writer of this hymn wished he could preach like Peter or pray like Paul. Write a verse or draw a picture of something you wish you could do as well as someone else does.

# EIGHTH SUNDAY AFTER EPIPHANY

## From a Child's Point of View

Today's texts can be related to one another in a variety of ways. One way that has significant potential for children is that each text expresses confidence in the power, care, and love of God. The psalm celebrates being able to sing praises to God. Isaiah notes the trustworthiness of God's Word. Paul rejoices that God's love and power go beyond death. Luke 6 provides the "therefore," with several suggestions about obeying God and God's Word.

*Old Testament: Ecclesiasticus 27:4-7 or Isaiah 55:10-13.* The New Jerusalem Bible offers a beautiful translation of the Ecclesiasticus passage, which explains that what we say shows us for what we are. However, even in this clear translation, the only comparison easily grasped by children is that of the orchard. Still, if explanations of the function of sieves and kilns are included, children can explore the need to discipline our speech.

Isaiah's personification of God's Word is also hard for children to understand. The best use of this passage is to compare what God's Word tells about God (in this text) to what our human words tell about us (in Ecclesiasticus and Luke 6:43-45).

*Psalm 92:1-4, 12-15.* Verses 1-4 of this sabbath psalm of praise celebrate the joy of singing praises to God. Children can follow easily and share in the praising. If you explored the bush symbols in Proper 1, children will enjoy recognizing the repeat of the image in verses 12-15.

*Gospel: Luke 6:39-49.* Each of these teachings of Jesus involves a vivid image which must be understood in order to get Jesus' point.

Of all the sayings, the one about the fruits of the bush is plainest to children. In the polarized language of Proper 1, good bushes bear good fruit and good people do and say good things. Bad bushes bear bad fruit and bad people do and say bad things. This standard is not to be used to evaluate others, but to encourage us to say and do the good things that will number us among God's good people.

Using the same language, children can see that it is better to live in a strong, flood-resistant house than in a flimsy one. The houses will become "flags" (like the healthy and barren bushes) for the good and bad people. The understanding of faith as a kind of dwelling place will come in later years.

Be careful about the splinter/log comparison. The mental picture of a person with a log in her eye trying to get a splinter out of someone else's eye amuses children. But at this point in their mental development, few children can move beyond the funny picture to Jesus' point about judgment.

*Epistle: I Corinthians 15:51-58.* This summary of chapter 15 is filled with too many strange symbols, abstract words, and detailed theological concepts to be understood by children as it is read. What children can hear and respond to is the mood of happy conviction that we do not need to fear death or worry about loved ones who have died. The powerful and loving God is in control of our deaths and will carry us through. If this message is presented simply to children before they can interpret the details of the passage, as their mental abilities grow, they will find in the passage a confirmation of what they already know.

## Watch Words

Vocabulary should not present any problems today—unless you focus on resurrection. If you do, remember that *resurrection* needs to be used with several short, simple words and phrases such as "after we die" and "a new kind of life."

## Let the Children Sing

"Come Christians Join to Sing" and "All Creatures of Our God and King" reflect both the psalm and Epistle readings, and offer every worshiper a chance to sing—at least the Alleluias.

## The Liturgical Child

1. If the flowering plant and dead branch are still available from the sixth Sunday After Epiphany, display them again. Refer to the display to:

- Illustrate Psalm 92. Point to the display, recalling its significance before reading the psalm.
- Recall the comparison of the bushes from Proper 1 to set the stage for a discussion of Luke 6:43-45.
- Remind children of the bush "flags" of Proper 1 in order to introduce today's "flags," the two houses.

2. Use Psalm 92:1-4 as a Call to Worship, followed immediately by "Come Christians, Join to Sing" as a parallel hymn of praise.

3. Invite five readers of a variety of ages to read one of the wise sayings of Jesus from the Gospel lesson. Each reader begins by saying, "Hear what Jesus said . . .":

Reader 1: verse 39
Reader 2: verse 40
Reader 3: verses 41-42
Reader 4: verses 43-45
Reader 5: verses 46-49

## Sermon Resources

1. In the children's classic *Charlotte's Web*, Charlotte, the spider, faces her life and death with an attitude that Paul would recognize and approve. Cite Charlotte as an example or tell part of her story. Chapters 21 and 22 include a conversation between Wilbur, the pig, and Charlotte about her death and the account of her death.

2. To help children sense the security Paul feels in facing death, tell stories about doing new, rather scary things with a trusted friend who has already done these things. Talk about going down a steep hill on a sled, riding a roller coaster, or going away to camp. Having an experienced friend along does not erase all the fears, but it helps. Similarly, dying with Jesus, our experienced, resurrected friend, is not so scary. We can trust him as we go into a new, unknown experience.

3. At the beginning of the sermon, challenge older children to work the puzzle on the worksheet and to listen for each of the words in the sermon. Then be sure to use the words when speaking about our confidence in God.

4. Be an artist. Use the praise-poem outline on the Worship Worksheet as the format for your sermon. Make it a six-point sermon. Introduce each point in a sentence that begins with one of the letters of PRAISE, then expound on it. At the end of the sermon, summarize your points by reading the entire poem. As the children leave the sanctuary, take a moment to respond to any poems they have written.

# PRAISE GOD!

Write a praise psalm. For each letter in the word **praise**, write one sentence praising God.

**P** _____

**R** _____

**A** _____

**I** _____

**S** ing to God because _____

**E** _____

God loves us always.
God takes care of us always.
Nothing is more powerful than God.

Follow the word trails to find 5 words we use in worship to talk about God.
Shade the letters as you find them.

1. _____

2. _____

3. _____

4. _____

5. _____

Answers: 1. confidence  2. rely  3. believe
4. faith  5. trust

# LAST SUNDAY AFTER EPIPHANY/TRANSFIGURATION OF THE LORD

## From a Child's Point of View

We seldom choose to tell children the two stories that are the focal point of today's texts because they lead children to ask uncomfortably unanswerable questions:

Why did God speak to Moses and not to the others? Was God playing favorites?

If I were really in the presence of God, would my face shine? I love God, so how come my face doesn't shine?

Why doesn't the face of anyone in our church shine? Is it because we are not good enough, or was this a special magic trick God did for Moses and Jesus? Did it really happen that way?

Few answers to such questions will satisfy literal-minded children. Children can, however, become familiar with these strange, interesting stories and explore a few key ideas that may seem unrelated to the stories now but will prove related as the children grow older.

*Old Testament: Exodus 34:29-35.* Children are better able to follow the story if they know that Moses had been on the mountain talking with God for forty days and was bringing back the Ten Commandments written on stone. (The Good News Bible translation is clearest about what Moses was carrying.)

The unstated message of this story is that if you live in God's presence, it will make a difference that others will notice. Moses' shiny face can be seen by adults as a symbol of his attitude toward life and his behavior. While children cannot make this connection, they can understand that know-ing God will make a noticeable difference in their lives. Because they know God loves them, they will love others. Their actions will reflect God's love. As their symbol-making powers grow, they will see a natural connection between this truth and Moses' shiny face.

*Epistle: II Corinthians 3:12–4:2.* Paul uses Moses' veil as a symbol of all the things we let come between us and God. Paul's argument requires more knowledge of Jews and the Law than children have. But if you restate Paul's message without the first-century details, children can hear Paul's warning not to let anything come between us and knowing God. For children, this means making time to be at church with God's people (because that is one good place to meet God), learning more about God by reading the Bible, and praying (sharing with God) with others and alone.

*Gospel: Luke 9:28-36.* On their first hearing, this story simply says to children that Jesus was special. God showed this with the light and the spoken message. That understanding is a fine place to start living with this story. Older children, if they know who Elijah and Moses were, can learn from this story that God was present with Jesus when he faced a hard task—going to Jerusalem to die. Knowing that God was present to comfort and encourage Jesus, children can be led to expect that God will be present to comfort and encourage them when they face difficult tasks. It would be helpful, however, to point out some phenomena in which we sense God's presence, other than light and voice messages (e.g., God comforting us through the words and presence of other people; a feeling deep inside that God is with us; remembering a Bible verse or singing a song about God).

*Psalm 99.* This psalm celebrates the God who shines around Moses and Jesus. To really understand the psalm, one needs to be familiar with Old Testament enthronement language and practices, and to know who Moses, Aaron, Samuel, and Jacob were. Few children do.

However, if children hear this passage introduced as a psalm that praises God, the King of the whole universe, and then are urged to listen carefully to hear what kind of king God is, they can share in the confident mood of the psalm and probably can understand some of the phrases.

## Watch Words

*Transfiguration* has become so obsolete that its dictionary definition refers only to this story about Jesus. It is easy and advisable to explore all the passages without using that word at all. If your tradition names this day of the church year Transfiguration of the Lord, let the term stand as the name of a specific day, rather than try to explain it as a description of what happened to Jesus.

## Let the Children Sing

"O Wondrous Sight! O Vision Fair" retells the story of the Transfiguration in fairly simple concrete language.

"Take Time to Be Holy" allows us to sing in short phrases about everyday ways to be close to God.

## The Liturgical Child

1. Read the Old Testament and Gospel lessons back to back. Invite the congregation to hear two stories that are very similar. Then read the Old Testament and Gospel stories in your best storyteller style. If you spend "time on the steps" with the children, take the lectern Bible with you and read both lessons there.

2. After introducing it as an enthronement psalm and inviting the congregation to imagine they are in a huge crowd, greeting "God, the King of the Universe," read Psalm 99 responsively. Arrange verses 1-4 and 6-8 in short phrases for responsive reading by alternate halves of the congregation. Plan to read verses 5 and 9 in unison. If there are two worship leaders, have one read with each half of the congregation to keep the pace upbeat and make the readings sound like crowd shouts.

3. Base the prayer of confession for the day on the ways we put a veil between ourselves and God. Children and adults "keep the veil up" when we (1) keep too busy with sports, homework, and television to participate in activities in which we might meet God; (2) avoid activities in which we might meet God, for fear our friends, or even our families might think we are weird and laugh at us; and (3) not even try to meet God because we are not sure how to do it and do not know what it would be like (i.e., we are scared).

Note: Children need to hear the lessons for the day before they can join in this prayer with understanding.

## Sermon Resources

1. When two-year-old Jessica McClure was trapped in a well for hours, rescue teams heard her singing Sunday school songs over the microphone they had dropped down the well to monitor her. No one knows for sure what was going on in her mind, but a legitimate case can be made that she sang those songs to comfort herself by remembering times she felt safe and loved—by others and even by God.

2. Invite worshipers to think about times they have sensed God's presence. Share some of your own stories. Be sure to include at least one story from your childhood. For example, I remember sitting on my mother's bed with my brother and sisters to learn the Lord's Prayer. When I peeked at Mother as we were praying together, I felt that she loved God very much and I knew deeply that God loved all of us.

3. Early in the sermon, encourage children to draw pictures of times they have sensed God's presence with them. Be ready to respond to these pictures as the children leave the sanctuary.

Listen carefully when Luke 9:28-36 is read. Draw a picture of what happened in this story.

You may want to read the story again in your Bible to remember the details.

Write a story or draw a picture about a time you felt God very close to you.

*Last Sunday after Epiphany* / © *1991 by Abingdon Press.*

# FIRST SUNDAY OF LENT

The Common Lectionary provides one set of readings for both Ash Wednesday and Good Friday. Year C (this book) provides material for Good Friday. Year A will provide ideas for Ash Wednesday.

## From a Child's Point of View

*Gospel: Luke 4:1-13.* Each of the three temptations Jesus faced invites a rich variety of interpretations. To children, the first temptation is the temptation to use our power to get what we want. Jesus' temptation, and that of many poor children today, is to be sure to get enough. For other children the temptation is to go for the biggest cookie, the lion's share of the fries, the prettiest dresses on the rack, and the best toys on the block. Jesus' response to this temptation is to remind himself that a life centered on being sure that we get the things we want and need is not much of a life (or will be a lonely, unhappy life, even if we do get most of the goodies).

The second temptation is to be "king of the world"—to get one's own way. In responding to this temptation, Jesus completely ignores the fact that he would have made the very best king of the world ever. Instead, he insists that he is not king of the world—God is. Therefore he will obey God's rules and do God's will. We are called to do the same when we are tempted to make everyone play the game we want to play, go to our favorite restaurant to eat, or watch the television show or video we want to see.

The third temptation for children is the temptation to use our skills and powers to be the center of attention—to show off. Jesus could have used his power to do showy miracles and great feats. Instead, he used it to heal and take care of others. We can use our brains to get the best grades in the class and win all the awards. Or we can use our brains to learn about God's world and find ways to be friends with others. Similarly, we can use our athletic abilities or musical talents to impress others, or we can use them to help everyone have a good time together. Whatever our talents or power may be, we are to use them with as much love and concern for others as Jesus did.

*Old Testament: Deuteronomy 26:1-11.* Children will not quickly understand this passage. The contradictory repetition of the ritual action is hard to follow, and the story recited in the creed probably will not be recognized without help—even by those who are familiar with the Exodus saga. But this is one case in which providing the needed help is well worth the effort—especially for older children.

Ten- to twelve-year-olds are very interested in the groups to which they belong. Many of them define themselves in terms of these groups: I am an American, one of the Jones family, a Scout—even one of God's people. Being part of a significant group that is "bigger than me" is appealing to these children. They appreciate the possibility of claiming the story of the group as "my" story and letting that story influence the way they act and the things they value. This passage invites children to claim the story of God's people as their story and to let it shape their lives.

*Epistle: Romans 10:8b-13.* The message of this passage for the children is that God saves and protects all who believe and will say so. The only way to be cut out of God's love is to say we do not want it. Conversely, if we do not stand up for God in what we say every day, we cut ourselves off from God. You will need to present these truths in your own words; Paul's words are too complicated for the children.

*Psalm 91:9-16.* Many children, especially those who have had fortunate lives thus far, hear this psalm simply as praise for God's care. But other alert, literal-minded children will question the relationship between this psalm and reality as they know it. There are no satisfying answers for these children. Explaining the text's probable source as a psalm for a king going into battle, or its use by Satan to tempt Jesus, may help adults, but it will not answer the children's questions. So it may be best to read the passage and let it stand as is until the children are older.

## Watch Words

*Confess,* to most children, means to admit wrong. In today's creedal lessons, it means to state one's beliefs. Since the word is used in every translation of the Epistle, it would be helpful to redefine *confess* before reading.

## Let the Children Sing

"Lord, Who Throughout These Forty Days," a natural choice for adults, is filled with Elizabethan *didsts,* sin jargon like *penitence,* and concepts such as Passiontide, which are strange to children.

"I Love to Tell the Story" celebrates the way we confess our faith. "For the Beauty of the Earth" confesses God's care in everyday terms. It also might be a good Sunday to sing the profoundly simple confession, "Jesus Loves Me." (No less than Karl Barth quoted this song when asked to summarize his faith and theology.)

## The Liturgical Child

1. Present the Deuteronomy passage dramatically. As a narrator begins reading the passage from a lectern, a person (possibly wearing a simple tunic) walks forward to the worship center carrying a basket of fruit and vegetables, and places the basket on or in front of the table. At the appropriate time, he or she faces the congregation to recite verses 5b-10, and leaves as the narrator completes the reading.

2. To parallel the Deuteronomy passage and to link our stewardship to our confessions of faith, plan for the congregation to say a creed (perhaps the storytelling Apostle's Creed) at the time the offering for the day is brought forward to be dedicated.

3. Lead the people in praying silently about their temptations. Give instructions such as those below, leaving silence between each one.

> As we come before God, let each of us pray. We each have long lists of things we want and think we need. Let us tell God about these things and ask God to help us avoid the temptations in them. (Pause)
>
> We all want our own way. We act as though we are king or queen of the world. Let us tell God the truth about how we try to get our own way at home and work and school. (Pause)
>
> Each of us has talents and abilities and gifts. Thank God for yours, and talk with God about the way you use those gifts to care for others, rather than to make yourselves look good. (Pause, then invite the congregation to join in the Lord's Prayer.)

## Sermon Resources

1. To recall the Exodus story, the base of the Deuteronomic creed, show a series of large teaching pictures that illustrate the story. (Look for these in church school closets.) Take the pictures into the congregation one at a time as you review the story during the sermon. In an informal congregation, the worshipers might tell the stories of some of the pictures. In formal congregations, the worshipers will enjoy a close look at the pictures as the preacher tells the stories.

During the rest of the sermon, challenge the children to draw pictures of events in their own faith stories—something that has happened at church, or a time when they felt God was taking care of them. Or they could draw their own version of one of the pictures you showed. Respond to the children's pictures as they leave the sanctuary at the end of worship.

2. Bring three props: a credit card (gold, if possible)—for wealth; a crown (check the Christmas costumes)—for power; and a foil-covered star—for fame. Display each prop on the pulpit as you preach about that temptation, to help the children tune in, at least briefly, on each of the three main points of the sermon.

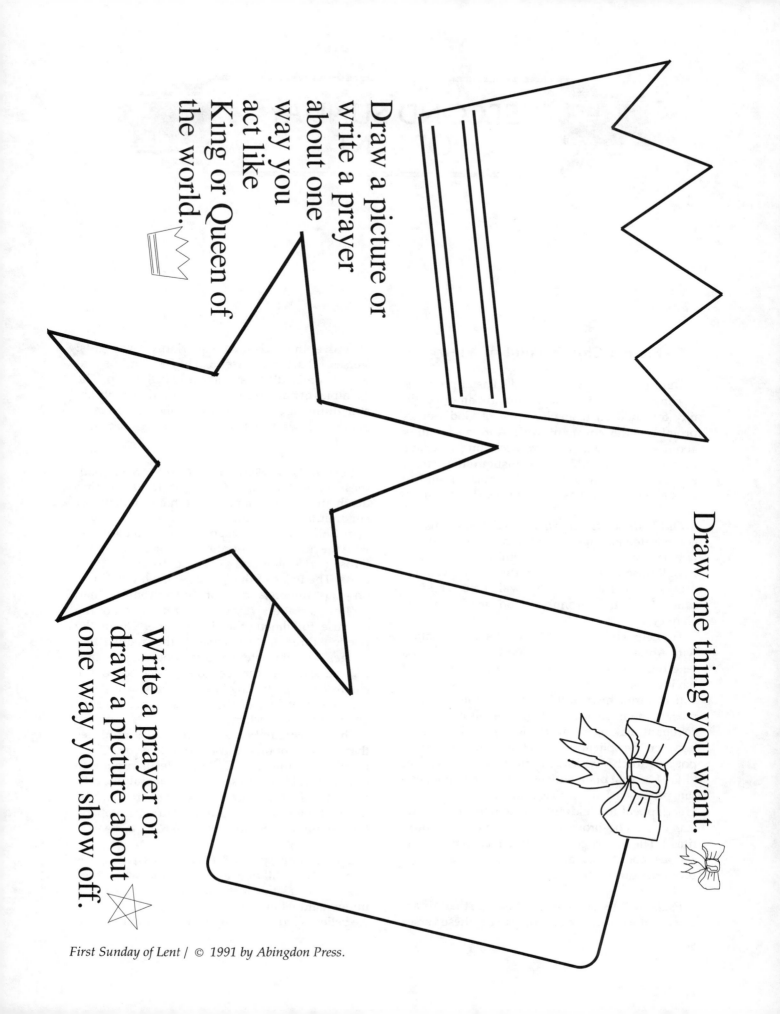

Draw a picture or write a prayer about one way you act like King or Queen of the world.

Draw one thing you want.

Write a prayer or draw a picture about one way you show off.

*First Sunday of Lent* / © 1991 *by Abingdon Press.*

# SECOND SUNDAY OF LENT

## From a Child's Point of View

During Lent we wait for God's Easter promises to come true. Today's texts provide an opportunity for children to explore one of God's other promises—the covenant with Abram—to think about what it means to live according to God's promises (Psalm 127, the Transfiguration story, and Paul's challenge to the Philippians), and to look ahead to the Easter promises (Luke 13).

*Old Testament: Genesis 15:1-12, 17-18.* This is a complicated passage for children, but a part of the familiar story of God's promises to Abram. Recalling some of the rest of this story (Abram's moves and Isaac's birth) will help children understand the promises God made in this chapter.

To help children follow God's conversation with Abram, read from the Good News Bible and take time to explain Abram's concern about not having a son.

If children hear nothing else in this reading, most of them will tune in to the details of the gory covenant-making ritual. The idea that God passed between the split animals in the form of a flaming pot and torch—which, in effect, said to Abram, "May I be split open and left to die if I do not keep the promises I have made to you today"—has great appeal to children. (Remember, this is the age of "blood-brother" rituals and tree-house rites.) The message to children is that God is serious about this and other promises. God's promises can be trusted.

*Psalm 127.* Verses 3-5 echo the value that Abram placed on sons. Boys may enjoy using these verses to prove their claimed superiority over girls. Verses 1-2 are more useful. They remind us that we rely on God's trust and care in all we do. The examples of building a house or guarding a city are straightforward and can lead children to create parallel verses about trusting God in their own activities.

*Gospel: Luke 13:31-35 or Luke 9:28-36.* Both these passages look forward to Jesus' coming death and resurrection, and both are difficult for children to understand.

In Luke 13, Jesus responds to Herod's threat with the resolve to continue his ministry and go to Jerusalem to fulfill God's promises by dying on the cross. The focus of this passage, however, is less on Jesus' understanding of God's promises than on Luke's readers' (that's us!) anticipation of the promise fulfillment that is to come. Given the poetic "three-day" language, the mother-hen images, and the references to prophetic history, this anticipation can be communicated to the children best by talking in your own words about the coming of Easter and the importance of Jesus' death and resurrection.

The Transfiguration story in Luke 9 promises that God supports those who live by God's promises. In this case, God gives Jesus support to face his coming death so that he may fulfill God's promises. If you read this passage, review the material for the Last Sunday After Epiphany (Transfiguration Sunday, pp. 60-62).

*Epistle: Philippians 3:17–4:1.* This passage is also hard for children to understand when they hear it read, but with adult help, they can understand its message—that we are to live as if we believe God's promises. If we believe that God is building a kingdom of love, we should live loving lives, rather than selfish lives focused on getting whatever we want at the moment. Good examples of living according to God's promises can be seen in Paul, Jesus, and Abram.

## Watch Words

*Promises*, especially God's promises to Abram, often lead us to speak of *covenants*. For children, covenant terminology may or may not be familiar. So if you use it, take care to provide definitions as you go. Or avoid misunderstandings by staying with the language of *promises*.

## Let the Children Sing

"God Will Take Care of You," which may be listed as "Be Not Dismayed Whate'er Betide," celebrates trust in God's promises. Although many children will not grasp all the language of the verses, the phrase repeated in both the verses and the chorus contains the heart of the message and enables even nonreaders to join in the singing.

"O Wondrous Sight! O Vision Fair" retells the Transfiguration story in song.

## The Liturgical Child

Your presentation of these rather complex passages is crucial to how well children will be able to "hear" them.

1. Before reading the Genesis passage, challenge worshipers (especially the children) to listen for the two promises God made to Abram. Either right after the Scripture reading or during the sermon, identify the promises and their source in the text so that children can check for themselves.

2. To clarify the break in Psalm 127, have two people read it. The first reader reads verses 1-2. The second reader reads verses 3-5. Have them stand so that the second reader can follow the first reader without interruption.

3. When reading Luke 13, imagine that you are an actor portraying the scene in the role of Jesus. Read the narrative lines in a matter-of-fact stage-director voice. Read Jesus' lines with great force to portray the humor when he called Herod an old fox and to communicate Jesus' pain in thinking about Jerusalem.

## Sermon Resources

1. To pave the way for talking about God's promises, cite some of the promises that are crucial to our relationships with one another. Teachers promise to teach their students what is true and important. When we join a sports team, we promise to attend practices and follow the set disciplines so the team has a chance to win. When two people marry, they promise to love and take care of each other and to be a family. Scouts, Indian Guides, and other clubs require that members make promises when they join.

2. Tell stories of several of God's promises, such as the promise of the rainbow, the promise of the Messiah, and the promise of the fulfillment of the kingdom of God's love on earth.

Shade each shape with a * in it to find 3 words you will hear, say, and sing in worship today.

Answers: faith, trust, promises

The psalm writer tells how God's care is needed for a strong house and a safe city. Read the poet's verses. Then, make up your own verses to tell how you need God's care in your life.

If the Lord does not build the house, the work of the builders is useless.

If the Lord does not protect the city, it does no good for the watchmen to stand guard.

If _____
_____ .

If _____
_____ ,
_____ .

IDEAS! Write about God's care for your schoolwork. Or, make up a verse about playing on a team or learning how to play a musical instrument.

*Second Sunday of Lent* / © *1991 by Abingdon Press.*

# THIRD SUNDAY OF LENT

## From a Child's Point of View

*Epistle: I Corinthians 10:1-13.* This passage, a call to repentance, is the centerpiece of today's lections. The message to children is that all of us are to obey God's rules. We all face temptations. God understands that we are not perfect, but God also expects us to try—and try hard—to do what is right. Verse 13 summarizes these points well.

Unfortunately for children (and for many other worshipers), verses 1-11 assume that readers know the complete story of the Exodus and wilderness wanderings. To understand Paul's points in verse 13, children will need to hear these stories in greater detail.

*Gospel: Luke 13:1-9.* Few children give death much general thought. Instead, they respond to specific experiences when their pets and people they know die. Therefore, although few children have considered the possibility that terrible deaths are repayment for terrible sins, many older children will be interested in the examples of death that Jesus cites and the problem they present. (They will, however, need help in fleshing out the sketchy biblical references.) The text also provides an opportunity to speak to the common childhood fear that "I have caused the death of (someone I love) by (something terrible I said or did.)"

It is hard for children to find the point in the parable of the fig tree without some help. In children's words, the parable says that God sets high standards for us but is willing to give us many second chances. The parable can be helpfully recast with coaches, as they decide whether to cut a player from the team.

*Old Testament: Exodus 3:1-15.* Children are fascinated by the idea that God spoke to Moses through a burning bush. In classroom discussions it is often hard to get past speculation about "what it was like" and "how it happened," in order to discuss what God said. Although they seldom admit it, many children wonder why God does not speak to them in such dramatic ways. Children need to be assured that God is not saving special communications for others who are better than they are.

When they do get past the bush to God's conversation with Moses, children appreciate God's plan to rescue the oppressed Hebrew slaves. It is good to know that God does not just watch what is going on but gets involved to change things that need changing. Children who are living in unjust situations appreciate the possibility that God will act to free them. Idealistic older children appreciate that God is doing something for people who need help, and all the children hear that God will not let wrongs (theirs or those of others) go unchallenged. This knowledge gives the call to repentance a sense of urgency.

Aside from today's theme, children are interested in God's name. I AM WHO I AM or I WILL BE WHO I WILL BE sounds like a meaning-filled Indian name. Children, either privately or as part of a backyard club, often adopt such names for themselves. So they are willing to learn what this name says about the God who claimed it.

*Psalm 103:1-13.* This psalm provides security in facing the call to repentance. It promises God's loving forgiveness, even when we do not deserve it. This is good news to people of all ages. Children will, however, need vocabulary help with the sin and forgiveness terms in order to understand many of the phrases.

## Watch Words

Be attentive to the words used to talk, sing, and pray about sin and forgiveness. Many of the traditional words are no longer part of everyday conversation. This means that children need both explanations of and practice in hearing and saying these words in your worship setting.

When speaking of *sin*, use with care the words *transgressions*, *trespasses* (even if your congregation uses the word regularly in the Lord's Prayer), *immorality*, *iniquity*, and *evil*. Remember that for most boys, *offence* is the team with the football and that today's definition of *trespass* is to go uninvited on private land. *Sins* and *wrongs* are just about the only words that require no explanation.

Avoid, when possible, *chide*, *rebuke*, and *requite* to speak of God's judgment of sin. *Punish*, *repay*, and *scold* are actions children recognize.

*Mercy* and *vindication* are not everyday words. And the *redemption* of coupons, the only redemption with which most children are familiar, is not a good parallel to God's activity; *forgiveness* and *pardon* are better words.

## Let the Children Sing

Read hymns about repentance carefully. They are so filled with "sin" jargon that none can be suggested for children without reservation. To help children claim a favorite repentance hymn of your congregation, explore it in the sermon or in a children's time before singing it.

"Let My People Go" is a familiar spiritual that retells the Exodus story. Some of the vocabulary in the verses is obsolete, but the familiar chorus is appealing to children.

"Lord, I Want to Be a Christian" is one song in which all of us can sing our commitment to do better. "O Jesus, I Have Promised" is more complex, but it can be sung by older children with a little encouragement.

## The Liturgical Child

1. Dramatize Exodus 3:1-15:

● Enlist three readers to present the passage: the first reads the narrative verses; the second reads Moses' lines; the third reads God's lines. Omit the "he saids."

● Present the passage as a play. Prepare one actor (perhaps in costume) to take the part of Moses and another actor to read God's part. As you begin reading the passage, "Moses" makes his way to the front of the sanctuary toward a floral burning bush (perhaps a green plant with red blooms). "God" may be visible in another lectern or may read out of sight of the congregation. Follow the dialogue of Exodus. (Ask "Moses" to memorize his part.)

2. Give special attention to regular prayers of confession and pardon in your worship today.

● In your call to confession and assurance of pardon, explain in simple terms what is happening or put into children's language the kyrie or response before the congregation sings it.

● Or use Psalm 103:8-13 as the assurance of pardon, following a prayer of confession.

3. Recite I Corinthians 10:13 as a charge to the congregation before the benediction.

## Sermon Resources

1. Set up a rhetorical form in which to tell the Exodus stories cited in I Corinthians 10:1-13. For example:

God gave the Hebrew slaves freedom . . . (tell about crossing the Sea of Reeds). But did the people trust God and live as God's people after this? No . . . (tell about the grumbling about food). We are not to do as they did.

God gave the Hebrew slaves food in the desert . . . (tell the story of the quail). But did the people trust God and live as God's people after this? No . . . (tell about the grumbling about eating only meat). We are not to do as they did.

(Repeat this format with stories of manna, water, God's presence in the pillar of fire and the cloud, and the giving of the Ten Commandments.)

Break out of this format to explore Paul's call to repentance in verses 12 and 13.

2. Talk about sins of which children are capable: cheating; taking what does not belong to them (especially "borrowing" from brothers and sisters); calling names, teasing, or "cutting someone out"; telling lies (or improving upon the truth) to keep out of trouble or to impress friends; breaking promises; and so on.

Find 8 words about sin and forgiveness. Find 3 people of the Bible named in worship today.

```
C L F Z C H C
O U O B E Y O
N K R L S Y M
F E G G A K M
E S I N V P A
S K V S E A N
S P E Q Z R D
M A N A D M
Q U E B Z O E
L L S D R N N
M O S E S R T
```

Draw a picture or write a prayer to show God one change you want to make this week. You may want to change the way you act. Or, you may want to do something to make life better for another person.

God, I want to change . . .

Amen

*Third Sunday of Lent* / © 1991 by Abingdon Press.

# FOURTH SUNDAY OF LENT

## From a Child's Point of View

*Gospel: Luke 15:1-3, 11-32.* Most church children will be familiar with this story since it is included in much church school curriculum. The message of the story is that God is like a father who keeps on loving his child no matter what the child has done. The promise to children is that nothing they can do is so bad that God will give up on them. Children who feel they never meet their parents' high standards, children who are constantly in trouble with parents and teachers at home and school, and children who do not have loving parents draw special security from this promise-story.

Be careful about using "father" language. Remember that the parable says God is *like* a father, not *is* a father. God is also like a loving mother, an always-there-for-you grandparent, or a special aunt or uncle. To help children stretch their understanding that God is more than any of our images, and to protect those children who do not have loving fathers, avoid phrases which imply that God *is* a father.

Any child who has a brother or sister can appreciate the older brother's position. It always seems that the other one is getting away with murder. Older children feel that younger siblings go to bed later than they did at the same age, are given less demanding chores and rules, and are "let off" more easily when the rules are broken. Frequently, they are right. Parents often learn as they raise a first child that they need not "sweat the small stuff." Expectations of the younger children are relaxed. Family schedules change as the shape and age of the family as a whole change. And of course, different children have different needs. All this is hard for children to see and interpret as fair, loving behavior. It is easy to decide that "they love her more than they do me" and to cry "Unfair!" with the older brother.

The challenge to the preacher is not to convince children that they are equally loved (some are not), but to urge them to be friends with their siblings—even if they are spoiled and petted. Children are not to judge their siblings harshly, but to judge them with love.

*Epistle: II Corinthians 5:16-21.* This is what happens when a trained preacher (Paul) puts the meaning of Jesus' parable into his own words: The simple is made beautifully profound in ten-letter words. Although Paul's big words and complex sentence structure are intimidating at first glance, all that children need in order to understand Paul's message is a good definition of *reconciliation*. The Good News Bible provides the best definition: "God . . . changed us from enemies into his friends and gave us the task of making others his friends also." In other words, God (1) has treated each of us with all the forgiving love the father bestowed on the lost son; and (2) asks us to reach out to other "lost sons" as the father asked the older brother to welcome the returned brother.

*Old Testament: Joshua 5:9-12.* Before reading this passage, remind worshipers of the story and purpose of manna. With this background, children can hear that God kept the promise. God fed the people until they were able to eat the food of the Promised Land.

*Psalm 34:1-8.* This is a praise psalm composed by David after he escaped from Abimelech by pretending to be crazy. It is easy to imagine David safely back with his followers, celebrating his escape and his sanity by creating, on the spot, a verse of praise for God that begins with each letter of the Hebrew alphabet. One can almost hear his followers calling out the letters, with David shouting his verses for them and God to hear. It's a happy picture of spontaneous praise, a good example for children to follow as they learn to praise God every day.

## Watch Words

*Reconcile, reconciliation,* and *reconciling* are key words in these texts, especially in II Corinthians. This word group is worth introducing, defining, and using again and again to build familiarity. The Good News Bible translates these words as phrases about "making enemies into friends." *Peacemaking* and *peacemaker* are good parallel words.

## Let the Children Sing

"For the Beauty of the Earth" and "Now Thank We All Our God" praise the God who is Lord of a world united by love.

"Let There Be Peace on Earth, and Let It Begin with Me" gives us the opportunity to commit ourselves to the ministry of reconciliation.

The words of "In Christ There Is No East or West" and "Blest Be the Tie That Binds" are difficult for children. Make the message of either song visual by asking everyone in the congregation to hold hands or to put a hand on the shoulder of the person holding the hymnbook.

## The Liturgical Child

1. To emphasize the acrostic form of this praise psalm, use two readers. The first simply calls out the Hebrew letter on which each verse is based. The second then reads the verse. The New Jerusalem Bible names the letters for each verse in the margin and offers a clear translation.

2. As the parable is read, have three actors pantomime the action. Although it is possible for children to do pantomiming with some practice, teenage or adult actors can express feelings with their faces and bodies more forcefully and with more insight. The richness of their performances will add to the understanding of worshipers of all ages.

Begin with all three actors at the front of the church. The younger son can "run away" down the middle aisle (perhaps throwing party confetti), "eat with the pigs" near the back of the church, then walk "home to meet his father" in the chancel.

3. If you sing "In Christ There Is No East or West" or "Blest Be the Tie That Binds" as a closing hymn, begin the charge and benediction before hands can be dropped. Say something like this:

God in Christ has changed us from enemies into friends. We are God's friends, and we are friends to one another. Now go out into the world, supported by God's love and the love of your friends in this congregation. Make friends with other people. Reach out in love to draw others into God's worldwide family. Let there be peace on earth, and let it begin with us. Amen.

4. Remember to pray about spring vacations (from school) the week before they occur. Pray for safety, a good time, a chance to be outside, and so on. Remember as you pray that not all children will leave town on exciting trips.

## Sermon Resources

1. Tell stories in which children take the lead in peacemaking. School children in Illinois welcomed AIDS victim Ryan White after another community had forced him and his mother to move. Every summer, Catholic and Protestant children, who would not speak to one another at home in Ireland, visit America together. In the process they form friendships they can use to build understanding between warring groups back home.

2. List some of the sinners God loved and used: tricky Jacob, braggy Joseph, hate-filled Jonah, Saul/Paul, and Jesus' disciples (a temperamental fisherman, a fiery troublemaker, a cheating tax-collector). The stories of these people are further proof of God's love. They challenge us to befriend the "impossible" people we live with at home, at school, and in the community.

3. One verse of "Jesus Loves Me" particularly fits the story of the loving father:

Jesus loves me when I'm good,
When I do the things I should.
Jesus loves me when I'm bad,
Even though it makes him sad.

Paul's message is printed backwards. Reverse the order of the letters and the words to find out what Paul said.

".OSLA SDNEIRF SIH SREHTO

GNIKAM FO KSAT EHT SU EVAG

DNA SDNEIRF SIH OTNI

SEIMENE MORF SU

DEGNAHC TSIRHC

" CHRIST _____

_____

_____

_____

_____

II Corinthians 5:18

Write a prayer about someone who is hard for you to love.
OR
Draw a picture of yourself making friends with a person it is hard to love.

Remember this person as you pray, "forgive us . . . as we forgive others" when you pray the Lord's Prayer.

Fourth Sunday of Lent / © 1991 by Abingdon Press.

# FIFTH SUNDAY OF LENT

## From a Child's Point of View

*Old Testament: Isaiah 43:16-21.* Knowing the historical context of the passage is essential to understanding Isaiah's message. Isaiah was speaking to people who were being carried into exile, to assure them that God would not forget them, that this was part of God's plan, and that a wonderful new deed was going to happen. To fully understand Isaiah's message, listeners must know both the Exodus story and the Exile story. This means that few children will grasp what is going on by simply listening to the reading.

However, if the situation is presented as a leader speaking to people who are being carried away from their homes by a conquering army, the child can understand Isaiah's message of hope. Two dimensions of this message speak particularly to children.

First, children can explore the fact that God is working even in unhappy, awful events. The people suffered as slaves in Egypt before they could go into the Promised Land. The Jews had to go into exile before they could rebuild. Jesus had to die on the cross before there could be a resurrection. This reality is good preparation for walking through the dark events of Holy Week.

Second, children can be alerted to look for signs of God at work around them. If God can be at work among people being led away to exile, certainly God can be at work in classrooms, on playgrounds, and in families.

*Psalm 126.* All the references to the return from exile and the foreign wilderness images make this psalm hard for children to understand. If the psalm is presented using the reading plan in "The

Liturgical Child," some of the older children will catch the flow of the poem—from "God, you rescued us in the past!" to "God, we need your rescue again," to "We know you can do it, God." Otherwise, this is a psalm for older Bible students.

*Gospel: John 12:1-8.* Most children like both giving and receiving gifts. They will work for hours crafting a birthday or Christmas gift for a special friend or loved relative, so naturally they are sensitive about how their gifts are received. This is the story of an exquisite gift of love given by Mary to Jesus, who accepted it and protected her and her gift from Judas' mockery. To children, it says that God accepts and values their gifts, just as Jesus accepted and valued Mary's gift.

Although pouring expensive perfume on a person's feet sounds strange to us today, children can follow the story with little explanation. It will, however, help the younger ones if, before the reading, they hear that this Mary was not Jesus' mother but a special friend who also was named Mary.

*Epistle: Philippians 3:8-14.* This is difficult reading even for adults. Few children will be able to follow Paul's complex sentences and thoughts. Plan to present Paul's message in the sermon. Themes to develop for the children include the following:

1. Paul knew what was important and what was not. Read verses 4-7 for Paul's list of "garbage." For Paul, being Jesus' disciple was the most important thing. He spent his whole life living as Jesus lived—telling others about God, even when that got him into trouble.

2. Paul did not become a missionary evangelist to earn God's love or to impress God. Instead,

Paul traveled and started churches as a gift to God. Just as Mary gave her gift of nard to Jesus because she loved him, Paul showed his love for God by preaching and starting churches.

## Watch Words

The vocabulary in today's readings and themes is fairly simple. Be careful in selecting "exile" and "refugee" vocabulary. *Exile,* especially, may be a new term for the children. Help them decode all the poetic images in Isaiah and Psalm 126. Beware of the temptation to speak about Paul's message in big theological terms such as *sanctification.* If you must use these terms, take care to explain them in everyday-living terms.

## Let the Children Sing

To sing about giving God our gifts, choose "Take My Life and Let It Be Consecrated." (Before singing, define *consecrated* as "a way of saying that we are giving ourselves to God.")

If spring is beginning, sing a hymn of praise to the God of creation—"I Sing the Almighty Power of God" or "All Things Bright and Beautiful."

"Tell Me the Stories of Jesus" is a familiar hymn that is good for the fifth Sunday of Lent.

## The Liturgical Child

1. Present Psalm 126 in three sections, with each being read by a different reader or group within the congregation. Identify the sections by the titles below to help worshipers follow the thinking of the poet:

> Remember (verses 1-3)
> Help! (verses 4-5)
> Hope (verse 6)

2. To set the Isaiah passage in context without going into great historical detail, invite the worshipers to imagine that they are refugees living in a foreign country, wishing they could return home. Then read the passage. (The Jerusalem Bible offers a particularly straightforward translation.)

3. If your worship will be focused on gift giving, place on the worship center a large beautifully wrapped gift box with a slot cut in the top. During the offering or at the end of the service, invite the children to put in the box pictures of what they want to give God. Youths and adults also may be invited to put in the box slips of paper on which they have written about gifts they intend to give God.

## Sermon Resources

1. Devote the sermon to telling the story of the Isaiah passage—perhaps from the view of a Jewish family watching as the nation is being destroyed and the family is taken into exile in a foreign country with new food and new ways. Talk about what different members of the family would miss most. Then read Isaiah's message. Imagine how this message might have been received by the refugees. What comfort could they find in believing their exile was part of a plan that would end in good? Identify and challenge worshipers to identify dead-end places where God could be at work today.

2. Challenge worshipers to think about the best gift they ever received. Tell about one special gift you have received. Who gave it to you? What made it special? (Note: The best gifts draw giver and receiver closer together.) Mary's gift was her way of showing Jesus how much she loved him. Paul showed his love for Christ by preaching, teaching, and even suffering in prison for talking about Jesus. Challenge worshipers to identify the gifts they give and could give to God.

3. Use Eric Liddell's story (Liddell was the hero in the movie *Chariots of Fire*) to illustrate the effect of knowing what is important. Liddell, after training for months to race in the Olympics, refused to run, even when the king insisted, because the race was to be held on Sunday. He believed that racing on Sunday was disrespectful to God. He loved to run, but he knew God was more important than any race.

God said,

Watch for the new thing I am going to do. It is happening already - you can see it now!

(Isaiah 43:19)

Draw or write about something you think God is doing now in your world, your town, or your church. Listen to the sermon for ideas.

Mary gave Jesus perfume. Paul became a missionary as his gift to God and Jesus.

Draw or write about a gift you want to give God.

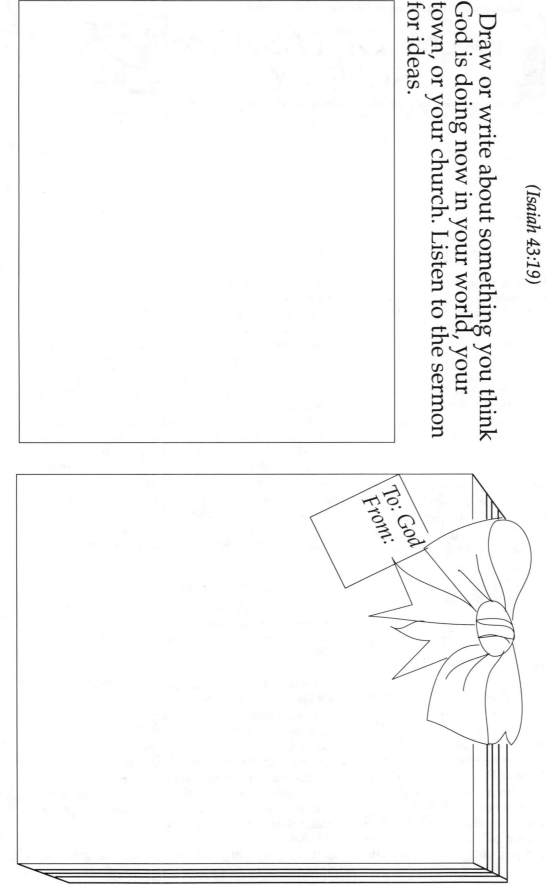

To: God
From:

# PALM OR PASSION SUNDAY

Note: Read all the materials for Holy Week and Easter Sunday now, even those for days on which your congregation does not gather for worship. Material in each section may be useful in preparing for other sections.

In choosing whether to celebrate Palm or Passion Sunday, give special consideration to children. Often children are rushed from the palm processional to the Easter sunrise. Adults hesitate to explore with them the violent Passion events. Many congregations neither expect nor plan for children to participate in Holy Thursday or Good Friday worship. Consequently, because they have not shared in the pain of the betrayals and the crucifixion, children are unable to experience fully the Easter joy. Instead of protecting children from the darkness of the Passion, we diminish the joy of resurrection. So if children will not worship with the Passion story during the week, you would do well to celebrate Passion rather than Palm Sunday.

## From a Child's Point of View

*Gospel: Luke 19:28-40 (Palm).* Luke's account of the triumphal entry mentions neither children, palm branches, nor the word *Hosanna*. The differences in this account and the other Gospel accounts are instructive for careful Bible students. Unfortunately, traditional Palm Sunday hymns include what Luke does not mention, and most worshipers, whether young or old, will "hear" these things in Luke's account anyway. Since there is little for children to gain in recognizing these differences, it is probably best to celebrate

the story of the "combined account" of the Gospels.

The key theme in both Luke's account and the "combined account" is that Jesus is King. Many recent theologians, especially feminists and those in the third world, rightly point to problems in this authoritarian picture of our relationship with Jesus. But children live in a world in which people constantly, and of necessity, tell them what to do and how to do it. A king or teacher or parent is needed for the present. In fairy tales and other children's literature, the king (or queen) is the one who has the right to give the orders, to tell everyone else what to do. This person, like a parent or teacher, is judged bad or good only by the way he or she chooses to use that power.

So the key point of this set of texts is that Jesus, who could have demanded his right to be served by his subjects because he was and is King, chose instead to die for the people he ruled. It is a powerful description of God's love, and a challenging description of how we should treat those we lead when we are the oldest in the group, the patrol leader, the team captain, the class president, and so on.

*Gospel: Luke 22:14–23:56 or 23:1-49 (Passion).* Older elementary school children need basic facts about crucifixion. One fifth-grader, after a very detailed discussion of Roman whips and nails, observed, "The movie I see every year at Aunt Ruth's kind of jumps from Jesus carrying his cross up the hill to the tomb on Easter. I always figured that Jesus was so weak that carrying that cross up the hill had killed him. But he was quite a man to stand all that stuff, wasn't he?" So the gory details do make an important difference.

The betrayal of Judas, Peter's three denials, and

the flight of the other disciples are personal injuries that all children can appreciate. The loyalty of friends, especially best friends like Peter, is highly valued. Most children have experienced painful betrayals by friends. Many have been embarrassed or hurt when a friend told a secret (as Judas told where to find Jesus). Most children have known the disappointment when a friend broke a promise to write from camp or to share a seat on the bus every day (like Peter's boast that he would stick by Jesus always). Although their experiences are minor compared to those Jesus experienced, the pain is similar enough to be meaningful to the children.

*Epistle: Philippians 2:5-11.* The language of this hymn is complicated for children to follow. But its central message speaks clearly to the childhood concern that "I not miss out on anything that is rightfully mine." Often this concern is presented as a demand for justice or fairness, but behind this demand is a drive to get "my share of the goodies." Therefore, the fact that Jesus refused to insist on what was rightfully his is significant. Without getting tangled in how Jesus preexisted with and in God, children can recognize that Jesus should have been treated royally and given the best of everything. Instead, he spent all his time taking care of others.

He healed people, even when it got him into trouble. He made friends with people others ignored or treated badly even when this embarrassed important people. He argued with leaders who claimed that God loved only people who did what the leaders told them to do; Jesus said that God loved everyone. Finally, when he had to choose between being killed and changing his loving ways, he chose to keep on loving. God then raised Jesus from death, made him more powerful, and gave him greater fame than any earthly king ever had.

There are two points in this passage for children. The most important is that Jesus loves each of us enough to give up what rightfully belongs to him in order to care for us. Second, we are called to follow Jesus' example and take care of others rather than worry about whether we are getting everything we deserve.

*Isaiah 50:4-9a, Psalm 118:19-29 (Palm); Psalm 31:9-16 (Passion).* Each of these passages parallels Jesus' Holy Week experience. As each is read, children will catch words and phrases that remind them of either the triumphal entry or the crucifixion. The Gospel or Epistle readings will, however, be the focus of the children's attention.

## Watch Words

The word of the day in hymns and prayers is *Hosanna!* It is a fun word to say and sing because it is a greeting meant only for Jesus.

Be sure the children know the difference between Jesus' *Passion* and the lusty feelings the word *passion* usually describes today. Remember that *crucify* and *crucifixion* are terms children will encounter only in church. Translate big words like *atonement* and *salvation* into short, concrete, everyday words and phrases.

## Let the Children Sing

"All Glory, Laud, and Honor" or "Hosanna, Loud Hosanna" are Palm Sunday hymns that children can sing easily, either as a children's choir or in the congregation.

Sing "This Is the Day" (*The United Methodist Hymnal*) responsively between choir (or leader) and congregation as the Call to Worship.

If you focus on the kingship of Jesus, close with "All Hail the Power of Jesus' Name." Though the ideas in the verses are difficult, the repeated chorus, "Crown him Lord of all!" can be sung by even the youngest worshiper.

"O Sing a Song of Bethlehem" calls us to sing our way from Christmas to Easter in four verses, and thus is a good Passion Sunday hymn to help children connect the baby to the man.

## The Liturgical Child

1. If your worship will include a processional with children carrying palms:

● Provide each child with a palm branch, rather than one strip of palm leaf. (Try to get a mental picture of a crowd waving those stringy palm leaves and laying them on the road for Jesus' donkey to walk on! Those people used full branches.) Most local florists can provide branches for a nominal fee.

● Include the minister(s), choir(s), and others

in the processional so that it isn't a "cute children's thing." Remember that Luke says it was adults who thought of this parade and led the way.

● Instead of processing into the sanctuary at the beginning of worship, before the story can be told, hold the palm processional at the end of worship. By then worshipers will have heard the story and explored its meaning, and now can be challenged to go out into the world to proclaim Jesus as their King. Ushers (perhaps children) can give a palm branch to each worshiper—beginning with the minister(s) and choir(s), then the other worshipers as they leave their pews.

● Suggest that the palms be displayed in homes all Holy Week (perhaps on the dinner table or in a vase on the TV), as a reminder that Jesus is our King.

2. For Passion Sunday, devote the entire service to a "Walk Through Holy Week with Jesus." Alternate Scripture readings with hymns, or sing hymns followed by a prayer. Some of the hymns can be choir anthems:

Triumphal Entry—Luke 19:28-40
Last Supper—Luke 22:7-23
The Betrayal and Arrest—Luke 22:47-53
Trials—Luke 22:66–23:25
Crucifixion and Burial—Luke 23:32-46, 50-56
Summary: Philippians 2:5-11 (This may be the
     base for a very brief meditation.)

Check the Holy Thursday and Good Friday suggestions (pp. 84-85) when selecting hymns for this service.

## Sermon Resources

1. Prominently display two crowns: a golden crown (perhaps from the Christmas pageant props) and a crown of thorns. In the sermon, explore two kinds of kings. The first lives in a palace, is strong enough to scare off enemies, and makes rules for the country. Paint a picture—not of an evil king, but of one who is authoritarian. Then describe the king that Jesus became by spending his life taking care of his people and finally dying for them.

2. After describing how we treat kings (we do whatever they say, we try to please them, we give them the best of everything, we bow or defer to them), explore who and what we tend to treat as "king of our life." Children often let a special adult, such as a teacher or professional sports figure/hero, become their king. In some neighborhoods, a child may become king of the block and totally run the show (this king may be an overtly evil gang leader or a benevolent natural leader to whom the other children always defer). The scriptural challenge is not to let anyone but Jesus be King in our lives. Jesus and his ways are to be more important than any other child or adult leader.

Draw a picture of one story about
King Jesus in each empty square.
Listen to today's scripture readings
and sermon for ideas.

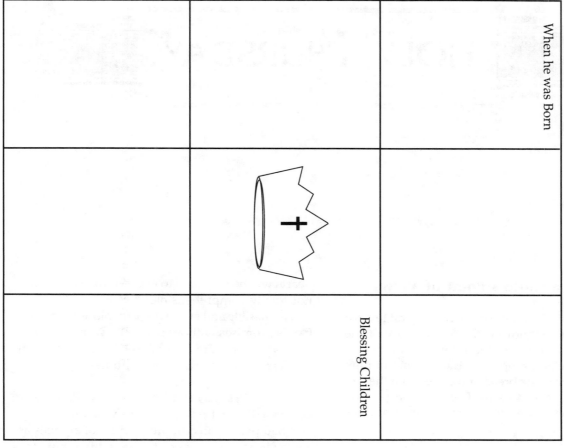

When he was Born

Blessing Children

Find and circle 9 Holy Week words.

Start here...

A B C R U C I F Y M S Q F O R G I V E N E S S L L O V E M K S J E S U S Q B R E A D M N R S P A L M R O C R O S S K S M S M S I N M S G O D

Answers: crucify, forgiveness, love, Jesus, bread, palm, cross, sin, God

# HOLY THURSDAY

## From a Child's Point of View

*Gospel: Luke 22:7-20.* This is the central text for the service. For children, this is the story of the first communion, rather than the story of the last supper. It tells us how and why communion began. We break the bread and drink from the cup because Jesus asked us to. Communion (among other things) is a way to remember Jesus and his great love.

*Old Testament: Jeremiah 31:31-34 (GNB).* Three statements in this passage stand out with great appeal and magnetism for people of all ages. ''I will be their God, and they will be my people'' promises loving closeness and security. ''None of them will have to teach his fellow countryman to know the LORD, because all will know me, from the least to the greatest'' paints a picture of knowledge that comes through relationships, not through teachings. Any child who is tired of having to ''learn about something'' from teachers welcomes the promise of being able to know God personally, rather than learning about God second-hand. ''I will . . . write [my law] on their hearts'' is even more personal. The promise is more than knowing about God, or even knowing God personally. God will live inside us. God's will is to be written deeply in us.

From the age of four or five, children develop a growing understanding of the way we use the word *heart* to talk about our deepest, truest commitments. They learn to put their hands on their hearts when they say the Pledge of Allegiance, to say ''cross my heart'' as a kind of oath, and to cut out valentine hearts for those they love. So, to think of God's will as being written on our hearts will be plausible to even young children, if not totally comprehensible.

It is possible and even wise to explore all three of God's promises without using the word *covenant*, unless you are sure the children are familiar with the term from church school studies.

*Epistle: Hebrews 10:16-25.* This book/letter was addressed to Hebrew Christians who understood and had participated in the sacrifice of animals as sin offerings. Therefore, to make his point, the writer uses the sin offering as a point of reference. To children today, these offerings are so foreign that even when they are explained, they make little sense. The writer's message, however, does make sense. The message is that there are three ways to live ''with the covenant written on your heart'': (1) to worship with God's people; (2) to tell others what we know about God and Jesus; and (3) to love (or take care of) one another. All three are concrete, everyday acts, of which children are capable as they respond to God's love.

*Psalm 116:12-19.* This text also demands appreciation of ritual sacrifices—wine libations. When the worship rituals and other texts of the day offer so much to children, this difficult passage probably will be passed over by them.

## Watch Words

Use *covenant* only if you are sure the children have explored it in church school. It is too rich a word, and there is too much going on to introduce it meaningfully during Holy Thursday worship.

## Let the Children Sing

"Let Us Break Bread Together on Our Knees" is the simplest communion hymn, and is especially meaningful when communion will be celebrated while kneeling at the rail.

Although children cannot make sense of many of the words of "Let All Mortal Flesh Keep Silence," they will sense the sheer awe of the occasion in the music.

If children are familiar with "Be Thou My Vision" from other programs of your congregation, it can be a way of celebrating the covenant "written on our hearts."

## The Liturgical Child

1. As the Gospel is read, the table is set with grace and drama by the table setters. A practice session for both reader and table setters is essential to coordinate movements and timing.

Verses 7-13: Spread a tablecloth and put in place all items except the unbroken loaf and the chalice. If you serve from individual cups in layers of trays, place the trays on the table at this time.
Verses 14-16: No action. Listen to Jesus.
Verses 17-18: Bring in chalice and set in place.
Verses 19-20: Bring in loaf and set in place.

2. Worship and celebrate the sacrament seated around tables as Jesus and his disciples did at the Last Supper. Hold the entire service in the church hall. Place the tables in a large horseshoe, adding one or two rows in the middle if needed. Cover the tables with white tablecloths, place candles on the tables, and set the places with printed orders of worship and hymnals. At the center of the horseshoe, place the communion elements.

If you use candles, plan to light them during a period of silence or musically supported preparation for worship after the worshipers are seated. This allows the worshipers to enter in friendly conversation and get settled around the tables before the mood of the service is set.

To more closely reenact the Last Supper, commune by the ancient method of intinction. A loaf is broken and passed among the worshipers; each person breaks off a piece to dip into the cup as it is passed around. Whatever method you use, try to use a loaf, rather than wafers, and do fill the chalice in the presence of the worshipers.

3. Create a responsive prayer of confession based on the Ten Commandments. Worshipers read the Commandments aloud, one at a time (from a carefully chosen translation); a worship leader replies with a prayer about the ways we do not keep that Commandment (or fail to live with it "written in our hearts"). For example:

*People:* You shall have no other gods before me.

*Leader:* But there are so many important things we must do, God, and so many things we want to do. There are clothes and homes and toys and trips and jobs and awards we want so badly. Sometimes we write so many wants and dreams on our hearts that they become our gods—instead of You. Forgive us, and write your will in big letters on our hearts.

4. Review the tenebrae directions in the liturgical suggestions for Good Friday (p. 85). If there will be no Good Friday worship, consider using the tenebrae in the Holy Thursday service after the celebration of communion.

## Sermon Resources

*Keep the sermon brief.* The heart of this service for the children is the celebration of the sacrament in the context of the story of the Last Supper. For worshipers of all ages, it is a time for feeling and doing, rather then studying and conceptualizing.

No Worship Worksheet is included for this day because the service should be so story- and action-oriented that papers and pencils would be in the way.

# GOOD FRIDAY

## From a Child's Point of View

*Gospel: John 18:1–19:42 or 19:17-30.* The story is the focus of the day. It is a simple, very graphic story. Jesus was betrayed by a friend, denied by his best friend, slapped across the face by a soldier simply for answering a question, whipped, treated cruelly by soldiers who dressed him in a robe and smashed a crown of sharp thorns upon his head, and finally, crucified. Throughout it all he remained gentle, loving, and forgiving. The story needs little explanation. It speaks on its own to people of all ages.

What the story says to children is that God still loved those people, even after they did such horrible things to Jesus. (God proved that love with the resurrection.) For younger children, it is enough to hear the story of the crucifixion and to know that God's love and power is stronger than the worst things the cruelest enemies can do. Older children can begin to identify the reasons people wanted to kill Jesus. Jesus loved everyone, even those the "good" folks did not want to have around. Jesus called on everyone to share whatever they had with anyone who needed it, and many people did not want to share. Some of the older children will begin to realize that we are capable of that same selfish response to Jesus' love.

Though it is a riveting story, it also is a long one and includes several passages in which children's attention can wander and be lost. So if you read the entire text, read it in sections, interspersed with liturgy. It is also possible to omit some of the abstract trial conversations.

*Epistle: Hebrews 4:14-16; 5:7-9.* The concept of Jesus as the Great High Priest requires both knowledge of and appreciation for the Old Testament system of animal sacrifice. Although it is possible to present knowledge about this approach to sin and forgiveness to children, this type of sacrifice is totally foreign to them. They generally ask questions like these: "If we are expected to forgive each other 'for free,' how come God has to have a special gift to do it?" "How can killing an animal make God happy?" "Why did God need Jesus to die in order to forgive us?" There are no answers that satisfy young minds. Appreciation of this theology will have to wait until their mental abilities develop enough to allow abstract thought.

Chapter 5:7-9 does offer one point for older children. Jesus was in trouble because he was too loving. He knew he was in trouble and that he was going to be hurt. He asked God not to let that happen, but he also kept on loving. He refused to stop loving. He lived by God's great Commandments, and for that he was killed. We are called to be as obedient as Jesus was. (Note: Good Friday is a day to celebrate *God's* love, rather than to call on worshipers to be more loving. Our best love never will be as powerful as God's love. So this point is probably best saved for another occasion.)

*Old Testament: Isaiah 52:13–53:12.* If this passage is introduced as one that always makes people think about Jesus, children will hear specific phrases that remind them of Jesus and his suffering. The prophetic nature of the passage is not particularly meaningful to children.

*Psalm 22:1-18.* If this passage is introduced as a psalm Jesus may have prayed on the cross, children will hear occasional phrases that remind them of what happened to Jesus.

## Watch Words

The child's word for *scourged* is *whipped*.

*Crucify* and *crucifixion* are words heard only at church and mainly during the Easter season. Be sure to define them so children know what you are talking about.

Beware of "atonement" language such as *high priest, sacrifice, mercy, grace,* and *salvation.* Avoid speaking of the cross in symbolic ways (e.g., hold fast to "the cross"). Instead, tell what happened in concrete, everyday terms.

## Let the Children Sing

"Were You There When They Crucified My Lord?" is the best hymn for the day because it tells the story in simple language, with music that has deep emotional quality.

This same emotional quality allows "O Sacred Head Now Wounded" to speak musically in spite of its difficult atonement vocabulary.

Avoid hymns with much atonement language, such as "Ah, Holy Jesus," as well as "In the Cross of Christ I Glory," in which the cross is presented in symbolic terms.

## The Liturgical Child

1. Begin the service with the sanctuary decorated as usual for Lent. For the call to worship, remove the flowers, purple paraments, and any other decorations. Do this in silence during the singing of the first hymn, or while speaking informally about the solemnity of the day, telling why each item is removed. (Older children serving as acolytes may help with this.) After the crucifixion narrative is read, drape a strip of black fabric across the arms of the central cross (if it is within reach).

2. Tenebrae is a candlelight service in reverse. The service begins with all candles lit. Readers then read sections of the Passion story. After each section is read, snuff out one candle, until the room is completely dark. Experience darkness for about a minute. Then light one candle as a sign of the hope of the coming resurrection. Worshipers leave in silence.

The following readings trace the story (streamlined a bit, with children in mind).

| | |
|---|---|
| John 18:1-14 | Jesus is arrested |
| :15-18, 25-27 | Peter's denials |
| :28-32, 38b-40 | Jesus is tried by Pilate |
| 19:1-6 | Jesus is sentenced to death |
| :17-22 | Jesus is crucified |
| :23-24 | Soldiers gamble for Jesus' cloak |
| :25-27 | Jesus cares for his mother |
| :28-30 | Jesus dies |
| :38-42 | Jesus' body is buried |
| Total darkness | |
| John 3:16-17 | "God so loved the world . . ." |

3. Place the tenebrae candles in a row on a long table, with a snuffer at each end. Select readers of all ages (with practice, young children can read the shorter passages). Seat the readers at the table so that the readings and candle snuffings can proceed in order from the ends of the table toward the center. The center candle should be the last to be snuffed and the one to be relighted.

Meet with the readers before the service so that all can take their places quietly on cue. Have the younger readers practice in the sanctuary so that they can be easily understood. Plan ahead to be sure that the last readers have sufficient light in order to read.

A tenebrae can be part of a longer service, or songs and prayers can be interspersed with the readings to form a Good Friday liturgy. Obviously, a tenebrae is more effective at night or in a room that is easily darkened.

## Sermon Resources

This is a day for minimum preaching and maximum storytelling. Tell stories about love that "won't give up." Talk about a person going to great lengths to care for a sick pet. Describe the efforts of a child to befriend a very unlovable neighborhood outcast. Tell about parents who stand by very difficult teenage children. Then tell about Jesus, who loved us even unto death, and who rose, proving that God's love cannot be overcome.

No Worship Worksheet is provided for today because the service should be so story-oriented and dramatic that papers and pencils would be in the way.

# EASTER

## From a Child's Point of View

*Gospel: John 20:1-18 or Luke 24:1-12.* Both stories of the discovery of the empty tomb can be read to children with little explanation. The response of the children is, however, different from that of adults. For children, Easter joy has more to do with the victory of God's powerful love over the forces of evil than with resurrection from death.

It is hard for children to understand death. Most children, even those who have experienced the death of a close relative, have trouble grasping the physical finality of death. Children who grow up in Christian churches, hearing the resurrection faith that God loves us even beyond death, do not easily share the fear of death described in the New Testament. Psychologists tell us that even teenagers have little meaningful understanding of their personal mortality. So it is hard for children to get into the celebration of resurrection from death. This part of the Easter message will mean more later in their lives.

In childhood, the central message of Easter is that God refused to let the hate of Good Friday be the last word. Considering everything that had been done to Jesus, God deserved to become angry and punish the people severely. But God did not do this. Instead, God continued to love the people who had betrayed, denied, and killed Jesus. And God refused to let Jesus stay dead. Jesus rose from death to prove to us that God's love is more powerful than the worst evil and that God will continue to love us, no matter what terrible things we do. So for children, the empty tomb is God's biggest surprise, and Easter joy is our delighted response to the discovery that even

though it looked as if the "bad guys" had won, they had not. God and God's love had defeated the forces of evil and were more in control than ever.

*Old Testament: Isaiah 65:17-25.* The rich poetic images of Isaiah's vision of God's dreams for the world are like coded messages for which literal-minded children have no key. The Good News Bible decodes some of these images as part of its translation and therefore is easier for children to follow. Even if read from this translation, the vision is challenging for children, but if it is presented as the dream of the Easter God who has defeated and continues to defeat evil, this passage becomes a glimpse into the future toward which God is working. Children will hear in specific phrases the possibilities to anticipate.

*Acts 10:34-43.* (During the Easter season the Common Lectionary suggests a reading from Acts as an alternative to the Old Testament reading.) Taken in context, Peter's statement in Joppa is about the fellowship of God's family, which crosses all human boundaries of nationality, race, and so on. But for Easter Sunday, it is a summary of the good news about Jesus and an opportunity for listeners to view themselves as witnesses, like Peter. Children who have celebrated the events of Holy Week are ready to respond by becoming witnesses. At the very least, they can recite the story in worship and claim it as their own. Some also can recognize the need for Christians to share the story with others.

*Epistle: I Corinthians 15:19-26.* Chapter 15: 19-26 is a difficult passage for children. That we should all die because Adam and Eve ate the apple seems terribly unfair. That God should punish us for what Adam and Eve did seems inconsistent with our insistence that God is loving. In their teen years, youths will begin to understand that what links us and our fates to Adam and Eve is that all of us disobey, in spite of our very best intentions. But this link is beyond the comprehension of most younger children. So read this passage for worshipers who are old enough to grasp the fear of death and so have the mental ability to feel linked both to Adam and Eve and to Christ.

*Psalm 118:14-24.* To children, this is a collection of short praises to the powerful God who saves us. Many of the praises require little explanation. Others, such as the verses about the rejected stone, include images that require detailed explanation. Today is not a particularly good time to explain these images, so it is better to let the psalm speak as it can to the worshipers celebrating God's Easter power.

## Watch Words

Enjoy the Alleluias! *Alleluia* wraps into one word these messages: "Hurray for God!"; "God, you did a great job!"; "Thank you, God!"; "Knowing you makes us happy, God!"

Use *resurrection.* It is a good word for children to hear and to recognize as belonging to the church. But do not expect children to find much meaning in the word until their understanding of death matures.

## Let the Children Sing

"Jesus Christ Is Risen Today" is probably the best Easter hymn for children. Even the youngest can join in on the Alleluias. (Challenge them to count the Alleluias for Easter fun.) Older children will pick up more of the short phrases of praise which precede the Alleluias every time they sing the song.

Children enjoy the contrasting feel of the verses and the chorus of the old gospel hymn "Up from the Grave He Arose." This hymn emphasizes the surprising nature of Easter.

Avoid hymns with lots of "resurrection" and "salvation" jargon.

## The Liturgical Child

1. Children can sense Easter joy before they can explain it. So fill the sanctuary with flowers. Hang white and gold paraments. Play joyful music. Add instruments such as brass to draw special attention to the music.

2. Encourage the presence of children at sunrise services held outdoors in a garden or cemetery. Focus on telling the story, singing an Easter hymn, and praying brief prayers of praise and thanksgiving. Save sermonizing for indoor worship later in the day. The location and timing of a sunrise service adds new reality to the empty-tomb story and makes the day stand out as a very special day for our church.

If crowds at mid-morning worship services are a problem, a story-oriented sunrise service to which children are particularly invited can open seats in the later service and thus allow worship at that time to be more adult-oriented.

3. Invite worshipers to read Acts 10:37-43 as a creed in which they respond with Peter to what God has done in Jesus.

## Sermon Resources

1. Like the rest of Holy Week, Easter for children is a time for storytelling and praising, rather than for critical thinking and sermonizing.

2. To focus the sermon on God's surprises, tell stories of God's surprises in the life of Jesus. Begin with God's decision to be born among us in a barn and to announce the birth to shepherds. Tell how Jesus befriended Zaccheus, a greedy tax collector. Tell about the time Jesus surprised people by proving that they had enough food for everyone in the crowd. Describe Peter's surprise and embarrassment when Jesus, his hero and God's leader, washed Peter's feet. Finally, tell of Jesus' death and the surprising way God announced his resurrection to women, rather than to important men. Create a rhetorical refrain, such as "God said, 'Surprise, I love you'" with which to conclude each story.

# Happy Easter!

Today our worship is filled with Easter words. Find them in the puzzle.

Draw a butterfly ____ each time one of these words is said in worship.

Draw a flower ____ each time one of the Easter words is sung in worship.

At the end of the service, this page will be an Easter garden.

Fill in the blanks with the correct Easter words.

R __ __ __ __ __ __ E

__ __ __ __ U __

__ __ __ __ R __

__ __ R __ __

__ __ E __

__ __ __ C __ __ __ __

__ __ __ __ T __

__ __ __ I __

__ __ __ __ O __

__ __ __ __ N __

**EASTER**

alive          stone          Jesus
Mary          Christ          risen
alleluia       tomb           Peter
forgiven      sunrise

*Easter / © 1991 by Abingdon Press.*

# SECOND SUNDAY OF EASTER

## From a Child's Point of View

*John 20:19-31.* This passage includes two related, yet separate Easter stories.

John 20:19-23 describes Jesus' first postresurrection encounter with the disciples. His appearance tells us two things about his resurrected body. First, he appears inside a locked room; his "new" body is not like the physical body he had before death. Second, his body bears the wounds of crucifixion; his body is still the same. This is the same Jesus who was killed on Friday. Children will be curious about this.

During this encounter, Jesus reassured his disciples that he was indeed alive, and then he put them to work. The message to children is that Easter is not an ending; it is a new chapter in God's work. On Easter evening, Jesus is already looking ahead. He gives his disciples the gift of the Spirit and sends them out, saying, "As the Father sent me, so I send you."

To help the children identify what the Father sent Jesus to do, explore key stories about Jesus' ministry. Their challenge is then to find ways to do that kind of work today. Just as Jesus fed the hungry crowd, children can work to help relieve hunger. Just as Jesus befriended the friendless, children can make friends with the lonely people they meet, and so forth.

The story of Thomas reassures children that the Risen Lord is still the kind, understanding Jesus. Thomas, who was left out of the first encounter with Jesus, raises the kinds of questions any child might raise. Jesus is not offended by the questions, but honors them and offers to let Thomas touch the wounds, if that's what it takes to answer his questions. In so doing, Jesus blesses all our questions. No honest question is too silly, disrespectful, or unworthy to be asked and answered (or at least discussed).

*Acts 5:27-32.* This passage gives an example of the disciples doing as Jesus instructed. They are being witnesses to what God has done through Jesus. For children, the heart of this passage is Peter's statement, "We must obey God rather than men." This is a brave stand. It calls on children to be as heroic as Peter in obeying God's laws and doing God's will, rather than going along with the crowd when the crowd is not going God's way. The "crowd" is most often other children who play together in informal settings, but it also can include their own families, school classes, or even congregation. (Children can become the conscience of their communities.)

*Psalm 2.* This psalm is included among today's lections as a meditation on the Acts text. It celebrates the worldwide lordship of Christ over all nations. If the psalm is dramatically presented, children can grasp the psalmist's point; but that point will not be the focus of their attention today.

*Revelation 1:4-8.* This passage includes lots of imagery with Old Testament roots, which are beyond children. Two phrases, however, do stand out for children. The first is the set of phrases about God, who is "Alpha and Omega," who "was and is and is to be." These are the answers to the questions, "What was there before God?" or "Who made God?" These answers challenge children to begin thinking of God as bigger than they can imagine. Such conversations lay the foundation of children's theology and provide great security. (If we are in the care of such a power, we are safe.)

The second phrase that grabs children's attention is the description of Christians as "a kingdom of priests," or as Protestant children might say, "a kingdom of ministers." This parallels John's sending of the disciples and can be explored in much the same way.

## Watch Words

The words of today's texts pose no problems for children. Avoid generalizing the messages of the texts with big words about the omnipotence of the preexistent God.

## Let the Children Sing

Singing "Come Christians Join to Sing" is a good way to keep the Alleluias going the week after Easter (and throughout the Easter season).

"Rejoice, the Lord Is King," with its repeated chorus of "Lift up your heart, lift up your voice," celebrates the Lord who is King.

## The Liturgical Child

1. Present John 20:19-31 with three readers. The worship leader for the day introduces the passage and recalls what happened in verses 1-18. A second reader then reads verses 19-23. A third reader picks up with verses 24-29. The first reader then concludes by reading verses 30-31. Changing readers for the different stories within the ongoing narrative helps keep the children's attention.

2. Give Acts 5:27-32 your best dramatic reading. Read the high priest's question in an authoritarian voice, looking down your nose at the disciples from one side of the lectern. Then turn slightly as you read Peter's brave, enthusiastic reply.

3. To present Psalm 2 dramatically, ask the choir to sing Pat McGeachy's lighthearted paraphrase of the psalm, set to the tune of "Little Brown Jug" (*A New Song* can be ordered from Pat McGeachy, 621 Brook Hollow Road, Nashville, TN 37205). Or give the psalm a very dramatic reading. Face the congregation for verses 1-6, turn toward the worship center or central cross for

verses 7-9, then turn back toward the congregation for verses 10-12. To pull out all the stops, memorize the psalm so that your hands can be used to emphasize the words.

4. If you sing the Gloria Patri regularly in worship, take time either just before singing it or during the sermon to explore the meaning of "As it was in the beginning, is now, and ever shall be, world without end." This is on-the-job worship education.

5. Create a benediction based on John 20:21. For example:

> Peace be with you. As the Father sent me, even so I send you . . .
> > to heal those who are sick and dying . . .
> > to befriend the friendless in Jesus' name . . .
> > to tell of God's love . . .
> > (etc., based on points of the sermon)
>
> As you go, remember that the peace of God is with you, and the power of the Holy Spirit will uphold and direct you because you are the Easter People, a kingdom of priests for God. Amen.

## Sermon Resources

1. These texts and those for the following Sundays suggest a sermon series about Easter People. Explore who the Easter People are, what they do, and what they are like. Challenge worshipers of all ages to see themselves as Easter People. Consider giving each worshiper a small token, perhaps a plastic or metal cross to carry in a pocket each day during the coming weeks, as a reminder that each of them is one of the Easter People. Ask the choir to sing Avery and Marsh's song, "Every Day Is Easter Day," today and several times during the series.

From today's texts we learn that Easter People experience God's peace (John), obey God first (Ps. 2 and Acts), and are sent to serve (Rev. and John).

2. Tell stories about people who chose to obey God rather than people. Include stories about well-known people such as Martin Luther King. Also, describe activities in your congregation that show you to be Easter People: volunteer work (serving as a kingdom of priests); mission projects (carried out by youth groups); and specific events which give a peace-filled feeling (perhaps a congregational weekend retreat in which children participate).

The New Testament was first written in Greek. Use the key below to translate this Greek verse into English.

καθὼς   ὁ   πατὴρ

_____   _   _____

ἀπέσταλκέ   με,

_____   ___ ,

κἀγὼ   πέμπω   ὑμᾶς.

_____   _____   ___ .

John 20: 21b

Translator's key

καθὼς = as        ὁ = the
κἀγὼ = I also    πατήρ = father
με = me            ἀπέσταλκέ = sent
ὑμᾶς = you       πέμπω = send

Listen carefully to the reading of John 20:19-31. Draw a picture of Jesus meeting his disciples on Easter evening. Make their faces and bodies show their feelings.

# THIRD SUNDAY OF EASTER

## From a Child's Point of View

*Resurrection* means new life. Today's texts include the stories of two people who received new chances at life from the resurrected Jesus; a psalm about how God saves or heals us; and a poetic image of Jesus, "the (resurrected) Lamb."

*John 21:1-19 or 21:15-19.* The message of this interesting fishing story is that although Peter denied knowing Jesus three times, Jesus gave him another chance. Children need to know that God and Jesus give many second chances to those who love God but sometimes "chicken out" or make mistakes.

In order to understand the story, children need to be reminded of Peter's triple denial and how Peter felt.

*Acts 9:1-20.* The story of Paul's conversion on the Damascus road is another interesting story that children can follow without explanation *if* it is read with dramatic flair.

The story makes two points to children. First, Paul's conversion is another Easter surprise—almost a joke played by God. God's strategy for ending the persecution of the early church was to turn the leader of the death squad into a Christian missionary! This is not a strategy many Christians would have suggested—even in jest. Some had trouble believing it when it happened. In turning Saul into Paul, God alerts us to look for new life in strange places and people. If God could turn Saul around, there's no guessing what other Easter surprises might be in store for us. Read the story to celebrate God's incredible power and sense of humor.

Second, the story promises forgiveness. If God is willing to forgive Saul, who killed Christians, and put him to work in the Easter kingdom, then perhaps there is a chance for us. To children who are frequently in trouble or feel they never measure up to what is expected of them, this is a very hopeful story.

*Psalm 30:4-12.* This hymn of praise for God's recurring gift of new life is too abstract for children. However, if presented as a hymn that Peter or Paul might have sung after being given a new chance by Jesus, older children can understand a few phrases.

*Revelation 5:11-14.* This passage is a coded message written during a time when a person who carried a piece of paper with Jesus' name on it could be fed to the lions. Children cannot understand the atonement theology which makes the lamb a good symbol for Jesus. But they can be told that "Lamb" is a code word for Jesus and that "one who sits on the throne" is a code for God. With this information, they can enjoy the challenge of decoding John's Easter message (God and Jesus are worthy of praise by everyone in the world).

## Watch Words

Do not let the word *Lamb* lead you to use other "slain lamb" language in worship today. Children can understand *Lamb* only as a code word for Jesus.

In talking about the second chances that Peter and Saul received, speak of *forgiveness* and of being *changed* rather than of *salvation* or *conversion*. (For most children today, *conversion* is a football term, or what you do with metric system measurements.) So unless your congregation uses the word regularly and specifically defines it, avoid using it today.

## Let the Children Sing

"Come Christians Join to Sing" continues to be a good Easter-season choice.

"Blessing and Honor and Glory and Power" can be fun to sing because it uses the Revelation code for simply worded praises to God. Point out before singing that this would be a good hymn to sing if Christians were being persecuted by those who did not know the code.

## The Liturgical Child

1. There is great dialog in John 21. Read it as it would have been spoken. Shout out the exchange between the fishermen in the boat and Jesus on shore. Decide how you think John would have said, "It is the Lord!" and speak the line accordingly. As you read verses 15-19, show Peter's embarrassment, hesitation, and self-disgust in your voice, and then let Jesus' forgiving love be apparent. Such a reading will make the whole text (1-19) a story that children can enjoy and appreciate.

2. Before reading John 21, remind the congregation of Peter's three denials and alert them to listen for Jesus' three responses. As you read each question, answer, and command sequence, hold up one, then two, and finally three fingers as clues.

3. Pray about apparently hopeless situations in which new life (or an Easter "turn around") is needed. In addition to noting community and worldwide issues, pray for people at school and at work with whom it is really hard to get along, for peace on school buses, and for problems between brothers and sisters who must share rooms and do chores together.

4. Create a litany of confession and petition in which the worship leader describes a variety of hopeless situations on personal, community, and international levels. To each case, the congregation responds, "Lord, forgive us, and help us find your Easter surprise here." Only the response needs to be printed in the bulletin. For example:

*Worship Leader:* Lord, each of us knows some people who get on our nerves. Something about the way they act just drives us a little crazy. We would like to find a way to be friends with these people, or at least be kind to them, but they bring out the worst in us. We say cruel words almost without thinking. We treat them in ways that surprise us. We'd like to do better.

*Congregation:* Lord, forgive us, and help us find an Easter surprise.

## Sermon Resources

1. *The Great Gilly Hopkins*, by Katherine Paterson, is an award-winning children's novel about a ten-year-old terror with one-in-a-long-line of foster parents. (The book is available in the children's section of most public libraries and generally available in bookstores.) Read part of or summarize the whole story's Easter-like changes. Then retell the stories of Saul's change of direction, Peter's forgiveness, and Jesus' resurrection. Gilly, Peter, Saul, and Jesus are all Easter people.

2. Ask the worshipers to produce the Easter tokens they were given last week. (Have the ushers ready to pass out tokens to those who do not have them.) Challenge worshipers to think about the week ahead and identify the difficult people and situations they will encounter. Then instruct them to carry their tokens with them again this week as a reminder that all hopeless situations and people are possible Easter surprises. Suggest that reaching into a pocket to hold the token can help us continue to work with God in frustrating situations.

Shade in the spaces with a ✽
inside to find . . .
a word that describes Easter People.

Draw a picture of a person who needs
an Easter suprise.

what Jesus says to Easter People.

Write a prayer for this person.

Answer: forgiven; follow me

# FOURTH SUNDAY OF EASTER

## From a Child's Point of View

*John 10:22-30 and Psalm 23.* These passages are based on the image of God or Jesus as a good shepherd. It was a great image in Jesus' day, and it can be meaningful today *if* we know a little bit about shepherds. Most urban children do not. To them, a shepherd is as likely to be a large, sometimes fierce dog as a person who cares for sheep.

Psalm 23 is based on the care that a shepherd must provide for totally defenseless sheep in a hostile environment. Not only must they be protected from wild animals, but they must be rescued from problems they got into but cannot get out of. For example, sheep can become tangled in thorn bushes or lost from the herd. When they wade into a fast-moving stream to drink, their wool can get so heavily soaked that they lose their footing, fall, and drown. It is the shepherd's job to protect the sheep from attacking animals, keep them together in safe pastures, and find still, shallow water so they can drink safely. Good shepherds will risk their lives for their sheep. As Easter People, we know that God in Jesus did and does the same for us.

To understand John's passage, children must know that shepherds often kept all the sheep of their village in one fold (fenced yard). When it was time to separate the flocks, all the shepherds called their sheep, each using a unique call. The sheep of each flock recognized their shepherd's call and left the sheepfold only with that shepherd.

Easter People recognize Jesus' call. So when they hear the call to love one another and to love God, they follow. Other people (like the Temple authorities) stand around and say it is smarter to keep what you have than to share, or that some people really are not worth loving. Those people do not recognize Jesus' voice. Jesus promises that God is able to care for all who do follow.

The good-shepherd image offers children security. God knows them personally and is taking care of them.

*Acts 13:15-16, 26-33.* This passage has no shepherd imagery and no clear message about God's care for us. Instead, it is a summary of the good-news story of Jesus and therefore is appropriate for the Easter season. Although the passage presents no particular problems for children, it probably will not grab their attention as much as the other passages for the day.

*Revelation 7:9-17.* This is a continuation of last Sunday's coded message to Christians under persecution. Every child (and Roman soldier) knows that if you wash something in blood, it turns red, not white. That's what makes the phrase "people in the robes made white by being washed in the blood of the Lamb" such a great code. To crack this code at its full depth requires appreciation for animal-sacrifice theology, which is beyond the thinking of children. So simply present the phrase as a code for all Christians. To enjoy the clever humor, imagine with the children a soldier who tried to make sense of the passage but did not have the key to the code.

Having cracked the code, children will be ready to explore God's promises to the people in the white robes in verses 15b-17 and the rest of Revelation. In children's terms, the promise is that God loves and takes care of each of us. Some terrible things may happen to us or to the people we love. We may need to make some brave stands that might make others angry with us (or, if we live in especially dangerous times, kill us). But in the end, we will find that God was with us all the way.

## Watch Words

Use only the "shepherd" words (*rod, staff, sheepfold, still waters*) with which the children are familiar, or explain the words as part of worship.

Avoid using "lamb" imagery such as the *blood of the lamb, slain lamb,* or *cleansing blood,* beyond the simple code word *Lamb.* These "atonement" terms are beyond the mental development of the children.

Clearly describe Jesus as the *Good Shepherd* and as the *Lamb.* Help children see that these are two ways to describe Jesus, rather than two contradictory statements.

## Let the Children Sing

To keep the Alleluias going, sing one of the Easter hymns with an Alleluia chorus.

Sing "The Lord's My Shepherd," Psalm 23, taking time to point out that it is Scripture set to music; or as a second choice, use the hymn "Savior Like a Shepherd Lead Us." Children have trouble with the complex theological language of "He Leadeth Me" and "The King of Love My Shepherd Is."

## The Liturgical Child

1. Psalm 23 is so well known and loved that congregations tend to read it in unison with more feeling than most unison readings arouse. It is often somewhat familiar to older children and therefore is easier for them to read with the congregation. If pew Bibles are not available, print the psalm in the worship bulletin to enable group reading.

2. Use Psalm 23 as an outline for the congregation's prayers of petition, for example:

Verses 1-2  Pray for the hungry and homeless.
Verse 3a  Pray for people who need to be restored—criminals in prison, addicts, people who have been cut out by those around them.
Verse 3b  Ask for guidance to do the right things at home, at school, at work, in our town, and in our world. Note specific issues in which God's guidance is needed now.
Verse 4  Pray for those who are facing death or illness.
Verse 5a  Pray for all who are living in war between nations, races, or in families.
Verse 5b-6  Offer prayers of thanksgiving and praise, citing examples of God's loving care.

Both the Scripture and the prayers can be voiced by one worship leader; or one leader can read the psalm phrases, to which a second replies with the prayers; or the worship leader can read the psalm phrases, the congregation responding with either printed or spontaneous prayers.

## Sermon Resources

1. Easter People know an important secret: Though at times it appears they are losing, God and the Easter People will be the big winners in the end. To explore John's coded reminder of this secret in Revelation, recall a popular children's movie in which the main character is constantly in terrible trouble and seems certain to lose or die, but escapes at the last moment. Compare that story to the situation of the early Christians who were being imprisoned, tortured, and even killed. Just as the movie character might have given up when things seemed worst, it would have been easy for early Christians to forget the Easter secret and give up. John wrote to remind them of the secret, to encourage them to "hang in there," and to give them hope. John's message is a good reminder for us, too.

2. Mention the Easter token again. Challenge worshipers to use it this week to remind themselves of God's love and care for them and others. Suggest that the token might comfort them if they got into seemingly hopeless situations, and remind them to watch for others in hopeless situations who need our prayers and supportive help.

Draw a picture of a shepherd taking care of sheep. Show these things:

lost sheep    hungry bear

thorny bush    stream

Draw a picture of someone (maybe you) taking care of another person.

Unscramble the letters in each word to find an Easter message from Jesus.

"YM PESHE ERAH YM COVIE, DAN I WONK

" — — / — — — — — / — — — — I

MEHT, NAD ETHY WLOFLO EM."

— — — — , — — — / — — — — / — — "

Answer: My sheep hear my voice, and I know them, and they follow me.    (John 10:27 )

*Forth Sunday of Easter/ © 1991 by Abingdon Press.*

# FIFTH SUNDAY OF EASTER

## From a Child's Point of View

*John 13:31-35.* Knowledge of the context is key to appreciating this text fully. The disciples and Jesus were gathered in the upper room to celebrate Passover. Judas had just left to betray Jesus. Knowing this, Jesus announced his death and gave the remaining disciples a new commandment. They were to love one another as God/Jesus had loved them (all the way to the cross).

John's intricate, abstract words in verses 31-33 will make little sense to children. But the new command in verses 34-35 is plain. And when it is set in context, children can understand that the kind of love Jesus is talking about is not a happy feeling, but a way of treating people. Loving as Jesus loved means putting ourselves on the line for others. Jesus insists that Christians will be recognized by the loving way they treat others.

*Psalm 145:13b-21.* This is the last section of an acrostic which praises God. In these verses, the focus is on praising God's loving care. Because the verses speak in generalizations, they are hard for children to grasp. Older children will understand a few verses, but all children will enjoy the poetic fun of praising God with an alphabet poem. The psalm may be most meaningful for children when it is used to encourage them to create their own acrostics to praise God's care of them and their world.

*Revelation 21:1-6.* The Revelation code images in this text, such as "a city dressed as a bride coming down from heaven" and "water from the fountain of life" are too much for children to translate. However, the message from "the one who sits on the throne" is simple. A time is coming when God will live with people and take such care of them that there will be no more tears, and every need will be met.

*Acts 14:8-18.* This passage probably was included with this group of texts because of Paul's statements about God's loving care in verses 15-17. The passage as a whole is also a funny story to tell within the faith family as we celebrate God's Easter surprise.

It seems that Paul and Barnabas, after healing a lame man, were welcomed as the very Greek gods they hoped to discredit. The picture of the two missionaries chasing after the crowd to keep them from worshiping Paul and Barnabas is comical. This story gives us the chance to laugh gently at the failure of all of our best efforts, and to remind ourselves that God works through us, even when we can't seem to do anything right. For children, this is a chance to see Paul, one of the great early Christians, "give it his best shot and blow it." He stood up in public, preached the good news, and even healed a lame man. But instead of convincing people to learn about God and Jesus, Paul's work led them to welcome him as one of their gods. Things simply did not work out as he had hoped. Paul's backfiring effort to share God's love can give us the courage to try and fail, knowing that God will work through us, just as God worked through Paul and Barnabas.

## Watch Words

In speaking of God's loving care, avoid *providence*. Those children who recognize the word probably would identify it as the capital of Rhode Island. So talk in specific terms about God's loving care.

## Let the Children Sing

To celebrate God's love, sing "For the Beauty of the Earth."

To commit yourselves to keeping Jesus' new command, sing "They'll Know We Are Christians by Our Love" or "Lord, I Want to Be a Christian."

Keep the Easter joy alive with "Come, Christians, Join to Sing."

## The Liturgical Child

1. In introducing Revelation 21:1-6, remind worshipers of the identity of "the one who sits on the throne" in the Revelation code, and alert them to listen carefully to everything "the one who sits on the throne" says. Raise one hand, with your index finger pointed up (the teaching pose in early Christian art), while reading each of the messages. This will help children hear the straightforward message of the passage without tripping on all the poetic images that surround the message from "the one who sits on the throne."

2. To create a litany prayer of confession, one person or group recites, "Jesus commanded, 'Love one another even as I have loved you,' " to which a second person or group replies with prayers that confess the ways we fail to love as Jesus commanded. Include confessions of our failures to love within families, among friends, and especially in relating to people we do not like. Confess communal as well as personal failures to love. In the assurance of pardon, remind worshipers that Jesus loves and forgives us always.

3. If there is a group of clowns in your congregation, and if your congregation has encountered them previously in worship settings, invite them to pantomime the story of Paul and Barnabas as it is read. You will need at least five clowns: Saul, Barnabas, the lame man, and at least two for the crowd.

## Sermon Resources

1. Begin to explore God's promises in Revelation 21 by listing things that make us cry. Babies cry when they are wet, hungry, lonely, hurt, angry, and any other time they do not have what they want or need. Young children cry less frequently than babies: when they are hurt (but they can be brave about small hurts); when they become really angry (throw a temper tantrum); and when they see something sad. Teenagers are more likely to cry because of hurt feelings. Grown-ups cry when very sad things happen to them or to people they love. We all tend to cry at funerals and when good friends move away. Teenagers and grown-ups cry at movies. Some people even cry when they are very, very happy (but these are not the tears we are thinking about today). Describing all these tear-producing situations can set the stage for thinking about ways to love those who are in tears and for recalling God's promise that one day there will be no more tears.

2. Ask how many people still have their Easter tokens. Recall previously made points about what it means to be Easter People. Then present Jesus' new command as the identifying mark of the Easter People. Scouts, sports teams, and even schools have badges and uniforms that identify their members. Christians do not have a badge or uniform. They are to act with such love that people around them will recognize them as Christians. Suggest that the worshipers carry their tokens with them this week as a hidden reminder that their actions should be so loving that others will know they are Easter People.

3. If you preach about God's loving care, direct the children's attention to the acrostic on the Worship Worksheet and challenge them to create their own alphabet poem to praise God's care. Invite them to show you their work as they leave the sanctuary after worship. Suggest that nonreaders draw pictures of things or people for which they praise God. Promise that if the children listen to the sermon, they will hear ideas for their work (then be sure to include some).

Psalm 145 is an alphabet poem praising God. Each line begins with a letter of the Hebrew alphabet.

Write your own alphabet poem praising God. Tell how God cares for you and for this world. Write one word or sentence for each letter.

A _____

B _____

C _____

D _____

E _____

F _____

Because it is the fifth Sunday of Easter, cross out every fifth letter below to find Jesus' message.

```
L O V E
K O N E
A R N O
T H P E R E V L
E N A S B I H A
V O E L O V S E
D Y O R U J O H
3 4 4 R N 1 3
```

_ _ _ _   _ _ _   _ _ _ _ _ _ _

_ _ _ _   _ _   _   _ _ _ _   _ _ _ _ _   _ _ _ ;

Answer: Love one another even as I have loved you.  John 13: 34

*Fifth Sunday of Easter* / © 1991 by Abingdon Press.

# SIXTH SUNDAY OF EASTER

## From a Child's Point of View

*John 14:23-29.* This is a rich text, providing several themes that are important to children. All the themes are more powerful if the text is set in its context: the Last Supper.

First is the question of how to show our love for Jesus. Loyalty among friends is very important to children. Best friends prove their devotion by being together, wearing matching clothes, or joining the same teams. Children express their devotion to their heroes by collecting baseball cards, memorizing sports statistics, and wearing shirts that bear those persons' names. So the question, "How can we show our love for Jesus?" has some urgency. Jesus' answer is clear. We are to show our love not by what we wear or by memorizing all the facts about Jesus, but by following Jesus' teachings. (The GNB's "obey my teachings" makes more sense to children than the RSV's "keep my word.")

Second, Jesus promises those who love him and obey his teachings that God will be with them always. Again, this speaks to children's insistence that friends be loyal. Jesus promises them friendship that they can count on always. Nothing can come between them and God. Just as God was with the disciples through Jesus during his life on earth, so God will be with them (and us) in the Holy Spirit after Jesus is gone. God/Jesus/Holy Spirit will be so close, they will be inside us.

Finally, Jesus promises his disciples (whose world is about to be torn apart by Jesus' crucifixion) that his presence with them will result in peace and that peace will become a mark of the church. The other texts celebrate this peace (Ps. 67), tell how the church worked to preserve it (Acts), and look forward to the day when the peace will be complete (Rev.).

*Acts 15:1-2, 22-29.* This is one story of how the church worked out a conflict to preserve the peace that Jesus gave. Because the conflict dealt with circumcision, it is difficult to present to children. Those who do not know what circumcision is require an anatomy lesson that is difficult to present from a pulpit. Those who know what is involved tend to giggle.

So introduce the word before reading the Scripture: "To understand this story, we need to know a big word that may be new to some of us. The word is *circumcision*. This is an operation that only Jewish men and boys in those days had, in order to show their love for God. Many people who were not Jews had joined the Christian church, and they did not want that operation. The problem was that some Jewish Christians said that *all* Christian men and boys should have the operation. This was a problem that had to be solved." After this, use the term *circumcision* without comment. Curious children will demand fuller explanations from parents later.

Older worshipers can explore some of the details of the cultural conflict, but children will be more impressed by the trouble taken to solve the problem. In order to keep the peace of the church, the church in Antioch sent two of its leaders on a three-hundred-mile trip (each way) to discuss the problem with the church leaders in Jerusalem. They were to listen carefully and find answers. In response, the Jerusalem church wrote a letter, told Paul and Barnabas what to do, *and* sent two of its members to talk with the Christians in Antioch. This was a lot of trouble for everyone, but they thought it was worth it. It was important that they solve the problem so that there could be peace in the church. We are called to work as hard as these early Christians did to keep the peace in the church today.

This passage is also a case study of the church working to include people of different ethnic backgrounds. The visions of God's peace have always insisted that all nations be welcomed. Children have opportunities to work for inclusive peace every day. Their schools include children of different races and cultures, and their neighborhoods include kids who are cut out by others. To work for God's peace is to make a place for everybody.

*Psalm 67.* This harvest psalm acknowledges that God gives the peace, that nations are to share it, that peace and justice are related gifts from God, and that a good harvest is a peaceful blessing from God. This is a psalm for children to enjoy rather than to understand. The New Jerusalem Bible offers a particularly clear, beautiful translation.

*Revelation 21:10, 22-27.* This passage is John's coded glimpse of the city of peace that will finally come. Some older children will be able to crack enough of the code to discover that the presence of God and Jesus in the city will be so great that there will be no need for a church—the whole city will be a church. A few children will understand that people of all nations will be welcomed and will share their wealth. (The GNB's "wealth" or NJB's "treasures" brought to the city are clearer to children than RSV's "glory.") But many children will simply enjoy the fact that the Bible includes such cleverly coded messages and perhaps learn the code words they will be able to understand later.

## Watch Words

Use the word *peace* in such a way that children realize it includes justice and inclusiveness, not just absence of war.

## Let the Children Sing

"Let All the World in Every Corner Sing" is a simple praise hymn which reflects Psalm 67.

"Savior Again to Thy Dear Name We Pray" includes many of the themes of these texts in simple concrete language children can understand as they sing.

"Dona Nobis Pacem," a prayer for peace learned by many children at camp, would be effective sung as a round by several choirs of different ages, or as a congregational hymn.

## The Liturgical Child

1. To emphasize the way the church tried to settle the disagreement in Acts 15, ask an older children's or a youth class to pantomime the action. On opposite sides of the sanctuary, mount signs for "Jerusalem" and "Antioch." Five people stand beside each sign. As the passage is read, the Antioch group discusses the problem and sends two of its members to Jerusalem, where they are welcomed, listened to thoughtfully, and given a rolled-up letter. Then they are sent back to Antioch with two "elders," and the visitors read the letter to the Christians, who respond with joy. (This will require a brief practice to coordinate the reading with the movements and help the actors present their roles well.)

2. To read Psalm 67 as a litany, teach the congregation the response in verses 3 and 5. The worship leader then reads the other verses, pausing at appropriate times for the congregational response. (Consider printing the response in the worship bulletin.)

3. Pass the Peace at the close of the service. The worship leaders (perhaps with the help of ushers or prepared children) move down the aisles and shake hands with the person at the end of each row, saying, "The peace of God be with you." The worshiper responds, "and also with you," and turns to pass the wish to his or her neighbor, who them passes it on down the row.

4. Pray for situations in which God's peace is needed. In preparation, ask several children to identify such situations in their schools and the community.

## Sermon Resources

1. Make a last inquiry about the Easter tokens. Suggest that this week worshipers carry the tokens as a reminder that God's peace is with them and that they, as the Easter People, are called to work for peace.

2. Urge the children to work on the Worship Worksheet as they listen to the sermon for ideas. Invite them to share their favorite letter drawing and prayer with you as they leave the sanctuary.

Turn each letter in the word PEACE into a picture of a person "working for peace." Then write a prayer beside each picture. One has been done for you.

**P**

God, please help us to find homes for everyone.

**A**

**C**

**E**

# SEVENTH SUNDAY OF EASTER/ASCENSION DAY

Note: The Common Lectionary suggests using the Ascension Day lections on the Seventh Sunday of Easter. This option is chosen here in order to expose children to the story of the Ascension in a worship setting.

## From a Child's Point of View

*Acts 1:1-11.* The Ascension story is of interest to children for two reasons. First, it answers the literal-minded questions, "What did Jesus do after Easter?" and "Where is Jesus now?" The answer is that for forty days Jesus helped his disciples understand what had happened on Good Friday and Easter. Then he returned to God. Second, the Ascension is the story of Jesus passing the baton of responsibility to his disciples. As he returned to God, Jesus instructed the disciples to pick up and continue his work. They were to be Jesus' witnesses, and they were to expect God to send the Holy Spirit to help them with the task. The "two men in white" emphasize this change when they ask why the disciples are staring into the sky. There is work to be done. So on Ascension Day, we complete our celebration of what Jesus did and get ready to go to work as his witnesses today.

Older children are especially receptive to the challenge to be witnesses. Their parallel of the phrase "in Jerusalem, Judea, and Samaria and to the ends of the earth" is "at home, at school, in [your town], and to all the world."

These eleven verses are packed with a summary of the forty days after Easter, the promise of the Holy Spirit, a discussion between Jesus and the disciples about the messianic kingdom, and the Ascension story. The Good News Bible is by far

the easiest translation with which to keep up with all this action. Even so, you may need to reread verses 8-11 in order that children focus attention on the Ascension.

*Luke 24:46-53.* This is the easiest of today's three Ascension accounts for children. Reading it just before or after the Acts account will help children clarify what happened. The message is the same. The disciples (and we) are to take up Jesus' work after receiving the Holy Spirit.

*(OR) Mark 16:9-16, 19-20.* This is the less appropriate of the Gospel options—for textual reasons and for the children's understanding. It includes a jumble of rather disconnected stories which, in some places, are almost contradictory.

*Psalm 47.* The inclusion of this psalm with the Ascension texts is hard to explain to children. The psalm is all pomp-and-circumstance for the triumphant "king of the world." The Ascension focuses on the "servant King" who calls on his followers to take up his ministry. Adults can see the significance of this pairing of servant King and triumphant King, but few children can. For children, the psalm will be separate from the Ascension celebration.

On its own, Psalm 47 is a great reminder that God/Jesus is King of the universe, the greatest power that ever was or ever will be.

*Ephesians 1:15-23.* This passage is for grown-ups. The sentence structure is too complex and the

104

words too abstract for children. Children will hear Paul's basic message about Christ in the more concrete story of the Ascension.

## Watch Words

*Ascension* and *ascend* are not children's words, but use them today to describe this particular event.

Beware of using vocabulary about the triumphant king. Words such as *dominion*, *exalted*, and *subdued people* are foreign to children. Otherwise familiar words like *triumphant*, *victorious*, *conquering*, and *glorious* become meaningless when combined in long lists of adjectives or when used repetitively in varying combinations.

Take time to give the legal definition of *witness* so that children know what Jesus is asking his disciples to do.

## Let the Children Sing

Most of the hymns designated for Ascension Day are filled with triumphal language and theological jargon which are beyond children's understanding. The children will more readily celebrate Jesus' Ascension by singing "Come, Christians, Join to Sing," or even "Christ the Lord Is Risen Today." Sing the latter hymn one more time to conclude the entire Easter season.

"Open My Eyes That I May See" is a good hymn with which to accept Christ's call to become his witnesses.

## The Liturgical Child

1. Conclude your celebration of Easter by retracing the forty days of Easter. Reread several of the Easter lessons, matching them with different movements within your worship. Example:
John 20:1-10 (empty tomb)
Hymn: "Christ the Lord Is Risen Today"
John 20:24-29 (Thomas's encounter with the Risen Christ)
Prayers of Confession and Assurance of Pardon: Pray about ways we fail to live the Easter faith. If you used the Easter tokens, pray a one-sentence prayer about our failures, as high-

lighted by each use of the tokens. Jesus' response to Thomas becomes our Assurance of Pardon.
John 20:15-19 (Christ calls Peter to "feed my sheep")
Prayers of Petition
Acts 1:1-11 (the Ascension)
Sermon
Psalm 47 or hymn of praise to Christ

2. Create an Ascension litany celebrating Christ's work and committing yourselves to take up that work as his witnesses. The congregation responds after each statement. For example:

*Leader:* Jesus, though you were God and Lord of the universe, you were not ashamed to live among us and love us. You even died for us.

*Leader:* Jesus, you kept an eye out for people who needed healing. You touched lepers, put healing clay on blind eyes, told the lame to stand up and walk, and went looking for the woman who touched your robe, believing you could heal her.

*Leader:* You made friends with people everyone else avoided. You invited yourself to dinner with Zaccheus, the tax-collecting cheat. You included rough fishermen and political troublemakers among your disciples.

*Leader:* You taught us to forgive and love even our enemies. And you showed us how to do it as you forgave the people who betrayed you, denied you, and killed you.

*Leader:* When we remember what you said and did, we know you were showing us how good the world could be. Give us the courage and wisdom to follow you.

*Congregation:* Christ, we will be your witnesses and carry on your work at home, in (your town), and in all the world.

3. Be aware of end-of-school events, such as special parties or trips, and the concerns, such as grades, and the relief that summer is coming. Talk with children about their summer hopes (fun trips and release from homework) and summer fears (new camps, unwelcome baby-sitters or day-care set-ups; or tough kids on the loose in their neighborhoods). Lift up all these events and concerns in the church's prayers on the appropriate Sundays.

4. Begin the benediction with a paraphrase of the question asked by the two men in white, "Why are you standing here?" Then send the congregation out to be Christ's witnesses and promise the presence of the Holy Spirit.

## Sermon Resources

1. Tell stories about Christian witnesses. Let some or all the stories be about people or groups in your church. In telling what was done, help the listeners understand these efforts as responses to Christ's Ascension request that we become witnesses, so that they see themselves and others in the congregation as Christ's witnesses.

Cross out the extra letter in each word of Jesus' message.

# "YOUR SHALTL BEN OMY WAITNESSES"

Acts 1:8

Name or draw 1 place where witnesses are needed. Listen to the sermon for ideas.

Name or draw 1 way your church could be the needed witnesses.

Write a prayer about this need.

# PENTECOST

## From a Child's Point of View

*Acts 2:1-21.* This passage tells of the giving of the Holy Spirit and is the key story for Pentecost Sunday. Because children will have trouble following the text, they will depend on you to retell and interpret the story. Two points are of particular interest to them. First, the coming of the Spirit with wind and fire invites their imaginations to work on "what it was really like." (See Sermon Resources for suggestions for exploring the feel of the wind, fire, and Holy Spirit.)

Second, the miraculous ability of the disciples to speak foreign languages on that day, in order to tell the good news to travelers from around the world, points out that God intends that we be united. Peter cites Joel's list of all the people (sons and daughters, old men, and even slaves) who will receive God's Holy Spirit as further proof that we are to be united.

*Genesis 11:1-9.* This is the story of the Tower of Babel, understood by the church as God's response to sinful human pride when we try to make ourselves equal to God. It is read today as a contrast to the Pentecost story, in which people of all languages are drawn together by the Holy Spirit. But children will catch none of this as they hear the passage. The story line, with all its details about brick and bituminous mortar, is hard for them to follow. And God's words sound almost as if God were intimidated by human capabilities and that God therefore erected an obstacle (differing languages) to keep us under control. So read the story from the Bible and then retell it in order to present its intended points clearly.

*(OR) Romans 8:14-17.* (The Common Lectionary suggests that either Romans or Genesis be read this Sunday.) This is another passage that is hard for children to "hear" as it is read, but one which offers ideas that are meaningful to them. Its first truth is that the Holy Spirit is not scary, nor does it make us afraid of God. Wind, flames, and a Holy Ghost can sound spooky to children. If your tradition uses the term Holy Ghost, this is a good time to "define out" the Halloween connotations and explore God's presence as a positive, desirable experience. The second truth is that because God's Spirit lives within us all, we are all brothers and sisters, sharing Christ's glory and suffering in God's family.

*John 14:8-17, 25-27.* This is a sophisticated Greek discourse, put into Jesus' mouth by John. The repetitive statements in verses 8-11 will lose many children; they are likely to hear only occasional phrases thereafter. But this description of the work of the Holy Spirit is helpful for children because it shows that:

1. The Holy Spirit lives deep inside each of us.

2. The Holy Spirit helps us to know God's love and will, and reminds us about Jesus. The Holy Spirit is speaking when we know that God does not want us to do something (maybe to call someone mean names) or when we feel God calling us to action (perhaps to defend someone who is being teased, or to make friends with someone who is lonely). The Holy Spirit reminds us that God made us special and loves us—even on days when everyone else is treating us like junk.

3. Because the Holy Spirit lives in us, we can experience peace inside—even when it is not peaceful around us.

*Psalm 104:24-34.* This passage celebrates God's creation of the sea animals. The poet credits God's Spirit with both creating and caring for these animals. Before reading this lighthearted praise poem, alert children to the presence of a sea monster named Leviathan.

## Watch Words

Use the word *Pentecost* often to build familiarity with the name of this less-well-known holy day.

Choose your Holy Spirit language carefully. *Holy Spirit* or *God's Spirit* are probably the best terms for children. *Holy Ghost* sounds like a possibly friendly Halloween spook. *Comforter, counselor,* and *helper* are more helpful as descriptions than as names. *Breath of God,* if examined in relationship to the wind symbol, can become a meaningful way to explain and understand how God lives within us. Either stick with one term or use as many terms as possible, challenging the children to collect them, and explaining them as you go.

## Let the Children Sing

Sing "I'm Gonna Sing When the Spirit Says Sing" and offer original verses related to the worship theme. Or sing "They'll Know We Are Christians by Our Love."

Try "Breathe on Me, Breath of God," with its repeated phrase at the beginning of each verse (if you have explored the "breath of God").

To continue the praise of Psalm 104, sing "All Things Bright and Beautiful," "This Is My Father's World," or "I Sing the Almighty Power of God."

## The Liturgical Child

1. Decorate the sanctuary with flame-red paraments. Invite worshipers in advance to wear something red in honor of Pentecost. Use red flowers in the worship center. Print the bulletin on red paper or in red ink. To emphasize the gift of the Holy Spirit to all, drape around the shoulders of each worshiper a red crepe-paper stole decorated with Pentecost symbols to wear during worship. (An older children's class may make the stoles by gluing cut-out symbols on either end of 36-inch red streamers; the class can help distribute

them after the reading of Acts 2.) In the worship center, place a birthday cake for the church, decorated with red icing and twenty red candles. Serve it with red punch after worship.

2. Point out *Holy Spirit/Holy Ghost* in weekly responses such as the Gloria Patri and Doxology as you come to them. Note its significance in each song.

3. Invite the congregation to sing the one verse of "Spirit of Living God" as a response to spoken prayers for the church and the world. It may be sung once at the end, or several times as a response to specific prayers within the whole prayer.

4. After the benediction, ask children or ushers to give each worshiper a red flower as a reminder of the presence of the Holy Spirit in our life.

## Sermon Resources

1. To explore the significance of the fact that people of all nationalities heard the good news in their own language, paraphrase Acts 5-12, replacing New Testament countries with more familiar current ones. For example, "Are not all these who are speaking Mexicans? How can they speak to each of us in our own language? Germans and French and Japanese, people from Zaire and Argentina."

2. Explore the Pentecost wind and fire symbols so that children "get the feel" of God's presence. Recall experiences with "strong rushing winds." A stiff breeze in our face usually feels fresh and good. We feel strong as we walk into it. An autumn wind blows away the dead leaves of summer to make way for new growth next spring. Children often play in the wind with pinwheels, kites, and streamers (and often with the scarfs we wish were on their heads). Thus the wind of the Spirit can easily be perceived as a cleansing, invigorating, welcome presence.

Children who camp have the edge on appreciating fire as a symbol of God's presence. Just as a flame ignites a bright lantern (the lantern is a brighter light than a softly glowing candle), God's Spirit ignites wishy-washy, easily frightened people into brave folks who will stand up to tell the world the good news. Just as a campfire or fireplace is a source of warmth and comfort on cold nights, God's Spirit comforts us when people are treating us coldly. Just as a flame may be used to sterilize a needle when we remove a splinter, God's Spirit works within us to clean out bad attitudes, ideas, and ways.

Listen to Acts 2:1-21. Write the answers to the questions below in the Pentecost Puzzle spaces.

1. P __ __ __ __ __ __

2. __ __ __ E __ __

3. __ __ N __

4. __ __ T __

5. __ __ E __ __ __

6. __ __ C __ __ __

7. __ O __ __

8. __ __ S __ __ __ __ __

9. __ __ T

1. The spirit gave the people _____.
2. What was seen over people's heads?
3. What was heard and felt?
4. Who gave the first Pentecost sermon?
5. In what city did this happen?
6. Pentecost is the birthday of the _____.
7+8 What did God give on Pentecost?
7+9 What is another name for this gift?

Answers: 1. power 2. flames 3. wind 4. Peter
5. Jerusalem 6. church 7. Holy 8. Spirit 9. Ghost

Draw or write about a time when you felt the Holy Spirit very close to you.

# TRINITY SUNDAY

## From a Child's Point of View

The doctrine of the Trinity is very abstract and complex. Scholars have argued about it for centuries. Many adults have difficulty understanding it. Often on Trinity Sunday, worship takes an educational bent as pastors strive to help their congregations grasp this basic but illusive doctrine.

Three of today's texts that deal with the Trinity are way beyond the understanding of children. But that does not mean there is no way for children to participate in the worship of the Triune God. If the worship leaders are aware of children's understanding of the Trinity, some of the liturgy and the sermon can meet the children where they are, invite them to worship God as they now experience God, and challenge them to stretch their understanding.

All that we can reasonably expect of children is that they know the names of the three persons of the Trinity and sense that these three persons are somehow intimately related to one another. Children relate personally to God (who created the world and cares for them) and to Jesus (who lived among us, showed us how to live, and loved us enough to die for us). They voice questions about the relationship between God and Jesus, but few answers can truly satisfy their literalistic thinking.

Most children are less familiar or comfortable with the Holy Spirit. Older children can begin to interpret the warm community feelings within the congregation and their personal experiences of God's loving care as the work of the Holy Spirit. During their adolescence, as they acquire the ability for abstract thought and a sense of closeness to God as a prime desire, the Holy Spirit will become both understandable and significant. So talking of the Holy Spirit with children is a matter of planting a few seeds which, though they seem insignificant now, will blossom later.

Children can share fully in praising God, who created and cares for the world. They can confess and be pardoned by God/Jesus who loves and forgives them. They can lay their concerns before God, who cares deeply about each person in this world and calls us to do likewise. They can be led to think about what they already know about God and then stretch that knowledge a little. In the process, they may sense God's presence with them and their faith community.

*Psalm 8.* This is the one text for the day that is truly child-accessible. It is a response to the greatness of God the Creator. Children can respond to this greatness without dealing with the other texts. They can follow the poet's line of prayer, from praising God to wondering why God pays any attention at all to people, to meditating on the important place in the natural order to which we have been assigned by God.

## Watch Words

*Trinity* and *Triune* are unfamiliar. Although children are not ready to define the words, they can hear and accept them as "words we use at church in talking about God."

As you speak of God, be careful to choose words that in no way limit God. Especially watch pronouns that imply that God is only male. God is greater than either male or female. If you cannot

111

bring yourself to speak of God as Mother as well as Father, avoid both terms and talk of the many ways God loves us and cares for us. (It is hard work to edit exclusively masculine language out of our talks about God, but it is good theology, and it is important to an increasingly large number of women and their daughters. Trinity Sunday offers a good opportunity to work consciously on this task.)

## Let the Children Sing

"Now Thank We All Our God" is probably the best general praise hymn for the day. "Holy, Holy, Holy," with its difficult vocabulary balanced by the repeated opening phrase, is a good second choice.

Consider three hymns, one for each person of the Trinity. To God the Creator, sing "For the Beauty of the Earth" or "This Is My Father's World." Sing "Jesus Loves Me," "Tell Me the Stories of Jesus," or "Come Christians, Join to Sing" for the Son. And try "Breathe on Me, Breath of God" for the Holy Spirit, especially if you sang it last week as you celebrated the coming of the Holy Spirit at Pentecost.

## The Liturgical Child

1. Point out the Trinitarian statements in the responses you sing or say every week in worship (e.g., the Gloria Patri and Doxology).
2. Create a child-accessible confession such as the following, based on the three persons of the Trinity.

God, because we cannot see you, it is easy for us to ignore you or act as if you do not exist.

We look at the trees and rocks and animals and see only things for us to use. We "forget on purpose" that you made them and that we are to take care of them.

Jesus, we think so much about what we want and what we are doing that we forget what you taught us about loving other people.

Holy Spirit, our feelings of happiness and anger and sadness and joy are so strong that we sometimes do not even notice your presence with us.

We are sorry. Please forgive us. Amen.

*Assurance of Pardon:* God loves and forgives all who confess their sin. Just as God made and loves the trees and animals, God made and loves each one of us. Jesus loved us so much that he died for us. The Holy Spirit, God's strong, loving presence, promises to be with us always—even 'til the end of the world.

3. To help worshipers feel both the wonder and the thoughtful questions of Psalm 8, "line it out." A worship leader reads the psalm one line at a time, then the congregation repeats each line, matching the tone and emphases of the reader. A dramatic reader can help the congregation, especially the children, understand the message of the psalm as the phrases are repeated. (When books were scarce in colonial America, lining out was an every-Sunday approach to both reading the Bible and singing the hymns.)

## Sermon Resources

1. Divide the sermon into three sections to explore the three persons of the Trinity. After each section, lead a prayer addressed to that person of the Trinity. Then invite the congregation to sing a hymn related to this aspect of God. (See the list of possible hymns in "Let the Children Sing.")
2. Talk about "used to thinks." Describe some ideas about God you "used to think" but have now discarded. For example, I used to think that when God talked to people, they would hear a voice inside their heads. I have since learned that God speaks through the words of other people, through what we read in the Bible, and through feelings deep inside us. Describe some childhood "used to thinks" and some of your currently changing ideas about God. Encourage worshipers to identify ways their understanding of God has grown and to expect that their current understanding will continue to grow.

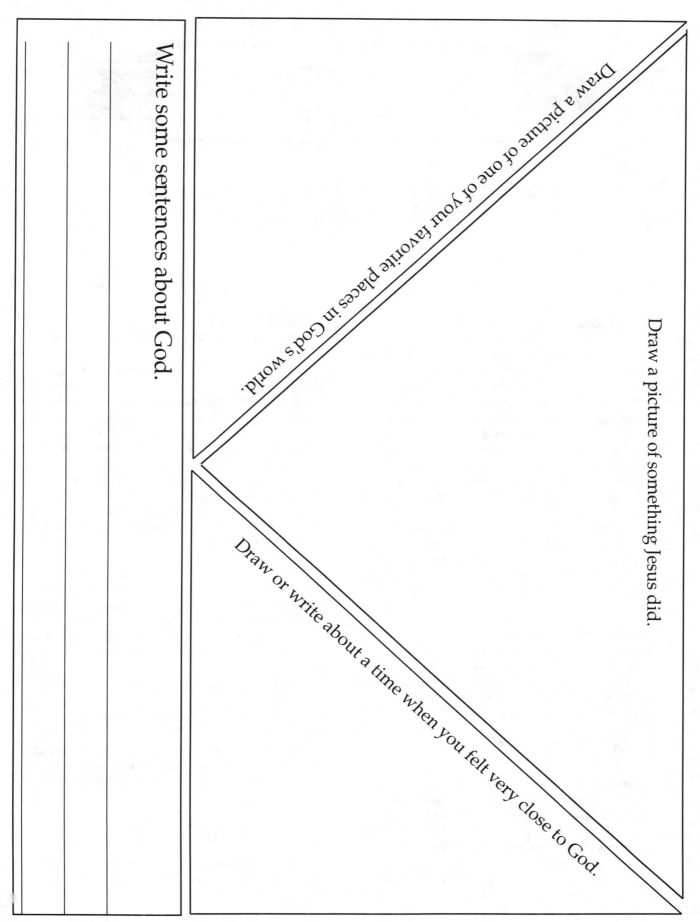

Write some sentences about God.

Draw a picture of one of your favorite places in God's world.

Draw a picture of something Jesus did.

Draw or write about a time when you felt very close to God.

*Trinity Sunday / © 1991 by Abingdon Press.*

# PROPER FOUR

## (Sunday between May 29 and June 4 inclusive, if after Trinity Sunday)

### From a Child's Point of View

*Old Testament: I Kings 8:22-23, 41-43.* These passages include two sections of Solomon's prayer for the dedication of the Temple. To understand the first section, children need to know the story of David's wish to build a Temple and God's promise about it. Knowing these things, they can join Solomon in praising God, who makes and keeps promises (covenants).

The second section acknowledges that God does not belong just to Solomon and the Jews (or just to us). God is Lord of the whole world. Part of Solomon's task (and ours) is to draw the rest of the world to God. Solomon did this by building a Temple that was open to people from everywhere. You might help children identify ways your congregation welcomes "foreign" people in God's name.

*Psalm 100.* This would have been a good psalm to sing at the dedication of Solomon's Temple. In fact, it is sung at the dedication of many sanctuaries today. Children can join easily in the short, simple praise phrases. It can help them to know that the "gates" and "courts" in verse 4 are parts of the Temple. A very rough paraphrase would be, "Come to church and into the sanctuary with praises for God."

*Epistle: Galatians 1:1-10.* The beginning of Paul's impassioned plea for Christian freedom from the Law is of some interest to children but has little preaching potential for them. Children like to receive letters and will be interested in the format with which first-century letter writers began their letters. Having been told about the format, children can follow Paul's introduction of himself (vss. 1-2*a*), the naming of the party to whom the letter is sent (vs. 2*b*), and the blessing (vss. 3-5).

Verses 6-10 are more difficult for children to follow. However, if The New Jerusalem Bible or the Good News Bible is read, older children will realize that Paul is really worked up about the gospel. It was so important to him that he was willing to curse those who presented what he viewed as a distortion of the gospel. (He cursed twice, just to make sure his readers did not think the first curse was a mistake.) His passion for the subject is what impresses children. They are called to care as much as Paul did about what God is doing in the world.

*Gospel: Luke 7:1-10.* This healing story is so tersely presented that children may misunderstand some of its details. The centurion's message about giving orders can cause children to think that the centurion thought he could order Jesus around, rather than that Jesus could order the slave healed without even being in the same room with him. That would make a big difference in the interpretation of Jesus' statement about the man's faith. Jesus was impressed by the man's total trust that Jesus could heal the slave, and that Jesus would heal the slave, even though the request came from a foreigner. So you may need to retell the story, elaborating on the key details.

### Watch Words

Define *centurion* unless you read the Gospel from The Good News Bible, where the man is introduced as a "Roman official."

114

## Let the Children Sing

"All People That on Earth Do Dwell" requires good reading skills. But since the tune is familiar, older children will be able to keep up fairly well. Some children will enjoy placing the hymn and psalm side by side, to identify their similarities and differences.

Sing about the church—"In Christ There Is No East or West" or "We Are the Church."

## The Liturgical Child

1. Read Psalm 100 as a litany. Pastor (or pastor and choir) can read responsively with the congregation, or two halves of the congregation can read responsively. Most hymnals include a responsive reading that can capture the mood of the psalm if it is read in the spirit of crowd cheers, but which can be deadening if read in monotones at dirge pace. Prepared leaders for each group can set an upbeat tone and pace.

2. To emphasize the psalmist's insistence that all the people of the world join in praising God, invite two or three members of the congregation who speak foreign languages to read verses 1-2 in those languages. (Consider including youths who are learning another language in school.) After hearing verses 1-2 read in different languages, the congregation reads the rest of the psalm in unison.

3. Pray responsively for the church. Pray for your own congregation, the churches in your area (either the churches in your town or those in your denominational district), your denomination, and the catholic church. Begin each section of your prayer with, "Lord we pray for . . . ," then offer specific prayers for the life and work of that part of the church. Include in your prayers people and ministries of which the children are aware (e.g., pray for the summer camp sponsored by your church). At the conclusion of each section, the congregation responds, "Hear our prayers for the church."

4. Pray your way around the world. Begin praying for the church in your country; then pray for the church in four or five other countries, in geographic sequence. Begin each stop on your prayer trip with, "Lord, we pray for your church in (name of country)." Then offer prayers about specific issues, ministries, and successes of the church in that country. The congregation responds, "Hear our prayers for the church in (name of country)." Conclude with a prayer for your own congregation.

## Sermon Resources

1. Preach about the church. Tell stories about your congregation. Tell stories of long ago and stories that include current members. Select stories that give an overview of the life and mission of this congregation. Be sure to include the story of the dedication of your sanctuary. (If appropriate, ask for a show of hands of those who were present at that dedication.) Use this as background to explore Solomon's feelings and prayers as he dedicated the Temple he built. Talk about how God has made and kept promises in both sets of stories. Finally, pray for the church, both catholic and local.

2. Use the format of Paul's letter to the Galatians as the format of your sermon. Follow the form of the greeting, and then speak to the congregation about the church (building on today's texts). Conclude with Paul's usual greetings (be sure to include some children or children's groups) and blessing. Present the letter as one Paul might have written to your congregation, or as a letter you are writing to them.

Psalm 100 calls people in every land to praise God. Draw faces, hair, and hats to turn these heads into praising people from other lands.

*Make a joyful noise to the Lord, all the lands!*
*Serve the Lord with gladness!*
*Come into his presence with singing!*
*Know that the Lord is God!*
*It is he that made us, and we are his; we are his people, and the sheep of his pasture.*

*Enter his gates with thanksgiving, and his courts with praise! Give thanks to him, bless his name!*

*For the Lord is good; his steadfast love endures for ever, and his faithfulness to all generations.*

Have you drawn a person from China or Egypt or Peru or Russia or India or Zaire?

Write a prayer for your church:
Tell God what you like about your church.
Pray for important work your church does.
Ask God's help for your church.

_____
_____
_____
_____
_____
_____
_____

Pray your prayer. Show it to your pastor as you leave worship.

# PROPER FIVE

## (Sunday between June 5 and 11 inclusive, if after Trinity Sunday)

### From a Child's Point of View

*I Kings 17:17-24 and Luke 7:11-17.* These two passages are very similar stories about the raising from death of the only sons of widows. Both make two important points. The first point is that God is powerful. God, working through Elijah and Jesus, can even bring dead people back to life. The second point is that God is loving and caring. In each case the raising of the son is a response to the widowed mother's plight. (At that time a woman depended upon her male relatives. A woman with neither husband nor sons lived in dire poverty.)

The widow's angry accusation of Elijah and Elijah's frustrated speech to God do not make sense to children. To accept the widow's speech, one must have some understanding of the Deuteronomic explanation of suffering and the role of anger in the grieving process. To understand Elijah's frustration, one must recall the story of the widow's help and of all Elijah had suffered as God's prophet. The easiest way to explain all this to children is simply to say that when we are really hurting, we sometimes say mean things. Because she was so upset about her son's death, the widow lashed out at Elijah and God. God understood and kept loving her. Because his friend the widow was so upset, and because he too grieved for her son, Elijah was upset also and told God so. God understood and kept loving him.

Because these stories link God's compassion with miraculous raisings, they may raise a difficult question in two forms. Intellectually curious children may ask, "If God has the power to raise these two sons from death, why doesn't God raise everyone?" Grieving children will ask, "If God could raise those people, why doesn't God raise (my loved relative)?" The only acceptable answer to either question is, "We don't know. That is one of God's secrets." This answer needs to be given with ample assurance that God loves us and cares for us, even when we don't understand. This assurance is critical for a grieving child—for whom this discussion best takes place not in worship but one-on-one, with lots of hugs.

*Psalm 113.* This is a meditation on God's power and love. If the short praise sections are presented separately, children can understand them. Verses 5-6 present an amusing picture of God being so great that it is necessary to stoop down to see heaven. The New Jerusalem Bible translates it:

> Who is like Yahweh our God?
> His throne is set on high,
> but he stoops to look down
> on heaven and earth.

*Epistle: Galatians 1:11-24.* Paul was trying to establish his credibility with the Galatians on their terms. To do so, he insisted that he received the good news straight from God, that he was not someone else's student. Such credibility does not mean much to children, who are constantly dependent upon the knowledge and teaching of others. They are more likely to hear in the passage a summary of Paul's change from persecutor to preacher. A particularly alert older child may ask the mechanical question, "How did God tell Paul the good news while he was in Arabia?" Unfortunately, Paul didn't tell us the answer to that one.

## Watch Words

*Widow* may be a new term for younger children. Explain it before using it to refer to the two mothers.

In speaking of death, use the concrete terms *died* and *dead* rather than euphemisms such as *passed on*. Stick to one or two simple terms, such as *raised* or *brought back to life* to describe what happened to the sons.

## Let the Children Sing

"I Sing the Almighty Power of God" (note that the Worship Worksheet is based on this hymn) and "For the Beauty of the Earth" are hymns through which children can praise God's love and power.

"Immortal, Invisible, God Only Wise" is filled with impossibly big words and strangely abstract phrases describing God. If your congregation sings it regularly, work through some of the verses during the sermon before singing it today. Emphasize that God is even more mysterious than these strange words and phrases.

## The Liturgical Child

1. Read consecutively the two stories about sons being raised from the dead so that all worshipers can note the similarities between them. It may help children pay more attention if the stories are read by two readers standing in opposite lecterns.

2. To help children hear the individual praise statements and to preserve the feel of Psalm 113, ask five readers to present it:

> Reader 1: verses 1-3
> Reader 2: verse 4
> Reader 3: verses 5-6
> Reader 4: verses 7-8
> Reader 5: verse 9
> All: Praise the Lord!

The first reader presents the call to praise. Each of the following readers cites one reason to praise God. Then all conclude with a shared praise. A class of older children or youths might prepare this reading, or you could gather an intergenerational group of readers. One short practice will be essential.

3. In your prayers, praise God for all the wonders of summer: special summer activities such as swimming, hiking, and whatever summer sport is central for your children; and for the change of pace that comes when school ends.

## Sermon Resources

1. Play with the how-great-is-God questions to explore God's great love and power:

"Who was there before God?" (Answer: No one. God always existed. You can't go back far enough to get away from God.)

"Who made God?" (Answer: No one. God always was and always will be.)

"How does God know what is happening everywhere all the time?" (Answer: We don't know how God does it, but we know God does.)

Make up more questions and answers. If you deal with such questions with an open, light-hearted attitude, children will gain a sense of security based on your certainty that God's love and power are bigger than we can imagine and sufficient to meet any need.

2. Invite worshipers to open their hymnals for ready reference while you work through some or all of the verses of "Immortal, Invisible, God Only Wise." No child will remember all the definitions or explanations. But children can sense that the words are more than we can understand because God is more than we can understand. They also can sense from you that the words and the God they describe are friendly mysteries, to be enjoyed rather than feared.

We know God as Father, Son, and Holy Spirit. So, multiply your age by 3.

———— x 3= ————
your age

Now write **God loves me always** that many times.

*Remember what you write. It is true!*

Draw a praise picture to show God some of the people and things you are thankful for.

# PROPER SIX

*(Sunday between June 12 and 18 inclusive,
if after Trinity Sunday)*

## From a Child's Point of View

*Old Testament: I Kings 19:1-8.* This is the first of three installments in the story of Elijah's trip to Mt. Horeb, God's message to him there, and the subsequent call of Elisha. In this section, Elijah is scared and running for his life. To understand what is going on, children need know only that Elijah had just killed all four hundred of Queen Jezebel's priests and that Jezebel was the meanest queen in the Bible. From the story, children learn that God was with Elijah, taking care of him when Elijah was in trouble, scared, and ready to quit. Children can expect that God will be with them, too, and will care for them when they are scared and feel hopeless.

*Psalm 42.* This psalm really belongs with Psalm 43, which is to be read next Sunday. (You may want to read both psalms on one or both days.)

The abstract language, poetic images, and geographic references make this psalm almost impossible for children to understand cognitively. Fortunately, the most understandable image—that of the thirsty deer—is in the first verse. It often catches children's attention before they get lost in the more complicated images that follow. If they hear this image, and if the rest of the psalm is read with deep feeling, children can catch its emotional sense. The refrain, especially if read from either the Good News Bible or the New International Version, summarizes these feelings and the psalmist's commitment to hope in spite of the gloomy situation.

*Gospel: Luke 7:36–8:3.* This is a story (7:41-42) within a story (7:36-50), followed by a tag-along story (8:1-3). And that is too much for one morning. I suspect that the intent is that we focus on the first set of stories and omit the tag-along (which probably was added in deference to the women's lobby).

Such a thing may be necessary, but a solid separate service could be constructed around the women who traveled with Jesus and his male disciples. Worshipers of all ages would be interested in learning who those women were and imagining how they must have gotten along together. A sermon about these women, set in a liturgy focused on discipleship and community, offers the hope that if Jesus accepted that bunch, then there is hope for us. It also calls us to welcome all kinds of people into our community of faith. Such a service would be quite child-accessible.

The story and parable within it are simple enough for children. The point is an important one: We do not need to earn God's love. God loved the sinful woman and the "good" Simon equally. The two were different only because the woman realized that God loved her in spite of what she had done. She was a lot more appreciative of God's love than Simon was. Simon had no right to look down on her.

To children who are continually graded at school, compared with other children by adults, and even judged by playmates when teams are picked for games, Jesus says that God loves you all equally. God loves the people who do not do their homework as much as those who do. God loves the people who are elected to class office as much as the kids who get bad marks in citizenship on every report card. God even loves the kids who are always getting into fights as much as those who are always kind and gentle. This is good news!

This is also a call to not think we are any better than people who do not make grades as good as ours, who are not as kind as we are, or who fail to meet our standards in any area. If God loves such people and accepts them, they should be good enough for us. In fact, Jesus tells us a sober secret: Sometimes people who have had to be forgiven many times are more loving than those who always have been good. It takes a while for children to grasp this secret, but it is a truth that those who are growing up as "good kids" especially need to encounter.

*Epistle: Galatians 2:15-21.* This passage will mean nothing to children when they hear it read. The sentences are too complex, and the vocabulary is both too abstract and too technical. But its message is very similar to Luke's message: God loves us. Jesus came to live among us and die for us to prove that God loves us. So we do not need to pile up good deeds or perfect-attendance awards to make God like us.

## Watch Words

Watch out for Paul's theological vocabulary. Avoid *justification*. Instead, speak of being friends with God.

Be cautious with *faith* and *grace* (most children recognize *grace* as a girl's name, as being able to do something with poise, or as a prayer said before eating). *Trust* is more familiar and communicates more clearly what Jesus and Paul were talking about.

Avoid Paul's use of *the Law* as catch words for trying to earn God's approval by keeping all the laws of the Old Testament. Elementary children are at the stage of moral development in which rules and laws are seen as good ways to live, work, and play together. They make moral decisions in reference to rules and laws. Paul's image is confusing because it sounds like a put-down of all rules and laws, rather than a challenge to the Pharisees' approach to the Law.

## Let the Children Sing

Use hymns that stress God's love for us and care for us in tight spots: "Jesus Loves Me, This I Know," "Now Thank We All Our God," "The Lord's My Shepherd," and "Be Not Dismayed Whate'er Betide" ("God Will Take Care of You").

## The Liturgical Child

1. Give a strong, dramatic reading of Elijah's story. Read Jezebel's threat to Elijah and Elijah's complaint to God as you think they might have been spoken.

2. Introduce the format of Psalms 42–43 (three major verses each, followed by the same refrain). The worship leader then reads the verses, with the congregation reading the refrains. (To help get into the feel of the psalm, invite the members of the congregation to imagine they are Elijah, running away from Queen Jezebel.)

3. Before reading Luke's story, place on the lectern a "flask of ointment" (perhaps a decorative perfume bottle) and eleven cardboard coins. Explain that each coin is worth 50 denarii. Separate one coin and count the other ten into a stack, pointing out that there are 50 denarii in one stack and 500 in the other. Urge the children to listen for each of these items in the story you will read from Luke. Point to each of the items as you come to it in the story.

4. For dramatic emphasis and clarity, present the story as a one-person play. As you read the narrative, face forward in the lectern. While reading the Pharisee's words, turn a little to one side of the lectern; while reading Jesus' words, turn a little to the other side. Imagine that the woman is kneeling on the floor a little behind Jesus. Assume the roles of Jesus and Simon with your facial expression, and even your hand movements, as you read their parts.

## Sermon Resources

1. To explore Elijah's experience, begin by talking about what scares people. Tell stories about being in storms or being lost (two big childhood fears) as well as stories about things adults fear. *The Diary of Anne Frank* offers excerpts about living faithfully with fear.

2. *Words by Heart*, by Ouida Sebestyen (available in most public libraries), is a powerful novel about a girl who learns to live by all the Bible verses she has memorized. Excerpts illustrate Jesus' points and Luke's points.

Draw a picture of something that frightens you.

Write a prayer about your picture.

Find the letters of one word in each kite. The words are Jesus' promise to us when we are frightened.

Answer: I am with you always.

*Matthew 28:20*

# PROPER
# SEVEN

*(Sunday between June 19 and 25 inclusive,
if after Trinity Sunday)*

## From a Child's Point of View

*Old Testament: I Kings 19:9-14.* Because children think literally, they interpret God's "speaking" in biblical stories as an audible voice. They also tend to remember dramatic stories in which God speaks out of burning bushes, or reassures fleeing slaves with a pillar of fire and a cloud. Therefore, they often believe that because they have not had such a dramatic experience or heard a "voice," that God has not spoken to them. For Elijah, God did not come in a dramatic wind, fire, or earthquake, but in "a still, small voice," "the soft whisper," or "the sound of a gentle silence." This text is therefore an opportunity to present to children the possibility that God can speak without an audible voice and to alert them to the ways God speaks deep within us.

A point that often goes unnoticed is that even after the wind, earthquake, fire, and "sound of gentle silence," Elijah still told God exactly how scared and unhappy he felt. Apparently he was not intimidated by God's presence, nor did God intend for him to be. We are invited to be as honest with God as Elijah was.

*Psalm 43.* This is a continuation of Psalm 42, which was read last week. Reread last week's commentary. In order for this cry for protection to make sense in today's worship theme, you will need to review with younger worshipers last week's story of how Elijah came to the mountain.

*Gospel: Luke 9:18-24.* For children this passage is two related short stories. In the first, Peter is presented as a hero who knows what he thinks and is not afraid to say so. While the other disciples are pointing their fingers at what others say, Peter makes his own statement. Children (and older worshipers) are called to follow Peter's example in standing up for what they think in daily life. For children, this means standing up for God's ways among their friends and at school.

It is hard enough to stand up and say what you think, but Jesus asks even more in the second story. He calls on the disciples to "take up your cross." For children to understand this call, they need to be reminded that the crucifixion was not an event which Jesus helplessly endured with patience. Jesus could have avoided being crucified. He could have run away. Or he could have stopped teaching and healing people. But Jesus loved us so much that he chose to go through with crucifixion for us. Therefore, when Jesus calls us to take up our cross, it is a call to suffer on behalf of others. Jesus is calling children not to endure bullies, difficult teachers, or mean peers, but to find ways to love those people in Jesus' name—even if it requires that they try some unpleasant things and endure some rough responses from those they try to love. Older children, in particular, respond to this call and are willing, with some adult support, to "take up a cross" on behalf of people they encounter.

*Epistle: Galatians 3:23-29.* This is a passage for adults. Its complex sentences deal in abstract language with an idea that is developmentally incomprehensible to children. Elementary children are at a stage of moral development in which ethical decisions are made by following or not following rules. They respond strongly to calls to follow God's rules, and they struggle daily with overcoming their own wishes and feelings in order to follow those rules. Paul's insistence that

Christians are beyond the Law (or rules) baffles them. It will make little sense until their mental abilities develop enough to allow identification of the principles behind rules. So read this passage for older worshipers.

## Watch Words

Be careful about using *the cross* as a catch word for self-sacrificing love. Children grasp the message more readily when it is presented in concrete terms about taking risks to love others.

## Let the Children Sing

Sing about God speaking to us through the Holy Spirit—"Every Time I Feel the Spirit"—and in creation—"This Is My Father's World." Singing "Open My Eyes, That I May See" is one way of committing ourselves to be alert for God's messages. Although the vocabulary of "Take Time to Be Holy" is a little difficult, older children can pick up several of the phrases about making time to listen for God.

Respond to Luke's call by singing "Lord, I Want to Be a Christian" as it is written, or by making up some verses such as "Lord, I want to speak like Peter," or "follow Jesus," or "take up my cross."

## The Liturgical Child

1. Review last week's suggestions about reading Psalms 42-43.

2. Create a litany prayer of confession in which the worship leader identifies the ways God speaks to us. After each "way," the congregation replies with an admission that we do not pay attention:

*Leader:* God, we wish you would speak to us, but we ignore the messages you speak all around us. Pictures from space show us the beauty and sweep of your creative power. Tiny flowers and intricate insects speak of your care for the smallest of things. The earth and the universe are full of messages about your power and loving care.

*People:* But we do not pay attention. Forgive us.

*Leader:* You speak to us through the people around us. If we listen carefully, often we can find your will in the advice of friends and leaders. If we care to, we can sense your love behind the love of those who take care of us. If we are alert, we will recognize people who are doing your work, and we will join them.

*People:* But we do not pay attention. Forgive us.

Add prayers about God speaking through the Bible, deep within us, and so on.

3. Use a similar format to shape the congregational prayers of thanksgiving and petition. Note specific ways you hear God speaking through the created order at this time of year. Pray for those through whom you sense God speaking. Be specific. Leave silent moments during which worshipers can pray for people through whom they sense God speaking to them personally. Pray about attentiveness and responsiveness to God speaking through the Bible. Close with prayers for alertness to God speaking within and around us.

4. Before the offering, invite worshipers to write the name of a person for whom they want to "take up a cross" during the coming week, or a promise to God about "taking up a cross" in a particular situation. Suggest that they put the folded slip of paper into the offering plate as a way of offering themselves to God. (Instruct the ushers to respect the privacy of these offerings.)

## Sermon Resources

1. Instruct worshipers to identify silently one person with whom they have difficulty. The person may be someone who hurts them frequently (perhaps on purpose), a bully who makes life difficult, or some other person at work or at school, in the neighborhood, or even in the family. Then suggest that they think of at least one way to take up a cross for that person during the coming week. Include time to pray for these persons during the prayers of the service.

2. Tell stories about taking up crosses. Include family stories such as a child giving up a favorite television show so that another family member can watch a show; children inviting an unpopular loner to sit with them and their group at lunch, and so forth.

God speaks to us in many ways.

Draw something larger than a house that tells you of God's power.

Draw a picture of something smaller than a softball that reminds you of God's love.

Write the letters on this word trail in the spaces to find a message from Jesus.

Start here

T A
K E
U
R
O S A P
C N
S A U
L L R
W O O Y
M E O D
F

" _ _ _ _ _ _ _ _ _ _ _ _ . "

Luke 9: 23

✝ ✝ ✝ ✝ ✝ ✝ ✝ ✝ ✝ ✝ ✝ ✝ ✝ ✝ ✝ ✝ ✝ ✝

Write a promise to God about a person who needs your love this week. Choose a person who may not love you.

# PROPER EIGHT

## (Sunday between June 26 and July 2 inclusive)

### From a Child's Point of View

Today's texts cluster around the theme of discipleship.

*Old Testament: I Kings 19:15-21.* This passage involves many specific historical details. But if children are retold the story of Elijah's flight, are reminded of Queen Jezebel's identity, and are encouraged to imagine how Jezebel would have responded to Elijah's anointing of a new king, they will realize that God did not come to Elijah in "the sound of gentle silence" to comfort him and let him off the hook. God had taken care of Elijah when he ran from Jezebel. Now God expected him to get back to work. To children, this says that God loves us and cares for us *and* expects us to be good disciples, even when it is difficult.

The concept of "the remnant" in this text can be helpful to preadolescent children. Ten- to twelve-year-olds often let groups, teams, and clubs shape their emerging personal identities. Ideally, there will be some groups with Christian values to which children can belong. But often Christian children feel that they, like Elijah, are the only ones with such values left in their schools or neighborhoods. It is tempting to children to set these values aside in order to join an established, visible group. To join Elijah as part of "the remnant" is a helpful, if not totally satisfactory, alternative. With adult support, children can develop a certain pride in belonging to the strong remnant that does not go along with other crowds when they abandon God's ways.

*Psalm 44:1-8.* This psalm celebrates God, the

Lord of history, in a way that is beyond the awareness of most children.

*Epistle: Galatians 5:1, 13-25.* These passages will not make much sense to children as they hear them read. However, with some help, they can grasp Paul's message in verses 14-25. (The emphasis on Christian freedom in vss. 1 and 13 will be understood in later years.) Paul begins with the command to love your neighbor as you love yourself (vs. 14). Then he presents a list of what happens when people do not follow this rule (vss. 19-21), and another list of what happens when they do follow this rule (vss. 22-23). This first list, in particular, is more clear in the vocabulary of the Good News Bible or New International Version. Although some items on the list may make children giggle, they need to hear Paul's condemnation of activities that television and today's culture seem to accept. Because they often are told not to act like animals, children enjoy Paul's comparison of the people who do not love to packs of destructive animals.

*Gospel: Luke 9:51-62.* This passage includes two separate stories. Verses 51-55 are a lesson in what to do when someone you have tried to love refuses to love you. Children will need background information on Jewish-Samaritan relations to understand the story, but they will need no help in understanding its "reality" message. The reality is that even Jesus was turned away by some people he tried to befriend. Children need to realize that the same probably will happen to them when they try to reach out to lonely, unhappy people at school and in their neighborhoods. When this happens, they are to be as forgiving as Jesus was.

Verses 57-62 report Jesus' conversations with

three would-be disciples. For children, the most compelling of the three excuses is the second. In a child's language, it is, "I am not ready to be a real disciple yet. When I grow up, I'll be one. But now I'm just a kid. All I can do is learn about Jesus." Jesus' response is that *now* is the time to be a disciple. Jesus needs children to do his work on the playground, in the swimming pool, the locker room, and all those other places where adults are not as influential. So children are called to be disciples *now*.

## Watch Words

In speaking of discipleship under difficult conditions, avoid terms such as *perseverance* and *forbearance*.

Avoid using *the flesh* and *the spirit* as tag words for life based on disobeying or obeying the command to love one another. Instead speak of *obeying* and *disobeying*.

Translate into today's vernacular the unfamiliar or obsolete words that describe sexual activities.

## Let the Children Sing

"Lord, I Want to Be a Christian," "Take My Life and Let It Be Consecrated," and "Breathe on Me, Breath of God" (in order of ease) are discipleship hymns children can sing.

"O Jesus, I Have Promised" will be hard for younger readers, but preadolescents often appreciate and claim for themselves this musical prayer.

Ask the children's choir or the congregation to sing "I've Got a Joy, Joy, Joy, Joy, Down in My Heart." Add verses that celebrate Paul's "fruits of the Spirit." A lighthearted congregation can enjoy even a final verse: "If the devil doesn't like it he can sit on a tack—and stay!"

## The Liturgical Child

1. To stage the three conversations in Luke 9:57-62, enlist the help of three would-be disciples (standing in a group at one side of the chancel) and Jesus (standing at the center). The worship leader (standing in the lectern) serves as narrator, introducing the passage and reading the intro-

ductory phrase for each conversation. Actors should memorize their parts, plan the emphasis and tone of their speaking, and work together to present the sequence smoothly.

2. Base a prayer of confession on Galatians 5:

Lord, when we read Paul's list of the results of living apart from you, we recognize many of them in our own lives. Each of us has done things of which we are deeply ashamed. (Pause for worshipers to offer silent confessions.) Though most of us have not practiced witchcraft, we have treated our own wants as gods. (Pause) Each of us has made enemies and waged war with them. (Pause) We know what it is to be jealous of what others have. (Pause) We are amazed at how quickly we can become really angry and lash out at others. (Pause) We often put our ambitions first, even before doing what is right and loving. (Pause) We have been part of groups that shut others out. Forgive us and help us change our ways to reflect your love. For we pray in the name of Jesus. Amen.

*Assurance of Pardon:* God does forgive all who repent and change their ways. We are promised that when we do love one another, we will find that love, joy, peace, patience, kindness, goodness, faithfulness, humility, and self-control fill our lives to overflowing.

## Sermon Resources

1. Tell a story about two children in a sports camp at your state university. Put them in a group with two campers from a different area of the state who are very pushy about playing "their" plays and are very loud in their support of opposing university teams. Tell how the two disciples reach out to these difficult outsiders by helping them find a practice field, eating with them in the cafeteria, and setting up plays in their favor during practice sessions. Let the outsiders respond by showing no appreciation for help in finding a field, making rude jokes about the disciples' favorite teams and players at the cafeteria table, and stealing a play from the disciples to cause their team to lose the game. After hearing this story, worshipers of all ages will be ready to walk in the shoes of Elijah, Jesus, and his disciples; they will think about discipleship that does not give up when faced with discouraging results.

Write and draw a comic book story about a disciple doing hard work at a swimming pool or on a team.

Title: _____

[four blank comic panels]

Disciples are people who love and obey Jesus.

Paul said that people who obey Jesus' command to love one another will have everything listed below. Write each word in the correct spaces. *Hint: Match a letter in the word to a letter in the word disciple.*

— — — D — — —

— — — I — —

— — S — —

— — - C — — —

— — I — — —

— — — P — —

— — L — —

— — — E — —

LOVE  JOY  PEACE  PATIENCE
KINDNESS  GOODNESS  HUMILITY
FAITHFULNESS  SELF-CONTROL

Circle the word that is left.

# PROPER NINE

## (Sunday between July 3 and 9 inclusive)

### From a Child's Point of View

*Old Testament: I Kings 21:1-3, 17-21.* This is the story of Ahab's murder of Naboth in order to take his vineyard. Children will need to hear the whole story (vss. 1-21) because it is probably new to them. The Good News Bible is the easiest translation for children to follow.

The message in the story is simple: God does care about us and the way we act. God will not allow Naboth's unjust death to go unnoticed, nor will God let Ahab continually get away with such terrible behavior. Younger children, who generally make moral decisions in order to avoid punishment or to claim rewards, respond quickly to this message. Older children may realize that not all evildoers are caught as Ahab was. Indeed, some seem to profit by their evil actions.

*Psalm 51:8.* This psalm moves from praise to recognition of sin, to acceptance of God's grace, to petition for help in avoiding sin. But its exquisite form is not apparent to children. Instead, they catch occasional phrases, especially in verses 4-6, that remind them of the message of Ahab's story.

*Epistle: Galatians 6:7-18.* This passage summarizes Paul's position on the circumcision debate, an issue children do not understand. But they can understand Paul's insistence in verses 7-10 that we will reap what we sow. To translate the harvest image for nonagricultural children, speak of the results of practicing (or not practicing) a sport or musical instrument, or of a summer spent in front of the TV, versus one spent playing on a team. The phrases "sowing the flesh" or "sowing the Spirit" are too abstract. Make them concrete by speaking about the results of spending your time serving others, rather than doing only what you want to do.

*Gospel: Luke 10:1-12, 17-20.* This passage provides balance for last week's readings about the frustrations of being a faithful disciple. When the seventy-two were sent out, they did their work with more success than they dreamed possible. Though they may not understand the details of Jesus' instructions to the group, children will catch the drift of the story and pick up on the excitement of the seventy-two as they return successful. A dramatic reading will focus the children's attention on the disciples' excitement, rather than on the problematic promise about walking on snakes and scorpions, or on the picture of the devil falling from the sky. Children, especially older children who are defining themselves by the groups they join, are encouraged to join the excited disciples doing God's work in amazing ways. (If they heard about "the remnant" last week, this story can be an indication that, at times, being one of the remnant is not a burden, but an exciting opportunity.)

### Watch Words

If you explore Ahab's story as a morality play, avoid obsolete words about sin and forgiveness such as *transgressions*, *abominations*, and *vindication*. Remember that if children have heard the word *righteous*, they probably heard it used in reference to unattractive self-righteousness. Also, be sure to tell younger children what a *vineyard* is.

Paraphrase Paul's terms *the flesh* and *the Spirit* in

129

Galatians with examples of modern activities that reflect each way of life.

Do not assume that children will understand the reaping and sowing language in Luke and Galatians.

## Let the Children Sing

Child-accessible hymns about sin are hard to find. The vocabulary and images in the most familiar ones make little sense to children.

"I Sing a Song of the Saints of God" and "We Are the Church" (Avery and Marsh) are upbeat hymns that celebrate the church at work together. "God of Grace and God of Glory" is harder, but children can join in on the repetitive chorus.

## The Liturgical Child

1. The story of Ahab has all the marks of a morality play. So take advantage of the children's summer schedules or a willing children's church school class to produce a simple morality play. With only one good rehearsal, as few as seven children can pantomime the story while the worship leader reads it (simple costumes and props help). You will need Ahab, Jezebel, Naboth, at least one town leader, two false witnesses, and Elijah. In rehearsal, help the children act with their whole bodies as well as with their faces.

When introducing the play to the congregation, describe morality plays and their simplistic messages. Later during the sermon, explore the problems this oversimplification leaves for us.

2. Base a prayer of confession on the story of Ahab:

> Lord God, Ahab and Jezebel seem absolutely terrible until we look at ourselves. When we are honest, we admit that, like Ahab, we sometimes are jealous of what others have, and we mope if we cannot have it for ourselves. Like Jezebel, we twist and even break the rules, in order to get what we want. We act as if we are somehow special and need not follow your commands. Like Ahab, we have done the wrongs others have suggested, hoping you would blame them and not us. Forgive us. Forgive us for the wrongs we do and for all the ways we deny them and try to cover them up. Amen.

*Assurance of Pardon:* The Bible tells us that when Ahab confessed his terrible sins to God and asked for forgiveness, God forgave even him. Jesus has promised that God will forgive us also when we confess. There is nothing so sinful that it cannot be confessed to and forgiven by the God who loves us so much that Jesus came to live and die and rise among us.

3. Create a praise litany citing "successes" within your congregation and within the larger church. Be sure to include some activities in which children participated. To each example, the congregation replies, "Praise God, who is doing wonderful things through us."

4. Before pronouncing the benediction, charge the congregation in the same spirit with which Jesus charged the seventy-two:

> As Jesus sent out the seventy-two disciples to teach, care for the sick, and make friends with the friendless, so I send you. Go out into (your town or area) to share God's love. Talk to those who will listen, take care of those who need help, and do your part to bring God's kingdom closer. As you go, remember that many people are waiting for you and will welcome you. Also remember that Jesus will be with you always. Amen.

## Sermon Resources

1. Tell or recall parts of the story of Pinocchio, who learned that he could not hide his sin. Compare the experiences of Ahab, Pinocchio, and ourselves in pretending that our sinful actions do not matter.

2. Tell stories of amazing successes in the church. For example, describe the mushrooming work of Habitat for Humanity. In less than thirty years, this house-building ministry has used volunteer labor and donations of materials and money to build thousands of houses for needy people in countries all around the world. (Read *No More Shacks* by Millard Fuller if you do not know this story.)

Or describe the effect of one Heifer Project—a flock of chicks sent by a children's church school class to a family in an underdeveloped country (eggs to eat, sell, and hatch into more chicks).

Or describe the results of work your congregation has done.

Turn each letter in DISCIPLE into a picture of a disciple at work.

D I S C
I P L E

Listen carefully to the story of Ahab when it is read from the Bible. Find 9 words from that story in the letters below. The words may go across or down.

```
L R S S I N X M K
A H A B J M U U Y
E V I N E Y A R D
L K C R Z Z A D F
I X O L E T T E R
J M V L B T D R W
A I E K E H R N Q
H N T M L I E S T
```

Words to find:
AHAB    JEZEBEL

MURDER    LIES

VINEYARD

SIN    LETTER

COVET    ELIJAH

# PROPER TEN

## (Sunday between July 10 and 16 inclusive)

### From a Child's Point of View

*Old Testament: II Kings 2:1, 6-14.* This passage has no particular message for children. It is simply a good tale about two faith heroes. From it, we learn how Elijah's life ended and that Elisha took up Elijah's work. Those children who have heard during the last few weeks about how Elijah ran from Jezebel and complained to God on the mountain will be pleased with God's recognition of Elijah's work. Going to heaven in a fiery chariot (a fancy, neat way to die) proves to children that Elijah was special to God. They also will appreciate Elisha's loyalty to Elijah and his bravery in asking Elijah for the power to take over Elijah's work. The use of the rolled-up coat to cross the river is mysterious and proves that Elisha will also be special. This is a story to approach with the same open wonder with which we approach Cinderella and the knights of the Round Table.

*Psalm 139:1-12.* This psalm invites children to bask in the security of God's loving care. According to the psalmist, God knows everything there is to know about each one of us and will be with us always, no matter where we go. For some children, God may be the only one they can trust so completely. Even children in secure homes occasionally feel (rightly or wrongly) that they are unloved or that "they love him/her more than me." In all these situations, the conviction that God loves them and is looking out for them offers hope.

Though the message of the psalmist is concrete, the Revised Standard Version language is difficult for children. The Good News Bible is much easier.

*Gospel: Luke 10:25-37.* The parable of the good Samaritan appears in much church school curriculum and therefore is familiar to children. Without knowing about Jewish-Samaritan relationships, young children can grasp Jesus' basic message that we are to treat as neighbor any person who needs our help. As older children learn the significance of the good neighbor being a Samaritan, they can use the parable to reevaluate their responsibility to people who are not in "their group." For fifth- and sixth-graders, who have strong group loyalties, this is an important task. Retelling the parable in modern settings and making up versions of the parable that include children the same age as those in your congregation are often ways to help children get the point.

*Epistle: Colossians 1:1-14.* This is the greeting (vss. 1-2) and opening prayer (vss. 3-14) of Paul's letter to the church in Colossae. Paul writes in cosmic, abstract terms about the faith of the Colossians. Basically, he is thanking God that the Colossians have responded to the good news and praying that God will give them the power to live as good disciples. But children will not be able to pull this meaning from the long, complex sentences and abstract terms. Given the richness of the other texts for the day, it is advisable to speak to children through those texts rather than through this one.

### Watch Words

*Samaritan, Levite,* and *priest* need not be defined in cultural terms. Offering modern parallels to each term is as, or even more effective.

## Let the Children Sing

Sing "Swing Low, Sweet Chariot," pointing out its base in the II Kings text. Then sing either "I Sing a Song of the Saints of God" or "For All the Saints." The former is easy for children. To introduce the latter, which is harder but one that children will encounter frequently in worship, suggest that they sing the hymn for Elijah and Elisha. Encourage them to sing the Alleluias, even if they miss some of the words in the verses.

"Let There Be Peace on Earth" and "Lord, I Want to Be a Christian" are two hymns with which to commit ourselves to being good neighbors.

## The Liturgical Child

1. Offer prayers of thanks and praise for faith heroes and heroines. Begin by mentioning several biblical characters (including Elijah, who stood up to Queen Jezebel for God; Elisha, who was brave enough to take up Elijah's work). Then thank God for and pray for some of the faithful people in your congregation and in the world today. Finally, provide silence for each person to pray for people who are faith hero/ines for them.

2. Base a prayer of confession on our failure to think and act in heroically, faithful ways:

> God, we admit that we are not as brave as either Elijah or Elisha. Not only would we be afraid to stand up to an evil queen, but we do not even stand up for you and your ways with our friends. We are quiet when we should speak up, and we go along when we should try to stop what is happening. We say we could do nothing to stop evil ideas and plans, when really we are just afraid to try. Forgive us. Give us the courage and strength to do heroic deeds and live heroic lives for you; for we pray in Jesus' name. Amen.

> *Assurance of Pardon:* Jesus calls us to repent—that is, to change our ways—and he promises us that when we do, God will forgive us and love us, and give us strength and power beyond our imagination. We are forgiven. So let us go and live heroically for God.

3. To give each person the experience of saying the first-person statements of Psalm 137, "line it out." (The worship leader reads the text one line at a time, with the congregation repeating each line.) Try the following lines: 1, 2, 3, 4, 5, 6, 7a, 7b, 8a, 8b, 9, 10a, 10b, 11, 12a and b, 12c.

4. During the church's prayers, pray aloud for the congregation's neighbors and offer times of silence in which worshipers may pray for their own neighbors. During one silent period, bid them to pray for each member of their families. After a general prayer for the congregation, bid worshipers to pray in silence for one member of the congregation whom they know has special needs. Follow the same procedure when praying for people in your community (groups such as the homeless and individuals encountered daily), and for the people of the world (victims of natural disasters and those caught up in political events). In all cases, speak of specific groups with specific needs.

## Sermon Resources

1. Tell stories of faith heroes and heroines, starting with Elijah (review the last weeks' stories) and Elisha and moving on to tell of others. (You may want to tell of people from different times or describe the activities of several different kinds of hero/ines: Martin Luther, who stood up for what he thought; Jane Addams, who moved into a violent ghetto to take care of poor children; Archbishop Oscar Romero, who stood up to the government of El Salvador on behalf of its oppressed citizens.) These stories may lead to identifying the disciplines that help us grow into heroic Christians.

2. Retell the good Samaritan story, setting it in your town and including people the children in your congregation have encountered. (If I were telling the story, a mugging would take place near the bus station. The mayor and a minister would pass by, but a homeless alcoholic would stop to help.)

3. In response to the good Samaritan parable, talk about groups and group loyalty. While celebrating the benefits of groups, point out how easy it is to ignore others beyond the group and actively hurt others with group-centeredness. Cite examples such as fans of rival soccer teams fighting, groups of close friends making fun ot those they do not accept in their group, and members of children's clubhouses causing trouble in the neighborhood.

Listen carefully when II Kings 2:1, 6-14 is read. Draw a picture of one thing that happened in the story.

Turn the story of the Good Samaritan into a comic book story that happens in your town.

The Attack

Who passed by?

Who passed next?

Who helped?

# PROPER ELEVEN

## (Sunday between July 17 and 23 inclusive)

### From a Child's Point of View

*Old Testament: II Kings 4:8-17.* This is the story of the time Elisha thanked a woman for her support by promising that she would have a son. It is a simple story for children to follow, but it offers no particularly striking message for them.

*Psalm 139:13-18.* This is the psalmist's praise of God, who created him and knows him thoroughly. The original Jerusalem Bible's translation is probably clearest to children. It emphasizes the psalmist's appreciation for the way he was made. To children, this psalm presents an opportunity to appreciate the unique talents and potentials that God has given them.

*Epistle: Colossians 1:21-29.* This passage will not mean much to children when it is read. But it includes a statement of Paul's goal in life to which children can respond very positively when it is paraphrased. Paul's goal is simply to tell every person in the world the good news of God's unconditional love. Such an enormous goal has great appeal, especially to idealistic, world-aware ten- to twelve-year-olds. They are looking for something important to which they can give themselves. So invite them to claim Paul's goal (which is one goal of the church).

Paul worked at his goal with the understanding that he was doing Christ's work and that when he suffered as a result of his efforts, he was sharing in the suffering of Christ on the cross. If children understand their own efforts to be forgiving and care for others as doing Christ's work, they will be willing to risk more and develop a higher sense of the worthiness of such deeds. Children can even begin to see, as a result of doing loving things, the similarity between their endurance of embarrassing names or taunts and Jesus' willingness to suffer at the hands of the soldiers.

*Gospel: Luke 10:38-42.* This is the story of Martha's complaint against her sister Mary. Most children, having fresh experiences with such sibling arguments, empathize with the sisters immediately. But the story is not really about sibling arguments. It is about choices. Each sister made a choice about what to do when Jesus arrived. No one forced Martha to go into the kitchen. So Martha had no right to complain about Mary. In the language used in parent-training courses, Martha needed to accept the "natural consequences" of her choice. Similarly, children who plead for piano lessons must then accept the reality that while they are practicing, someone else might be watching television.

Jesus also insisted that Mary had made the better choice. So children need to consider their choices carefully, because some are better than others. Just as Jesus thought it was better to sit and talk about important things than to worry about a fancy meal, it also is better for children to help a younger brother or sister get ready for church than to spend all their time worrying about what they themselves will wear. It is also better to visit a shut-in with their Sunday school class than to accept a last-minute invitation to go to the movies with a friend.

### Watch Words

There are few word traps in today's themes.

135

## Let the Children Sing

To sing of God's creative work in us, choose "Now Thank We All Our God," "He Leadeth Me: O Blessed Thought" (children pick up on the chorus first), or "God Will Take Care of You" (the repeated phrase and easy chorus overshadow the obsolete vocabulary of the verses).

Celebrate the great goals of the church with "We Are the Church." Commit to these goals by singing "Take My Life and Let It Be Consecrated."

Sing about making good decisions by choosing "Dear Lord, Lead Me Day by Day" or "Lord, I Want to Be a Christian."

## The Liturgical Child

1. Follow the psalmist in praising the wonderful way God has created us and cares for each of us:

Lord, we want to talk to you about how you have made us and how you shape our lives:

Creator God, you gave each of us a one-of-a-kind body. There are things we like about our bodies and things we wish were different. We confess that we sometimes eat and drink things that are harmful to our bodies. In the silence, let us each speak to God about our bodies. (Pause)

Lord of our lives, you gave each of us special talents and skills. Sometimes we forget to say thank you for them. Sometimes we need to talk to you about how we use these skills to love others. In the silence, let us each speak to God about our talents and skills. (Pause)

Loving God, you placed in each of us certain qualities. It is easy for us to list those with which we struggle. But we are less ready to notice the admirable qualities, the patience and kindness and generosity you have planted in us. In silence, let us each honestly thank God for those good qualities we recognize in ourselves. (Pause)

The worship leader concludes by prayerfully reading aloud Psalm 139:13-18, changing the singular pronouns to plural.

2. Create a litany that asks God's help in making wise choices. The worship leader briefly describes a variety of decisions. (Include decisions about how to treat people and how to use our time; decisions made by political leaders; decisions about cheating in games and at work, etc.) To each decision, the congregation responds, "Lord, help us choose well."

3. As the story of Mary and Martha is read, have three expressive adults pantomime it. (Adults will more fully express the feelings involved and will be proof to children that adults also engage in spats.) Pause in the readings so that Martha can show her growing frustration.

## Sermon Resources

1. People of all ages like to hear stories about themselves. So tell stories about how your congregation and the members in it are Christ's feet (delivering Meals on Wheels), Christ's hands (taking care of children in a mission day-care center), Christ's mouth (teaching church school classes or saying loving words to lonely people), and Christ's heart and mind (trying to find ways to end racism or reduce homelessness). Be sure some of the stories include children as stars. Include one story in which the hero or heroine suffers as a result of those efforts. Present these sufferings as a way to show that the person shares in Jesus' suffering.

2. To explore choices and their consequences, describe "Create Your Own Adventure" books. In these books, the story is interrupted frequently for the reader to decide which of two options the characters should take. Directions send the reader to different pages to find out what happened as a result of the characters' choice. Most children (third grade and older) have read at least one such book and enjoy rereading it to try out different combinations of choices.

A daring preacher with a relaxed mid-summer congregation could begin the sermon by reading part of one of these books, letting the congregation vote on the choices by show of hands. Then the story of Mary and Martha could be presented in the same format. (The first decision is what to do when Jesus arrives, followed by Martha's decision about how to respond to Mary's choice.) This sets the stage for an analysis of how we make and live with our choices.

Turn this body into a picture of you. Draw around it pictures of things you do well.

Write words that describe you in the frame.

When they arrived in the Promised Land, Joshua told the people to make a choice. Use the key to break the code and write Joshua's command in the spaces below. What was their choice?

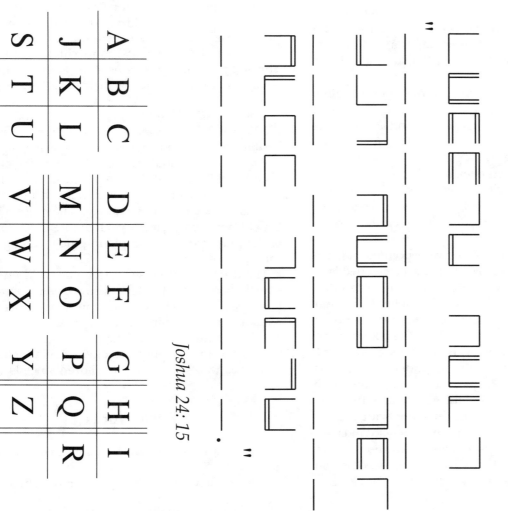

*Joshua 24: 15*

Answer: Choose this day whom you will serve.

| A | B | C | D | E | F | G | H | I |
|---|---|---|---|---|---|---|---|---|
| J | K | L | M | N | O | P | Q | R |
| S | T | U | V | W | X | Y | Z | |

# PROPER TWELVE

## (Sunday between July 24 and 30 inclusive)

### From a Child's Point of View

*Old Testament: II Kings 5:1-15b.* The story of Namaan's cure first attracts the attention of children because the heroine is a little girl. The fact that a little slave girl provided the key information about the cure and that Namaan and his wife took her suggestion seriously delights children, who often feel they have nothing important to contribute and that adults do not take their ideas seriously.

The importance of "little things" (a slave girl's information and a bath in a muddy river) is shown in two ways. First, it insists that God is at work in everyday events as well as in dramatic events. Children who grow up with the spectacular biblical stories often overlook God at work in the love of their families, the activities of their church, and the events of their own lives. This story encourages children to look for God at work in everyday events.

Second, as Namaan's servant pointed out, we should be as willing to do nonspectacular deeds as we are to do the dramatic ones. Children often undervalue their deeds of lovingkindness and playground peacemaking because they are not as dramatic as those in the Bible. They long to do heroic deeds and solve big problems in single strokes. They need to be reminded that God is working out the big plan through all our little efforts. Just as God used the information from the slave girl and cured Namaan—not with a great feat but with a bath in a muddy river—so God uses and values our efforts to love others and to share God's love with them. No loving deed is too insignificant to be noticed and used by God.

*Psalm 21:1-7.* This is a psalm of praise which Namaan might have sung after being cured. If he did, he would have prayed as if he were a king who has received what he asked of God.

*Epistle: Colossians 2:6-15.* This is part of a letter written to grown-ups about a grown-up intellectual problem. The children of Colossae were probably as unconcerned about this issue (except when it upset their parents) as are children today. The one point that makes sense to children is that Jesus is to be the center of their lives (vss. 6-7).

*Gospel: Luke 11:1-13.* This passage introduces the Lord's Prayer (vss. 1-4); it also offers a rather baffling parable and then a more sensible set of teachings about God's response to our prayers.

Older children will be interested in how this version of the Lord's Prayer developed into the one used in your church today. They also will benefit from comparing several different versions of the prayer and from exploring the meaning of each phrase.

The teachings in verses 9-15 invite children to stretch their understanding of how God responds to prayer. Many children assume that God can respond only by giving us what we ask for or by speaking audibly to us. This text suggests that God has as many options as does a loving father who tries to respond to his children's needs.

### Watch Words

*Leprosy* and its social isolation need to be described.

Even if they pray it regularly, most children

138

need help with the vocabulary of the Lord's Prayer. *Hallowed* needs to translate as *holy*. All the "kingdom" words—*kingdom, thy will be done, power, glory*—need to be tied together so that children can understand the whole as the prayer of the citizens of God's kingdom. Young children will not understand *daily bread* as including any food other than bread, unless they are introduced to this possibility. *Trespassing* is going into somebody's house or yard without permission; *debts* are financial bills. Children need help to connect these realities to sin and forgiveness. *Temptation* may be a big word to learn. Remember that for many children today, the only things that are *delivered* are mail, pizza, and catalog orders. So paraphrase "deliver us from evil" with something like "guard us from evil people and things."

## Let the Children Sing

*Sing the Lord's Prayer:*

1. Children's or youth choirs enjoy singing "The Lord's Prayer" to a West Indies tune. Many youths know this version. (It is printed in *Songs for Today*, a youth songbook by Augsburg Press, and it may be printed in other books.) A choir may sing it as an anthem; the choir and congregation may sing it responsively, the choir singing the phrases of the prayer and the congregation singing the repeated "hallowed be thy name."

2. The traditional version of the Lord's Prayer can be sung by the adult choir or by a soloist.

Choosing "I Sing the Almighty Power of God" is one way to celebrate God at work in the world. "All Things Bright and Beautiful" focuses on both big and little things.

## The Liturgical Child

1. Pray about "little things" in which you sense God's presence and power. Note storms, sunsets, and other weather events of the past week. Thank God for the Bible school, the church-camp experience for children, and other activities of your congregation in which you see God at work. Mention events in the community and human-interest events from abroad which indicate that God is at work among people every day. Then pray for the will and the wisdom to do "little things." Pray for the patience to say kind words when we feel tired and crabby, for the strength to keep forgiving people we need to forgive frequently (like brothers and sisters), and for the wisdom to find little ways to help relieve hunger and end homelessness.

2. Read the psalm after the Old Testament lesson. Invite worshipers to imagine they are Namaan, praying on their way home from the river.

3. Use the Lord's Prayer as an outline for the prayers of the congregation. The worship leader prays the Lord's Prayer aloud, pausing after each phrase for the worshipers' own related prayers.

4. Turn the Lord's Prayer into a three-part litany. Worship Leader #1 reads one phrase at a time. Worship Leader #2 adds prayers related to that phrase and the life of the congregation. Then in silence, the worshipers add their own prayers related to each phrase.

## Sermon Resources

1. Preach about God's work in the "little things." Last week you told stories about the work and life of the congregation. Tell more stories this week, focusing on the little ways you see God at work. Describe caring phone calls and visits, tray favors made for institutionalized people, the newcomers of all ages invited to church. Encourage people to value the little things others are doing in God's name and to look for little things they can do to share God's love and build God's kingdom.

2. To explore Luke 11:9-15, describe three kinds of gifts and compare them to three ways God responds to our prayers. The first gift is the surprise we had not even considered asking for, but which delights us. God often gives us such surprise gifts. The second gift is just what we wanted. Sometimes God gives us what we want and pray for. The third gift is not at all what we wanted, but something that becomes more valuable as we live with it. God may not respond to our prayers as we wish. Often, with time, we begin to value and understand God's response. But sometimes we do not.

In describing each gift, tell about similar gifts you have received. Include at least one childhood gift. To keep the children's attention, place three wrapped gifts on the pulpit. Point to and handle each one as you discuss it.

3. Older children appreciate a sermon that works through the phrases of the Lord's Prayer. Provide them with a printed copy of the prayer with the phrases printed in separate paragraphs, as you will deal with them. Encourage children to check them off as you work through them, or to write them in their own words next to the printed text.

Be a detective.
Look for evidence that God is at work at your home and church.
Draw one clue in each magnifying glass.

Below each line of the Lord's Prayer, write a prayer of your own for that subject.

Our Father, who art in heaven, hallowed be thy name.

Thy Kingdom come. Thy will be done on earth as it is in heaven.

Give us this day our daily bread.

And, forgive us our debts as we forgive our debtors.

And lead us not into temptation, but deliver us from evil:

For thine is the kingdom, and the power, and the glory forever. Amen.

# PROPER THIRTEEN

*(Sunday between July 31 and August 6 inclusive)*

## From a Child's Point of View

*Old Testament: II Kings 13:14-20a.* This passage, although it is an interesting story, offers no particularly important message to children. In fact, some fair-minded children may feel that the king should have been warned of the significance of the number of times he beat the arrows on the ground. It sounds like a somewhat underhanded trick, and even implies that God cannot be trusted to deal openly with us. Such concerns, however, need not prevent children from enjoying this as the colorful story it is.

*Psalm 28.* This psalm is difficult for people of New Testament faith because it is filled with the expectation that God will treat "us" (the good, or chosen) better than "them" (the wicked, or not chosen). To deemphasize this exclusiveness, especially with children, focus on verses 1, 2, 6, and 7, which express trust in God's care without reference to others. This is not difficult, since the complex structure of the psalm is not easy for children to follow. They will respond to lines lifted up for special notice in the liturgy and sermon.

*Epistle: Colossians 3:1-11.* This passage says to children that there is a difference between Christians and non-Christians. Christians know that God loves them because they know that Christ died for them. They also know that enjoying and sharing God's love is the most important thing in the world, and knowing this makes them act in certain ways. The most significant items for children on Paul's list of "un-Christian" activities are being greedy (note connection to Luke text), hurting others when we are angry, hating, insulting people (calling cruel names), using obscene language, and telling lies. Because of the complex sentences and difficult language, this message needs to be presented during the sermon in words the children can understand.

*Gospel: Luke 12:13-21.* This passage speaks as directly to materialistic children as it does to their elders. They might prefer to store Nintendo games, bicycles, dolls, and sports equipment in their barns, but they know that when they hoard things for themselves, they are acting just like the farmer in the parable. They also know that when they become obsessed with wanting some new toy or designer shirt, they are on the wrong track. Jesus' message to them is that all the things we think we must have are not really important at all.

## Watch Words

*Inheritance,* if you use the Revised Standard Version of Luke's text, needs to be defined as *property and money left after a person dies.*

If this text leads you to speak of *materialism,* explain what it is.

## Let the Children Sing

To celebrate the centrality of Christ, sing "Come, Christians, Join to Sing" with all its Alleluias, or "Fairest Lord Jesus," which, though it includes some abstract symbols, also includes many concrete nature images.

For your commitment to live disciplined lives,

sing "Be Thou My Vision" (if the children sing it in other church settings) or "Lord, I Want to Be a Christian."

## The Liturgical Child

1. Read Luke with great dramatic inflection. Take the part of each speaker by changing your tone of voice and expression, and by the use of your hands and body. As you read the parable, remember that Jesus was known as a great storyteller for his delivery, as well as his content. Let the words of the barn-building fool swagger. Decide what God's tone will be in speaking to the man. Use your hands for emphasis. Eye the congregation as Jesus would have, as he made his final point in verse 21.

2. Use Colossians 3:1-11 as the base for confession and pardon:

> *Leader:* Let us confess our sins to one another and to God.
> *People:* Lord, we say we belong to Jesus, but we do not live as if we do.
> *Leader:* We become so wrapped up in getting what we want that we will bend, or even break rules to get our way.
> *People:* Lord, we say we belong to Jesus, but we do not live as if we do.
> *Leader:* And we want so much! We see clothes, houses, cars, and all kinds of toys that we feel we must have in order to be happy.
> *People:* Lord, we say we belong to Jesus, but we do not live as if we do.
> *Leader:* Our feelings often rule us. When we are angry, we hurt others. We give in to hating people we do not like.
> *People:* Lord, we say we belong to Jesus, but we do not live as if we do.
> *Leader:* Our mouths show us at our worst. We stoop to name calling, foul language, and lies. Even we cannot believe what sometimes comes out of our mouths.
> *People:* Lord, we say we belong to Jesus, but we do not live as if we do.

> *Leader:* But God has not left us to live with our own failures and sin. God loves us. Jesus died for us. In Jesus, we are forgiven and become new people. God is constantly at work, remaking us. So let's overcome our greed.
> *People:* Let us set our hearts on living like Christ.
> *Leader:* Let's learn to control our anger and set aside personal and community hatreds.
> *People:* Let us set our hearts on living like Christ.
> *Leader:* Let's speak kind words, offer compliments and encouragement to others, and tell the truth in all situations.
> *People:* Let us set our hearts on living like Christ.
> *All:* Amen.

## Sermon Resources

1. Retell the parable of the barn-building fool, describing the acquisitive habits of a fictional family in your community. Describe both the items each member of the family thought he or she needed, and why it was so important to have those items. Walk through a hectic weekend spent shopping for and taking care of all the things the family owned. After sending the exhausted family to bed, ask the congregation to ponder what those people might have done differently, had they known that a tornado would destroy them and everything they had that night. This leads to questions about whether the family would have been better off if it had lived by that alternate plan anyway.

2. Describe "gotta haves" with which people of all ages become obsessed, and tell how those things affect us. Describe "gotta haves" which we really do not use once we have them, "gotta haves" that turn out to be bad for us (like a computer game that becomes the sole interest in our life), and "gotta haves" we enjoy but really could do without. Talk about how we, as Christians, manage the "gotta haves" in our lives.

Listen carefully when II Kings 13: 14-20 is read. Then draw a picture of one thing Elisha asked the king to do.

Each word in the message below is upside down and backwards. Turn the words forward and right side up to find Jesus' warning about keeping our lives right side up.

" GUARD YOURSELVES

FROM EVERY KIND

OF GREED .

— — — | — — — — | — — —

OF GREED .

— — | — — — — . "

*Luke 12: 15*

Answer: Guard yourselves from every kind of greed.

# PROPER FOURTEEN

*(Sunday between August 7 and 13 inclusive)*

## From a Child's Point of View

*Old Testament: Jeremiah 18:1-11.* This passage presents an image that is both familiar and challenging for children. Though they may not have seen a potter working at a wheel, most children have many enjoyable experiences working with clay. They understand the process of reworking a piece until you get what you want. But younger children especially will need help making the connection between potters working with clay and God working with us. The natural expectation of concrete thinkers is to visualize God reworking the shapes of our bodies. To get beyond this to Jeremiah's message, children need to hear examples of what God would change about us (e.g., God working selfishness into generosity, or a quick temper into a controlled one). Children also need to explore what this reworking is like. Obviously, God does not punch us down into a lump (or turn us back into babies) and start over again. God works on us by giving us teachers and examples in the lives of others. God gives us the messages of the Bible to help us know how to live. God is with us, helping us learn from events in our lives.

Although we often focus on God's shaping of our personal lives, God was speaking to Jeremiah about shaping the nations. Older children, having an interest in the larger world and focusing on groups to which they belong, are primed to hear that God shapes and reworks the lives of groups and nations.

*Psalm 14.* For children, this is a description of "bad" people. They gather from the psalm that "bad" people do not recognize God (vs. 1), do terrible things (vs. 1), take advantage of other people (vs. 4), and never worship at all (vs. 4). Such people also seem to be in the majority (vss. 2-3). This is all rather abstract, and given the other very significant texts of the day, it should not be the focus.

*Epistle: Hebrews 11:1-3, 8-19.* This passage is an attempt to define *faith*. For children, faith is trust. Abraham and Sarah trusted God when they were called to move to an unknown land, and also when God promised them a son, though they knew they were too old to have children. Abraham even trusted God's promise about Isaac so much that he was willing to sacrifice the boy. (Because children hear this last story from Isaac's point of view, they find it more frightening than reassuring. It raises questions about whether God would ask their parents to prove their faith by killing them, and whether their parents would do it. Children often overlook the fact that God refused to let the sacrifice take place. For this reason, consider omitting verses 17-19.)

We are called to trust God as Abraham and Sarah did. Today that means trusting that God loves us and made us with a good plan in mind for us. It also means we know that God is working to make the world a loving, happy place and that we are ready to help.

*Gospel: Luke 12:32-40.* In its opening verses (32-34), this passage continues the theme of last week's Gospel lesson, but it involves a number of abstract images (the Kingdom, purses that do not wear out, and the location of treasures and hearts) which must be worked through if children are to understand them.

The second part of the passage focuses on the

need to be constantly prepared for God's presence. Three prepared people are noted: servants prepared for their master's return from a wedding feast at any hour; a home owner prepared for a thief whose approach is known; and a Christian prepared for God's presence. Children need help to find each of these people in the somewhat run-together passage, but they can appreciate them when found. They also need specific suggestions about what to do in order to be prepared for God (e.g., use well the talents God has given them, be loving, worship God on their own and with others).

## Watch Words

The job of the *potter* and the function of a *potter's wheel* need to be described briefly so that the children can recognize the similarity between them and their own experiences in working with clay.

*Faith* is best paraphrased as *trust*.

## Let the Children Sing

The Jeremiah text all but demands the selection of "Have Thine Own Way, Lord." Although the concepts in verses 2-4 are beyond most children, there is no better Sunday on which to introduce this hymn.

Faith hymns tend to be filled with abstract jargon. For children, sing "Jesus Loves Me" or "The Lord's My Shepherd."

## The Liturgical Child

1. To bring Jeremiah's experience in the potter's shop to life, arrange for a local potter to work at a potter's wheel during the reading of the Scripture. Read slowly enough so the potter can demonstrate what Jeremiah saw, or take time just before the reading to discuss with the potter how pots are shaped and reshaped.

2. Before reading the Luke passage, alert the children to listen for the three prepared people. As you come to each of them in the reading, raise one, then two, and finally three fingers.

3. Create a litany prayer about being ready. The worship leader offers petitions for God's work

(name mission activities of the congregation, specific community concerns, and global issues, being sure to include some activities in which children participate). After each petition, the congregation responds, "Let us prepare the way of the Lord!"

## Sermon Resources

1. Give each worshiper a small lump of clay (the size of an egg) before the sermon. The physical experience of working the clay will sharpen Jeremiah's message. Having something to do with their hands also helps children listen to the sermon. The clay could be passed out by ushers or by a children's class as the sermon begins. Children's modeling dough from a discount store or potting clay from a craft store cost about the same and work equally well. Invite worshipers to leave their clay in a dishpan at the rear of the church, or take it home with them. Provide a stack of paper towels by the pan. (Most people will not need a towel, as clay dries quickly and will dust off their hands.)

2. Talk about who and what we trust. Describe our trust in appliance-repair people, doctors, pilots, drivers of vehicles in which we ride, the friend to whom we tell a secret, the baby-sitter with whom parents leave their children, or the teacher or coach who teaches us to play a musical instrument or to excel in a sport. Recall current commercials that ask us to trust their products. Talk about the kid who dares us to try something new (perhaps swinging across a creek on a rope or taking drugs). Compare trusting people to trusting God's love and God's call to be peacemakers and loving friends.

3. To explore Luke 12:32-34, bring some props:

● Pull out your wallet or purse. Show the congregation what is in it. Describe your feelings and what you would have to do if it were lost or stolen. Then reread Jesus' message and talk about safer purses.

● Bring several of your treasures (or pictures of nontransportable treasures). Include a variety, such as a collector's item, a hobby tool, a memento of a person or trip, a picture of your family, and so on. Describe the objects' value to you and how you would respond if they were "messed with."

Then talk about how protecting our valuables can turn us into defensive worriers and keep us from loving people and letting them love us. In the process, encourage worshipers to identify some of their treasures that may be getting in their way.

4. The motto of the Boy Scouts is Be Prepared. Compare what it means to be prepared as a Scout with what it means to be prepared as a Christian.

Shade each space with a dot in it to find 2 words that mean almost the same thing.

Draw some of your treasures in the treasure chest below.

Use each word in a sentence about God and you.

1. _____

2. _____

Write a prayer about your treasures.

1. _____

2. _____

Answers: faith, trust

# PROPER FIFTEEN

## (Sunday between August 14 and 20 inclusive)

### From a Child's Point of View

*Old Testament: Jeremiah 20:7-13.* This passage must be understood in context. Jeremiah had been beaten and chained to the city gate overnight for prophesying God's judgment of Jerusalem. His harsh words are understandable when the lament is heard as his words and feelings on his way home from this debacle. God had given him an unwelcome message, which he would have preferred not to preach, but he did. For his courageous preaching, he was ridiculed and deserted by his friends. Still, he trusted God.

For children, this is an inside look at a faith hero. It points out that it is not easy to do God's work. Public punishment, humiliation, and the desertion of friends are torments children can understand. It is reassuring that such treatment made Jeremiah, for whom a book in the Bible is named, angry and frustrated. Knowing how Jeremiah felt, children admire him for putting up with it and for trusting that God would work through it to bring justice. Children can even forgive Jeremiah for his less than admirable wish to watch God's revenge on his enemies.

*Psalm 10:12-18.* This psalm is a lament in the acrostic form. It is rather difficult for adults to follow the jumble of pleas as the poet adheres to the acrostic. Children will catch short phrases here and there. In summary, the psalmist hopes that God will overthrow the evil people and provide justice for the oppressed.

*Gospel: Luke 12:49-56.* This passage reflects Jeremiah's experience of the divisiveness of God's Word. Just as people did not like Jeremiah's condemnation of their nation and way of life, many who heard Jesus did not like his pointing out their self-centeredness, greed, and power games. Jeremiah was beaten and put into stocks. Jesus was crucified.

People who stand up for God's ways today should expect no different results. If you stand up to a bully to protect someone else, you might get punched. If you refuse to go along with a mean prank, the others might call you names and cut you out of the group. There might even be situations when you would need to stand up for God's ways against a member of your own family. That is really hard, *but* Jesus insists that it is necessary.

The tendency to soft-pedal this point with children does them no favor. They know that it is risky to stand up for God's ways on playgrounds, on school buses, and in backyards. Adult failure to acknowledge this appears to children to be a startling lack of perception of the realities children confront. It is far more helpful to recognize these realities and prepare children to cope with them by interpreting them in light of Jesus' message.

*Epistle: Hebrews 12:1-2, 12-17.* This passage, in its context in the letter to the Hebrews, calls people to be inspired by the faith heroes and heroines of the past to live faithful lives today. In context with the other readings for today, the passage calls readers to live faithfully in spite of the price (the divisiveness in Luke, the humiliations of Jeremiah). Whichever context you choose, children will respond to the idea that faith heroes are looking over their shoulder to encourage them and support them. To be as trusting as Abraham and Sarah, as loyal as Jeremiah, and as brave as Jesus—these are goals that have reality and power for children as they try to stand up for God's ways in their daily lives.

## Watch Words

Watch your "judgment" vocabulary: *evil* and *wicked* are seldom nouns but are generally adjectives today. So speak of *evil people* and *wicked plans*, rather than *the* evil or *the* wicked. *Vindicate, vengeance,* and *revenge* deal with *getting even.*

The *witnesses* of Hebrews 12 are more readily recognized as *heroes/ines* or *examples.*

## Let the Children Sing

Choose the following hymns (listed in order of ease for children) to celebrate the faith heroes: "I Sing a Song of the Saints of God," "For All the Saints Who from Their Labors Rest" (the younger readers will settle for the Alleluias), or "God of Grace and God of Glory" (the repeated chorus can be sung by all).

A good opening praise hymn for the day is "Come Christians, Join to Sing."

## The Liturgical Child

1. Know when school starts for your children and include that in your prayers on the appropriate week. Pray about excitement and fears. In smaller churches, pray by name for children entering school for the first time this fall and those headed for college. Pray for students and teachers and bus drivers and coaches.

2. Set Jeremiah 20:7-13 in context—verses 1-3 —before reading it. Then read it dramatically, as if you were Jeremiah, talking to God on your way home from the painful, embarrassing night. Shake your fist at God in verse 7. Shrug your shoulders in exasperation in verse 8. Look up a bit shyly to admit your thoughts in verse 9. Look from side to side for enemies in verse 10, as you complain about the plotting against you. Turn your hands up in resignation and acceptance in verses 11 through 13.

3. Praise God for faith heroes; pause for silent prayers from the congregation:

Lord God, we are indeed surrounded by people who have lived heroically faithful lives for you. The Bible is full of stories of everyday people who lived brave, loving lives. For Abraham and Sarah's brave move; for Jeremiah, preaching his unpopular message; for Jesus, willing to die rather than stop loving us, we thank you. Each of us praises you for those people in the Bible who are important to us. (Pause)

But still others have gone before us to show us the way. We remember Martin Luther, who challenged the church to keep its faith strong. We remember Christians who have died rather than give up their faith. We remember missionaries who have risked their lives to tell others of God's love. Each of us praises you for those heroes of the church who show us the way. (Pause)

Each of us also praises you for people we have known personally. For parents, or children, or Sunday school teachers, or friends who have been examples to us and have inspired us to live by God's ways. Hear our thanksgiving for these people. (Pause)

Even as we thank you for this cloud of heroes who surround and inspire us, we are aware of our responsibility. So we ask you for the courage, wisdom, and love to live as heroically as they did. Help us to make good decisions. Give us the power to do what we know you would have us do; for we pray in the name of Jesus. Amen.

## Sermon Resources

1. For children, getting what is wanted at the moment, or avoiding pain at the moment, often leads to ignoring what they know to be right. So Esau, who for the quick relief of his hunger gave up forever something very precious, is a good antihero. Tell his story for balance.

2. Include in the sermon a story or two about heroes in the history of your congregation. If possible, link the stories to a building, a tree, or an item seen regularly around the church. Or bring special papers or pictures from the church safe or from a member's home to give reality to the person and events described. Challenge children and adults to follow in the faithful footsteps of their congregational ancestors.

Draw or write about one place where a faith hero is needed today.

FAITH HERO NEEDED

Talk to God about ways you could be that hero.

Draw a picture of or write the name of one of your faith heroes in each frame below. Listen to the sermon for ideas.

Write a prayer about one of them.

Thank you God for _____
because _____

Help me to be like _____
by _____
.

# PROPER SIXTEEN

## (Sunday between August 21 and 27 inclusive)

### From a Child's Point of View

*Old Testament: Jeremiah 28:1-9.* This is an adult passage. Jeremiah speaks with subtle humor about the difference between prophesying welcome peace and prophesying unwelcome famine or disastrous war. It is a distinction that is beyond the awareness of children. The key image of the yoke in the passage is unfamiliar to most children. Those older children who are aware of the yoke as a symbol for discipleship will be puzzled by its negative connotations here. Today's Gospel text deals with the big theme of judgment in a more child-accessible manner.

*Psalm 84.* This is a pilgrim's song praising the Jerusalem Temple. The melodramatic language of verse 2 amuses children. (It is easy to imagine a group of people mopping foreheads, feigning faints, and intoning with mock seriousness, "My soul longs, yea, faints for the courts of the Lord!" (RSV).) Verses 5-7 require information about pilgrimages to the Temple. Verses 8-9 form a rather separate prayer for the king. Still, if the psalm is introduced as a prayer in praise of the Temple, and if the Temple is referred to as "the psalmist's church," children will catch meaningful phrases about being at church.

*Gospel: Luke 13:22-30.* This passage has an important message for children, but it is not one they will hear as the passage is read. The message is that God cares about what they do and holds them responsible for their actions. None of us can hide out from God in groups. We cannot expect that because our family has always gone to church, or because the crowd we run with has

never gotten into serious trouble, God will overlook the fact that we are not caring, loving individuals. God cares about what each of us does and says.

To help children begin to interpret the "narrow gate" correctly, describe people trying to get through a narrow gate into "God's place" while carrying armloads of clothes and toys they do not want to leave behind. Teenagers and adults will be able to think of nonphysical baggage (hostility to certain groups, commitment to their own self-centered plans, etc.). Children cannot. But working only with physical baggage, they can begin to get the message.

WARNING: Jesus meant to shake his hearers out of their complacency. But children can be frightened into insecurity by the image of knocking at the door and being told by Jesus to go away. Without some adult help, they cannot find Jesus' standards for entrance in this text. Those literal thinkers who are unsure about whether God has really spoken to them (as God spoke to people in the Bible) are left wondering whether God really knows them or would turn them away. So be sure to outline Jesus' message that we are responsible for what we do, and be clear about Jesus' call for us to live loving and caring lives.

Jesus' promise that people will be surprised by some who make it "through the gate" both assures children that God is aware of their small, unnoticed efforts and warns them not to judge other people too quickly.

*Epistle: Hebrews 12:18-29.* This passage presents deeply symbolic images of approaching God under the Law and approaching under Jesus' grace. The text is impossible to decode for children. Since the message behind the images is very similar to that of the Luke text, count on using Luke to explore the message with children. The warning about children being frightened by the "closed door" in Luke also applies to these stern images.

## Watch Words

Be careful with abstract "judgment" language and avoid as much of the image-filled language of Hebrews 12 as possible.

*Yokes* are not familiar items. If you talk about them, describe them and their purpose.

The *Temple* in Psalm 84 needs to be introduced as another word for *church*.

## Let the Children Sing

"We Are the Church Together" and "I Love Thy Kingdom, Lord" are Christian parallels to Psalm 84. The latter needs to be explored with children before singing.

During the next several Sundays, focus on themes of repentance and commitment. Choose one of the following hymns to sing several times during the series: "Be Thou My Vision," "Lord, I Want to Be a Christian," or "Take My Life and Let It Be Consecrated." Consider using one as a "hymn of the month" to build the children's familiarity.

The verses of "Go Forth for God" do not make much sense to children. But they enjoy the repetition of the first and last lines of each verse and can sing them (if nothing else) if the lines are pointed out by the worship leader.

## The Liturgical Child

1. To create a reading of Psalm 84 that children can understand with little explanation, read verses 1, 2, and 10 through 12 in the Good News Bible. Read it first as the prayer of the psalmist for the Temple. Then invite worshipers to pray the psalm by "lining out" a paraphrase in which "Temple" vocabulary is replaced with "church" vocabulary. For example: "How lovely is your church, Lord Almighty!" (In lining out, the congregation repeats each line after the worship leader, reflecting the leader's tone and words.)

2. Create a responsive prayer of confession which describes the various things we do, hoping that God will not notice or care. The congregation's response to each description: "But you do care about what we do and say." For example:

*Leader:* God, we stand before you in this sanctuary this morning claiming to be your people, and so we are. But we do not always act like your people. In school and at work, we often "forget" your rules just to get good grades or to look good to others.

*Congregation:* But you *do* care about what we do or say.

*Assurance of Pardon:* God *does* care about what we do and say. God cares so much that God lived among us in Jesus, to show us how to live and to forgive us for all our failures to do and say loving, caring things. In Jesus, we are forgiven and find the power to do loving deeds and say kind words.

3. Sing "Go Forth for God" as the last hymn. Then use the first lines of each verse as the Charge before the Benediction.

## Sermon Resources

1. Build a sermon around Psalm 84's love of the church and the verses of "I Love Thy Kingdom, Lord." Use the verses of the hymn as your sermon outline and invite worshipers to keep their hymnals open for ready reference. Explore the ideas of the verses and translate difficult vocabulary and images. Sing the hymn after the sermon.

2. Discuss excuses children (and older worshipers) frequently use to deny responsibility for what they say and do. Talk about what we are really saying and what Jesus says to us (see Luke text) when we offer such excuses:

"It doesn't matter."

"No one will notice."

"I'm just a kid."

"I really didn't mean to . . . ."

(as in "I really didn't mean to make her cry. I was just showing my friends this neat new trick, and . . . .")

"It just happened. I don't know how."

(as in "I don't know how the lamp got broken. We were just wrestling on the floor, and all of a sudden there was this big crash, and . . . .")

"(Someone else's name) made me do it."

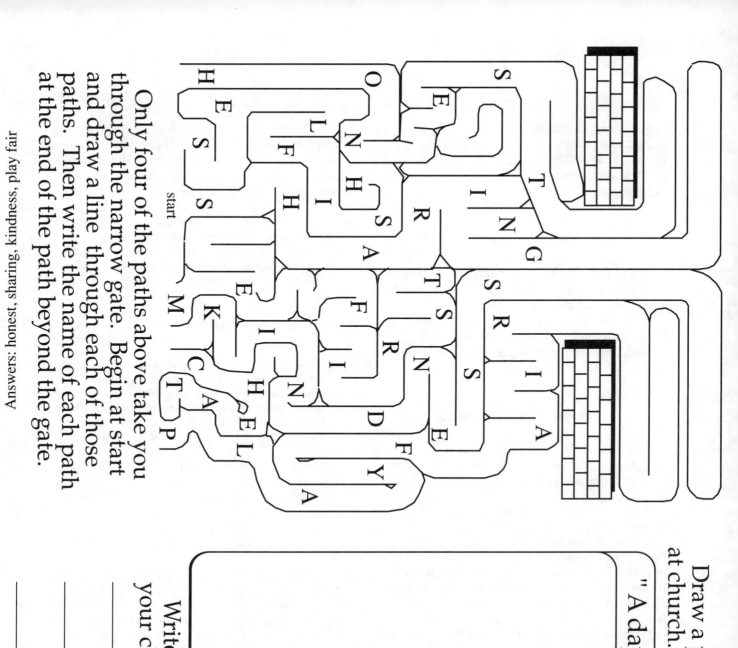

Only four of the paths above take you through the narrow gate. Begin at start and draw a line through each of those paths. Then write the name of each path at the end of the path beyond the gate.

start

Answers: honest, sharing, kindness, play fair

Draw a picture of what you like to do at church.

"A day in your courts is better than 1,000 elsewhere." *Psalm 84:10*

Write a prayer telling God about your church.

_____

_____

_____

# PROPER SEVENTEEN

## (Sunday between August 28 and September 3 inclusive)

### From a Child's Point of View

*Old Testament: Ezekiel 18:1-9, 25-29.* This passage, like last week's texts, insists that before God, we are each responsible for our own behavior. We cannot blame anyone else for the results of what we do. "God is just!" is good news for children who often feel they get blamed for what is not their fault. Ezekiel assures children that God will not do this. But Ezekiel also demands that children not hide behind others or blame others for what really is their own fault. Children often blame anyone older than they are for misleading them (e.g., "The teacher didn't tell us about that homework."; "The older boys *made* me do it."; "(name of older sibling or friend) said it was OK."). Or they blame younger children for dragging them down (e.g., "I tried to stop him, but he did it anyway."). Ezekiel insists that God is not fooled by such excuses.

Ezekiel also promises that if we change our ways, God will recognize our efforts. God will not hold our past failings against us, nor can we expect God to remember our past good deeds and overlook our current sin. So the promise is both good news and a stern challenge.

Children tend to be fascinated by the proverb about sour grapes. They enjoy the possibility that one person could eat something so bitter or sour that it would give another person the bad taste. But even older children are not able to grasp the relationship between the sour grapes and God's judgment. This message will need to be presented in straightforward terms, not poetic images.

*Psalm 15.* This psalm describes the person who is worthy of worshiping God (coming to church).

Even children realize that none of us fully meet these requirements. The psalmist is really talking more about God's greatness than about the entry requirements for worshipers. The psalm might be compared to a list of what a person would need to be like to be worthy of playing on a team with a great sports figure, or playing music with a great musician, or working with a great scientist. We read this psalm in worship, knowing that God welcomes us—even though we are not worthy.

*Epistle: Hebrews 13:1-8.* This is a series of minilectures about how to live. Children are frequently on the receiving end of such lectures and recognize them. The lectures are in verses 1 (on loving), 2 (on treating strangers kindly), 3*a* (on remembering prisoners), 3*b* (on caring for those who are not well treated by others), 4 (on honoring marriage), 5-6 (on love of money), 7 (on respecting leaders), and 8 ( a summary statement about Jesus). Children can understand them, but none of the lectures is developed in a way that speaks to their lives with particular clarity and force.

*Gospel: Luke 14:1, 7-14.* This passage tells two parables about parties. The first story is for party guests. Reminders of arguments about who gets to sit by Grandma, or who has to share the piano bench at a family reunion dinner, help children understand the feelings attached to seat assignments at first-century dinner parties. With this background, children can deal with the two levels of Jesus' teachings. They appreciate the practical fact that if you take a "good place," you will be embarrassed when you are asked to move. They can also appreciate Jesus' unstated message that where you sit is not that important anyway, and we should not be upset about such matters.

The second story is for hosts—of birthday parties, spend-the-night parties, trips to football games, and afternoons at the movies. Like adults, most children treat parties as chances to invite only those they want to invite. They choose their friends and those they would like to have for friends. Older children, especially girls, already recognize the possibility of inviting people who will "invite you back." Jesus suggests that a party is a chance to extend our friendship to people without friends, and to those who do not have anything to return. Because children often are given strict limits as to the number of friends they may invite to parties or outings, this is a call for tough, self-sacrificing living. Be aware that Jesus is asking more of children than of adults in this parable.

## Watch Words

Speak of God as being *fair*. Children will understand *justice* as a synonym for *fairness*.

Choose your translation of Psalm 15 carefully for simple, current vocabulary. The Good News Bible is easiest for children.

## Let the Children Sing

Sing "For the Beauty of the Earth" to recite God's wonders on a holiday weekend when people tend to be outdoors.

Because all of today's texts call us to responsible action, choose familiar hymns of commitment: "Lord, I Want to Be a Christian," "Be Thou My Vision," or "Go Forth for God" (see last week's notes).

## The Liturgical Child

1. If it is Labor Day weekend, pray about last picnics and other end-of-summer events. Pray about settling into fall schedules with school and after-school activities. Review the prayer suggestions regarding the beginning of school in Proper #15.

2. Base a responsive prayer of confession on Psalm 15. Read verse 1 as an introduction, then move directly into 2a. Pause for congregational response. Continue to read and pause after each of the following sections: verses 2b-3a, 3b, 3c, 4b,

5a, and 5b. The congregational response to each section is "Lord, this does not always describe us." The worship leader may read directly from a selected translation or may paraphrase some of the lines for clarity. Conclude with: "None of us is worthy to come into God's presence. We all have sinned and fallen short of what God intends for us. But in Jesus, God forgives us and welcomes us, and calls us to live in God's love and presence today and every day. So be it."

## Sermon Resources

1. To give worshipers the sensation of Ezekiel's sour grapes, ask them to imagine biting into a really sour pickle and then feel their lips pucker, their tongues curl, their teeth tingle. After several such taste experiments (perhaps sour milk or bitter grapefruit), everyone, including the children, will be ready to hear about grapes that were so sour that when the fathers ate them, the children tasted them. (Though children will not grasp the meaning of the sour grapes, they will participate in part of the sermon and will become familiar with an image they will later understand.)

2. Most children begin the school year intent on being good students. They organize their notebooks for great things and set up desk-study space at home. It is a time of trying hard and feeling responsible. Therefore, they are primed to hear Ezekiel's promise that each of us is responsible for our own actions—that what your brothers and sisters did when they had your teacher does not count. The grades other kids make are their own business. *You* are responsible for what you do.

3. Challenge worshipers to make a list of the five people they would invite to a super birthday party—for children, it might be a bowling and pizza party; for youths, a set of concert tickets; for adults, dinner in a fine restaurant. As they work, explore Jesus' insights into how we usually compile such lists. Next, ask the worshipers to think of two people in their class at school, at their workplace, or in their neighborhood, who probably never are invited to parties. After they have had a minute to think, reread Jesus' points about who to invite, and encourage everyone to imagine including one of those two outcasts on their list. Suggest possible impact on the new guest. Imagine what difference it would make at the party.

Cross out every fourth letter in each group of letters below to find words that describe people who worship God.

1. DOWKHATAISRAIGHOT

_ _ _ _ _ _ _ _ _ _ _ .

2. DONAOWRB
   ONGTTOFX
   RIEKNDSQ

_ _ _ _ _ _
_ _ _ _ _ _
_ _ _ _ _ _ .

4. DONAOTSX
   PREXADRS
   UMOPRS

_ _ _ _ _ _
_ _ _ _ _ _
_ _ _ _ _ _ .

3. S P E B A K T X R
   U  M  H  F  R  A  O  M  I
   S  H  K  E  A  R  X  T

_ _ _ _ _
_ _ _ _ _ _ .

Listen for these words in Psalm 15.

List 5 people to invite to a party.

1. _____
2. _____
3. _____
4. _____
5. _____

Draw a picture of what you would do at that party.

Now listen when Luke is read. What does Jesus say about parties?

# PROPER EIGHTEEN

## (Sunday between September 4 and 10 inclusive)

### From a Child's Point of View

*Old Testament: Ezekiel 33:1-11.* This passage includes two job descriptions—one for a watchman and another for a prophet. With some help, children can grasp the comparison between the two. The message is that just as we are responsible for the results when we refuse to follow the warnings of a watchman, we also are responsible when we refuse to follow the advice of God's messengers when they tell us how to live. For today's children, prophets include the messengers in the Bible, their preachers and teachers at church, and other adults who help direct their lives. Whereas youths and adults must decide which are true prophets and which are false prophets, young children accept as legitimate those who come to them in roles of authority. For them, the focus is on whether to obey these prophets or to disobey and pay the price. Ezekiel tells them that they are responsible for the results of their disobedience. He also tells them that God does not send all these messenger/prophets to put a lot of demands on them, but to let them know what it takes to have a good life.

*Psalm 94:12-22.* This psalm expresses confidence that God is on the side of justice and that God protects those who do what is right. Both these ideas are important reassurances to children as they face injustice at school and among friends, and as they make decisions about how to respond to choices between good and bad (but lucrative) behavior. Unfortunately, the vocabulary of this psalm makes it hard for children to hear the message as it is read. The preacher will need to deliver the message during the sermon.

*Epistle: Philemon 1-20.* This passage deals with a situation totally foreign to children. They have neither an understanding of first-century slavery nor appreciation for the social stand Paul was asking of Philemon. If asked what Philemon should do, their response is, "Simple! He should do what Paul asked, because Paul was the great teacher and leader of the church." So for children, this is mainly an interesting story. They are generally impressed with Onesimus' courage in returning to Philemon.

*Gospel: Luke 14:25-33.* This passage includes two concrete stories which illustrate a very "hard" lesson about discipleship. Children can understand the stories about the tower builder and the king going to war, but they will need help to interpret them and relate them to Jesus' point in verses 25-27 and 33.

Jesus was speaking to adults, not to children, when he demanded that they "hate"—that is, "be totally detached from" their families. He overstated his case to make the point that our discipleship is to take priority over *all* other loyalties and commitments, even those to family. For adults, this is difficult but possible. For children, who are dependent upon the love and care of their families, it is not even remotely comprehensible. It is also scary because of what it demands of children and what it suggests might be demanded of the parents upon whom they are so dependent. Children need to hear this verse with reassurances about Jesus' point. It helps to read it with verses 27 and 33, which insist that each of us must be a good disciple and that following Jesus is to be the most important thing in our lives.

## Watch Words

Do not assume that children know what a *prophet* does. Outline the task, to teach them and to refresh their elders.

## Let the Children Sing

There are few hymns related specifically to any of today's texts. The commitment hymns of the last few weeks continue to be good choices as the discipleship theme continues. "I Sing a Song of the Saints of God" celebrates the sainthood to which Philemon and we are called. Remember "All Things Bright and Beautiful," "Come, Christians, Join to Sing," or "I Sing the Almighty Power of God" for general hymns of praise.

## The Liturgical Child

1. Before reading the Ezekiel passage, point out that it includes a job description for a watchman (or sentry), who guards a city against enemy armies, and a job description for a prophet. Urge worshipers to listen for the responsibilities of each job. If your translation uses "sword" for enemy armies, introduce that code word before the reading.

2. In prayer, thank God for some of the prophets you recognize in the history of your denomination, congregation, and community. Also, allow silent time in which individual worshipers may speak to God about those who have been and are being prophets to them personally (people who help them know right from wrong).

3. Follow The New Jerusalem Bible in presenting Psalm 94 as a series of proverb-like statements about God's justice and support of good people. Print the verses in titled sections in the morning bulletin for a unison reading. Or have different readers (some may be older children) read each section while another person presents a large poster title for that section:

| | |
|---|---|
| Happy People | verses 12-13 |
| God Is with Us Always | verses 14-15 |
| God Has Protected Me | verses 16-17 |
| God Takes Care of Me in Trouble | verses 18-19 |
| God Is Always Fair | verses 20-21 |
| I Am Safe with God | verse 22 |

4. The book of Philemon catches the attention of children because it is the shortest book in the Bible. Take advantage of this interest by inviting worshipers to follow along in pew Bibles as you read the book aloud. Congratulate them at the end of the reading for having read a whole book of the Bible and encourage them to read others.

Before the reading, explain the situation that prompted Paul's letter and encourage worshipers to imagine themselves in Philemon's place—opening the door to his runaway slave who handed him this letter from Paul.

5. Before reading the Gospel text, alert children to listen for a story about a person building a tower and another story about a king going to war.

## Sermon Resources

1. Compare Ezekiel's watchman to modern-day watchmen, such as weather forecasters and media people who describe traffic snarls during rush hours in big cities. Identify children's modern-day messengers or prophets from God, including parents, teachers, and older friends who help them to know right from wrong and warn them when they are heading for trouble (e.g., parent warning toddler she will be burned if she touches the stove; an older friend who warns that "running with" certain people will surely get you into trouble).

2. Tell stories about starting things that cannot be finished: an unhappy eight-year-old who runs away from home without food or any idea of where to go; an overly ambitious science-fair project (perhaps dissecting a pig, which cannot be obtained); a boast about being brave enough to explore a deserted house. Proceed to ambitious discipleship stories: a commitment to set aside snack money each day for a hunger offering at church; a decision to keep on forgiving someone who continually teases you and makes life on the bus miserable; and so on.

Listen to Ezekiel describe a
**PROPHET.**
Draw a picture in the box below of a person
who helps you to know right from wrong.

OR

Write the name of that person down the
left side of the box. Beside each letter of the
person's name, write a word beginning with
that letter to describe the person.

( My Prophet )

Listen carefully when Philemon is
read. Then draw a picture or write a
story about what Philemon did after
he read Paul's letter.

# Then...

# PROPER NINETEEN

## (Sunday between September 11 and 17 inclusive)

### From a Child's Point of View

Today's texts deal with repentance and forgiveness. Hosea describes the disciplinary action God was about to take against Israel. Jesus speaks of God's joy over the straying sheep who is brought home and the coin that was found. Paul points to himself as an example of God's willingness to forgive even the most flagrant sinners.

*Old Testament: Hosea 4:1-3; 5:15—6:6.* Although this passage does not mention parents or children, it speaks of God correcting the people as a parent corrects errant children. It begins as a parent would, opening a disciplinary discussion: "(Name), we have a problem." Hosea 4:2 describes the problem between God and the people in terms that children recognize. Hosea 5:15–6:2 describes the sequence of punishment and restoration with which children are familiar. The children, however, need help to move from the poetic language of the verses to this punishment-restoration sequence. If Ephraim and Judah are defined as pet names for God's people, then in 6:4, children can hear God (the parent) say to the people the same phrase they have heard their parents use.

The empathetic responses in the natural order described in 4:3 and 6:3 will not make sense to children, but with some help, they can appreciate Hosea's call for love that is longer lasting than a morning fog (6:4b). Verse 6:6 simply states God's demands of the people. God wants us to know God (to be God's friends) and to love God and one another with a longlasting, everyday love.

*Psalm 77:11-20.* This is the most difficult of today's texts for children because it is filled with symbolic references to God's history with the Jewish people and poetic images from nature. If the psalm is read dramatically, children will pick up short phrases that describe God's power and loving care.

*Gospel: Luke 15:1-10.* This passage includes the parables of the lost sheep and the lost coin, tied together by Jesus' insistence that God rejoices over the repentance of one "lost" person. These parables frequently appear in church school curriculum and therefore may be familiar to most young worshipers. Children will enjoy hearing a familiar story read and explored in worship.

Because children think concretely, they need to work at these parables from two sides. They will not see the connection between these sides until their thinking matures. On the concrete level, children have experience with being physically lost. Psychologists tell us that the fear of being lost or abandoned is one of the deep, disturbing fears of childhood. So for them, the parables promise that God will never abandon them. Then with adult direction, they can explore Jesus' promise that they can never do anything so awful that God will not forgive them. Just as the shepherd goes after the one lost sheep, so God will come after them. Later, when children can comprehend being lost in sin, they will realize that these truths merge in the parables.

*Epistle: I Timothy 1:12-17.* This passage assumes knowledge of Paul's life that most children and some adults will not recall without help. So begin by briefly outlining Paul's persecution of the church, his conversion, and his missionary career. Verses 15 and 16 are the key ones for children, who will not follow the theological language in much of the rest of the passage. Reminded of Paul's story, children can see the truth of what he is saying and can conclude that if God could still love and use Paul after he repented of his persecution of the church, then there is probably nothing they can do that God will not forgive, when they repent as Paul did. This is reassuring. It also reminds children to forgive others as willingly as God forgives them.

## Watch Words

Remember that for children, *lost* describes physical abandonment. So avoid using it to describe being lost in sin. Instead, talk about *sin* and *forgiveness*.

Avoid *mercy*, *pardon*, and *grace*, in favor of *forgiveness*. Or choose to use one of those words and take time in the sermon to explore its meaning.

Instead of talking about Paul's *persecution* of the church, describe how he hunted and killed Christians.

## Let the Children Sing

Continue singing the chosen hymns of commitment.

To celebrate God's "good shepherd" love, sing the version of "The Lord's My Shepherd" most familiar to your children, or "Jesus Loves Me." Be sure to sing the following verse:

> Jesus loves me when I'm good,
> When I do the things I should.
> Jesus loves me when I'm bad,
> Even though it makes him sad.

Even though its first line comes from I Timothy 1:10, children will be baffled by the abstract language of "Immortal, Invisible, God Only Wise." Save it for a day when you are exploring God's greatness and have time to define and enjoy all the big words together.

## The Liturgical Child

1. Paraphrase the traditional prayer of confession based on the lost-sheep image:

> Loving God, who takes care of us as a shepherd takes care of sheep, we admit that we have wandered off like lost sheep. We have ignored your rules and teachings to follow our most selfish and mean desires. We act and speak without thinking that we might hurt others. We think only about how we feel and what we want. Forgive us. Lead us to kind actions and gentle words; for we pray in Jesus' name. Amen.

> *Assurance of Pardon:* Jesus said that God rejoices when one sinner repents. God welcomes us back home and helps us live more loving lives. We can depend on that. We are forgiven.

2. As another assurance of pardon, have worshipers read or "line out" I Timothy 1:15-16, claiming Paul's conviction of forgiveness for themselves. (In "lining out," the congregation repeats each line after the worship leader.)

3. Before praying the Lord's Prayer, highlight the phrase, "Forgive us our debts (trespasses) as we forgive our debtors (those who trespass against us)." Briefly outline the way the focal text of the day affects the way we pray this phrase (e.g., imagine what it meant to Paul to pray this phrase after being forgiven for killing Christians).

## Sermon Resources

1. If children are into the third or fourth week of school, compare Hosea's call to make commitments that last longer than a morning fog to the commitment to study hard that the children made when they began the school year. Talk about how easy it is to give up on a commitment to study, or to be kind and fair and forgiving, especially to people who make life difficult.

2. To illustrate the punishment and restoration sequence in Hosea, trace it in a story about a parent who disciplines a child. Perhaps it can be a story out of your past.

Trace a Path to find the lost sheep, lost coin, and lost person in this maze. Start over each time you find the thorn bush.

START

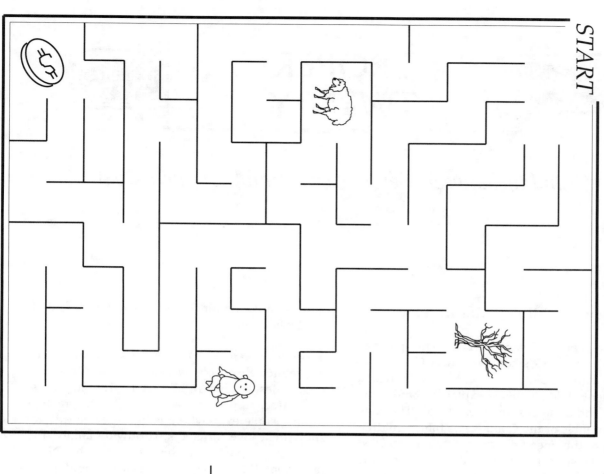

Listen carefully when Luke 15: 1-10 is read. Write each word below in the correct spaces.
( *Hint: Match a letter in the word to a letter in the word LOST or the word FOUND.* )

L — — — — —

— O — — —

— S — — —

— T

and

— F — — — — —

— O —

— U —

— N — —

— D

sheep      coin      sinner

loved      forgiven      repent

Paul      joy      shepherd

*Proper 19 / © 1991 by Abingdon Press.*

# PROPER TWENTY

## (Sunday between September 18 and 24 inclusive)

### From a Child's Point of View

*Old Testament: Hosea 11:1-11.* This passage continues last week's comparison of God's relationship with the people to that of a parent with a disobedient child. If this is explained before the reading, and if the passage is read from The New Jerusalem Bible or the Good News Bible, children will catch the meaning of a few image-filled phrases. Hosea's message is that although the people deserve to be destroyed because of the way they have acted, God has chosen instead to discipline them in order to help them come back to God. God's wish is that those people would realize how much God loves them and would learn to depend upon and love God in return. And God wants the same for us.

*Psalm 107:1-9.* This is the first section of a psalm whose format is interesting to children. It is a song for pilgrims to sing as they walk together toward Jerusalem (not unlike the songs we sing to pass the time on long car trips). Verses 1-3 are the introduction and are followed by sections that describe how God saves people in different kinds of trouble: those lost in the desert (4-9); prisoners (10-16); the sick (17-22); sailors in storms (23-32). Each section describes the distress of one group, explains how God saves them, and then calls on those people to praise and thank God (e.g., those who are lost in the desert are thirsty and hungry; they cry to God for help and are led by God to cities; for this they are called on to thank God). The fact that such a psalm is included in the Bible, and the possibility that other verses could be made up about people whose needs are met by God are

more stimulating for children than the content of the biblical verses.

*Epistle: I Timothy 2:1-7.* This passage calls on us to pray for all people everywhere. God loves all people. Jesus came for all people. Therefore, we are to treat all people well. For children, praying for all people everywhere is one specific way to show their love for God's worldwide family. By including verse 8 in this section, The New Jerusalem Bible suggests that we should pray especially for those with whom we have disagreements. This is a challenging discipline for worshipers of all ages.

*Gospel: Luke 16:1-13.* This passage includes a parable and four related teachings that are difficult both to understand and to apply to life. The parable (vss. 1-8a) describes the action and conversation of two "bad guys." Children need to be told that Jesus did not approve of what the servant did or of the master's compliment. Instead, Jesus was using their outrageous story to make four important points:

First, Christians should work as hard at doing God's work as the bad servant worked at stealing his master's money (8b).

Second, we should be generous in sharing our money and toys (9). People who share have many friends. And having friends makes a person happier than having money or things.

Third, if we use our money and things well (generously), God will entrust us with even more exciting and important work (10-12). Therefore, when you learn to share your small amount of money and numerous toys as a child, you will be prepared to use wisely the larger amounts of money you will have as an adult, in order to do responsible work in God's church.

Fourth, we are not to be greedy (13). Doing God's work is much more important than what we wear or what we eat or what we want for our birthday.

Children (and many adults) will not be able to grasp any of these points from the reading of the text, but will need to hear the passage explained during the sermon.

## Watch Words

*Mammon* needs to be defined as all the things money can buy. Jesus is warning us against *greed*.

Before reading Hosea 11, explain that *Israel* and *Ephraim* are names for God's people. Also, use *discipline*, instead of *punishment*, to emphasize the corrective nature of God's action.

## Let the Children Sing

"O God of Every Nation" unites the themes of Hosea, I Timothy, and Luke. Although the hymn includes many abstract words, they are words that are familiar. Singing this hymn frequently in worship will help children catch the meaning of more and more of the phrases. This might be a good hymn for the whole congregation to learn together.

"Have Thine Own Way, Lord," if familiar, is a hymn through which children can commit themselves to God's discipline.

Celebrate the saving God of Psalm 107 by singing "Now Thank We All Our God."

Ask a children's class, a children's choir, or the whole congregation to sing "He's Got the Whole World in His Hands," in response to I Timothy.

## The Liturgical Child

1. In the spirit of the I Timothy reading, take a prayer trip around the world. Pray for people of several different countries (in geographical sequence), and their needs. Print a world map in your order of worship and/or place a globe in your worship center.

2. Before the prayer of petition, give the worshipers a brief time of silence in which to identify people with whom they have problems.

Then voice corporate prayers, with pauses for individual prayers:

Lord, we pray for all the people of the world. We pray for our own country (Pause), for the leaders who are our heroes, and for the elected leaders with whom we disagree. (Pause)

We pray for (several friendly nations or groups with specific needs). (Pause)

And we pray for (unfriendly countries, terrorist groups, etc.). (Pause)

We pray for people we love and love to be with in our families (Pause), at school and work (Pause), and at church. (Pause)

We even pray for those people and groups who drive us a little nuts. (Pause)

Bring us all closer together. Help us to treat one another with loving respect, so that the world may indeed have peace. We pray in the name of Jesus, who loves us all, and who died that we might have life and love one another. Amen.

3. Focus prayers of confession on the different "I wants" and "I needs" that overly influence our lives.

4. After introducing the format of Psalm 107 and reading the first section, invite worshipers to create their own verses to describe God's rescue of some group of people. Post the results on a bulletin board or in the church newsletter. Most adults will work on this at home. Some children may work on it during the sermon (see the Worship Worksheet for a possible format).

## Sermon Resources

1. The Luke passage, with all its difficulties, suggests an open-Bible teaching sermon. Invite worshipers to follow along in pew Bibles, or have the text printed in the order of worship. Work through the parable and the four points, explaining the meaning of each one, and illustrate them with examples from childhood and adulthood. (If the text is printed in the order of worship, suggest that people underline key words and write [or draw] notes in the margins.)

2. Provide modern examples of discipline which, like God's discipline of Israel, are aimed at teaching important lessons. For example, tell the story of a child whose parents insisted that she earn the money to buy another bicycle when hers was stolen because she had left it in the front yard (after repeated warnings); or the story of a wealthy father who found his son a job pulling tobacco (or whatever local work is hot and hard) so he would experience how most people earn their money.

**MAMMON** is a fancy word for money and what money can buy. Jesus warned us not to love mammon. That is hard!

Draw pictures of mammon that you like.

OR

Write a word beginning with each letter in the word mammon to describe mammon that you like.

M

A

M

M

O

N

Write a prayer about one of them.

Travelers walking to Jerusalem made up songs about God rescuing people. Listen to Psalm 107. Then write a verse about a group God helps. (You may be in that group!)

Describe their troubles.

There were some _____ who _____

How did God save them?

In their sadness they called on the Lord and God saved them by

How can they thank God?

Let them thank the Lord for such constant love and

# PROPER TWENTY-ONE

*(Sunday between September 25 and October 1 inclusive)*

## From a Child's Point of View

***Old Testament: Joel 2:23-30.*** This passage includes two rather distinct sections. The first (vss. 23-27) is Joel's prediction of the end of the locust plague that has eaten the country into a famine. Good weather and good crops are promised for the coming year. With a little explaining, children can understand the images. But today's nonagricultural children do not appreciate the significance of Joel's promised relief.

The second section (vss. 28-30) is part of Joel's vision of the Day of the Lord. One of the benefits of that day is that God's Spirit will enable great dreams and visions. From this, children learn that God's Holy Spirit is the source of our best dreams for ourselves and for the world. In fact, one job of the Holy Spirit is dream-making. So our dreams are to be taken seriously as gifts from God. If this passage is read on Worldwide Communion Sunday, children and adults might identify and celebrate their dreams for a world that is well fed, healthy, and at peace.

***Psalm 107:1, 33-43.*** This psalm is the introduction and closing hymn of praise (an epilogue) to the traveler's song that praises God's care of people. Though children appreciate the fact that God is with God's people through thick and thin, they will have trouble digging that message out of the conflicting poetic images of this passage. The first part of the psalm is for kids. The rest is for adults.

***Gospel: Luke 16:19-31.*** This is the story of the rich man and Lazarus. The rich man's sin is not that he is rich, but that he, who had the resources to relieve Lazarus' suffering, was so caught up in his own self-interest that he did not even notice Lazarus' need. This happened in spite of the fact that he (and his five brothers) had read the Law and the Prophets, in which such self-centered oblivion to the needs of others is repeatedly condemned.

Children will need help to find this point in the story, but it is a point they need to consider. Even young children can learn to be aware of the needs of those around them. They can learn to "see" when their parents are tired and busy and find ways to help them, rather than make more demands. They can "watch" for unhappy children at school and try to support them. And they can understand this awareness of the needs of others as disciples' work, set out for us by God.

***Epistle: I Timothy 6:6-19.*** This passage contains a series of instructions and warnings about living the Christian life. The warnings are aimed at adult concerns and framed in abstract generalizations and theological jargon. Children will understand little when the passage is read. With help, they can hear the message of verses 17-19—that it is better to do good deeds than to collect neat things.

## Watch Words

Define *dreams* and *visions* as ideas about what could be. They are not weird experiences in which we see things that are not there, or see into the future in a magic way.

## Let the Children Sing

Before singing "Open My Eyes, That I May See," point out the repeated phrase "illumine me" and rephrase it in terms of recognizing dreams.

"Be Thou My Vision" fits several of today's themes. Consider highlighting the message of a key verse before singing it.

## The Liturgical Child

1. Present Jesus' story dramatically. Either have three readers (narrator, the rich man, and Abraham) read the passage, or enlist three older youths or adults (Lazarus, the rich man, and Abraham) to pantomime the action while you read. Plan with the actors a central location for the beginning of the story—a place to one side for "heaven," and a place to the other side for "hell." Simple costumes would help the children recognize the characters.

2. Invite worshipers to pray for members of their families, people they encounter every day, and people with special needs in the larger world. Begin each of the three sections with a corporate prayer, followed by silence for individual prayers.

4. Pray responsively about dreams for the world:

Leader: God, who created us and this world, you have promised that you will pour out your Spirit upon us with dreams of how the world could be and visions of how to attain these dreams. So we share these dreams and ask that you help us to bring them about.

We dream of a world in which everyone has enough food to eat and a safe, warm place to live. But we see pictures of people starving all over the world. In our own town, we know that people are living in shacks and on the streets. And we hardly know how to help.

Congregation: Lord, pour out your Spirit among us.

Leader: We dream of a healthy world. We dream of finding cures for cancer and AIDS. We dream of medical care for everyone, so that children do not die from curable diseases like measles.

Congregation: Lord, pour out your Spirit among us.

Leader: We dream of a beautiful world that is safe for all people, plants, and animals. We worry about all our garbage and polluted rivers and poisoned air. We want to save the whales and the elephants—and ourselves. But we cannot seem to find a way to do it.

Congregation: Lord, pour out your Spirit among us.

Leader: We dream of a world at peace. We hope for the end of racism, for the settling of old feuds between nations and tribes, for sharing between rich and poor, and even for peace in our families. But we have trouble setting aside our own selfish wants to work for the good of us all.

Congregation: Lord, pour out your Spirit among us.

Leader: Lord, be with us and these dreams you have given us. Give us the courage to make changes in the way we do things and to demand that others also make needed changes. Give us the strength to keep dreaming and working when it looks hopeless. And keep us open to new dreams and visions and possibilities.

Congregation: Lord, pour out your Spirit among us.

All: Amen!

3. If this is Worldwide Communion Sunday, use breads from around the world (San Francisco sourdough, Russian pumpernickel, pita bread from the Middle East, etc.) for the sacrament. The breads may be precut into bite-size pieces and mixed together in baskets to pass among the worshipers. Or the worshipers may break bread from one of the loaves. Link the variety of breads to Joel's promise of a good harvest and a well-fed world.

## Sermon Resources

1. Tell stories about people who work to realize dreams. Recall how the "I Have a Dream" speech of Martin Luther King, Jr., gave people the courage to work for civil rights. Describe the importance of being able to "see yourself doing it" in order to succeed in sports. Tell about children in the fifth-grade Sunday school class who worked successfully on their dream for a beautiful world by writing to the board of their church, asking that the church not use styrofoam cups and plates.

2. Introduce Time Out as a game that families can use to become aware of one another's needs and find ways out of unhappy situations. The game starts with one family member calling "time out" when he or she feels that people are bickering or that a blow-up is imminent. When "time out"

is called, they all stop what they are doing. Each person then can speak one sentence to express what he or she feels and wants at the moment.

Then the group agrees on what to do to get the work at hand done and to meet everyone's needs as much as possible.

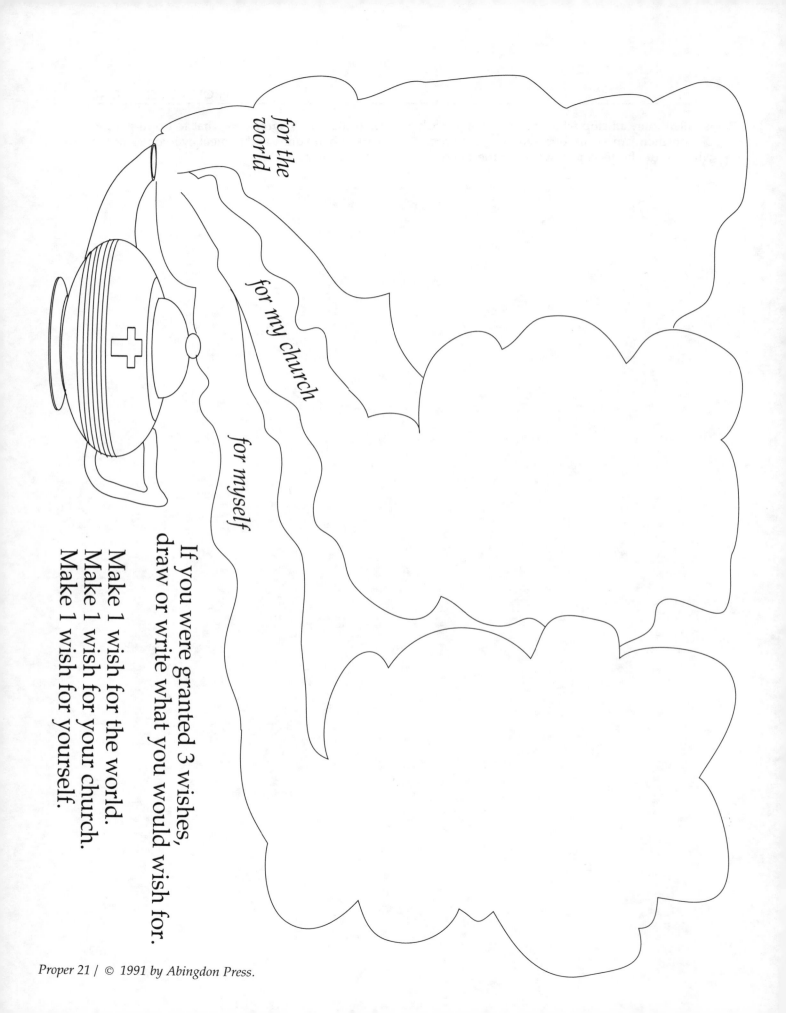

for the world

for my church

for myself

If you were granted 3 wishes,
draw or write what you would wish for.

Make 1 wish for the world.
Make 1 wish for your church.
Make 1 wish for yourself.

# PROPER TWENTY-TWO

## (Sunday between October 2 and 8 inclusive)

### From a Child's Point of View

The shared theme of these texts is that we are God's servants, working together to do God's will. If it is Worldwide Communion Sunday, the sacrament can be presented as the workers' Table, at which we share fellowship with disciples around the world and gain strength for our work.

*Old Testament: Amos: 5:6-7, 10-15.* This is Amos's promise that God will punish the people because they obstruct justice and oppress the poor. But it is hard for children to find this message. Verses 11 and 12 are the easiest to understand, and older children will catch more of the message if they are told before the reading that (1) trials were conducted at the city gate (so justice "at the gate" means that people receive justice from the police and lawyers); and that (2) "the house of Joseph" is a name for God's people.

Amos's message to children is that God does not overlook selfishness and does demand honesty and fair play. Children, like the people of Israel, need to take God's rules or standards seriously. God expects them to be honest at school and when playing games. God insists that they not take advantage of those who are younger or those they are to lead. God is against children taking what is not theirs and is also against hoarding what is theirs instead of sharing it.

For children, it is important to emphasize God's expectations, rather than Amos's promised punishment. Because they think literally, children may assume guilt for anything "bad" that has happened to anyone they love. The result is a guilty child fearful of God's punishment, rather than a brave child ready to live up to God's expectations.

*Psalm 101.* This psalm is a king's pledge to rule justly. Children will have trouble following most translations because they are filled with uncommon, abstract words. The Good News Bible's startlingly short, common words make the message plain for both children and adults.

The message is that God expects kings, presidents, and other leaders to follow the same standards outlined in Amos. Children are to expect this kind of behavior from political leaders and are to follow these standards when they are in positions of leadership (team captains, den leaders, etc.).

*Epistle: II Timothy 1:1-14.* This passage contains encouragement from an older preacher to a young man who is overly cautious about doing God's work. If invited to "read over Timothy's shoulder," children can hear Paul call them to use the gifts (talents, personal qualities, leadership positions among other children) which God gave them. They are to be brave and courageous in standing up for God's ways. They are to be willing to be teased or bullied for doing God's work. And while doing this, they are to remember that God loves and cares for them.

*Gospel: Luke 17:5-10.* This passage includes two separate teachings. The first is not to underestimate what we can do. Children often feel they can do nothing that will make a very big difference. They also feel overwhelmed when trying to do what is asked of them. Jesus claims that if they act faithfully, they will be surprised at what they can do.

The second teaching is that doing God's work (being fair and generous) is not something for which we should expect much attention and thanks. It is simply our job, as God's people.

## Watch Words

*Disciple* is the word/idea behind all of today's texts. A *disciple* is a person who does what Jesus taught.

Remember that *justice* is first understood as *fairness*. And *righteousness* is a big word for *doing what is right*.

*Faith* (like a mustard seed) does not require special knowledge, nor is it a magic possession. *Faith* is being willing to do God's will (even when you are not sure how it will work out).

## Let the Children Sing

*Sing Hymns of Discipleship:* "They'll Know We Are Christians by Our Love"; "Take My Life and Let It Be Consecrated"; "I Sing a Song of the Saints of God"; "Lord, You Give the Great Commission" (see Sermon Resources); "God of Grace and God of Glory" (words in the verses are hard, but children can sing the repeated chorus if alerted to it); "Let There Be Peace on Earth" (especially if it is Worldwide Communion Sunday).

## The Liturgical Child

1. If it is Worldwide Communion Sunday, review the bread suggestions in Proper #21. Let the variety of breads remind worshipers of the disciples around the world who eat many different kinds of bread at their Communion tables for the strength to do God's work.

2. Psalm 101 may have been part of the coronation ceremony. So ask worshipers to imagine they are hearing this address from a leader taking office. Read the psalm as if you were a king or president addressing your people. (In some congregations you could even begin by saying, "Thank you, thank you," as if quieting the ovation of an inauguration crowd.)

3. Base the charge and benediction on the II Timothy exhortations:

Just as Paul encouraged Timothy, so I encourage you to use the gifts God has given you—not cautiously, but with courage and power and self-control. Do not be shy about standing up for God's ways. Be ready to suffer for doing God's work. And remember that God loves you, has given each of you important work to do, and is with you always. Amen.

4. Pray as part of God's worldwide team working for justice and sharing. Name specific needs related to political justice, and to famines or other disasters. Also pray about fair play in children's games and sharing with family and friends. Pray for people who take risks to do God's work on playgrounds, in legislatures, and in offices.

## Sermon Resources

1. Paraphrase II Timothy for children as follows:

From Paul, an older preacher, to Timothy, whom I love very much, and whom God loves: I thank God for you every day. I remember everything we did together and look forward to being with you again. I remember how much you love God, just as your mother and grandmother loved God.

Because I remember all this, I also remind you that you have a job to do. God has given you the gifts to be a fine leader, and the church has elected you to be its leader. So do not give up. God does not want you to be too cautious about using your gifts. Instead, God fills you with power, and love, and self-control. So use those gifts!

Do not be ashamed to stand up for God's ways. If people tease you, call you names, or even push you around, you can take it. Look at me—I am in prison for doing God's work, but I do not mind. I know God will take care of me, even in prison, and I know that God will take care of you.

So remember everything you have learned about God's love and plan for the world. Follow my brave example. And most of all, remember that God's Holy Spirit lives in you and gives you power to do amazing work for God.

2. Use the new hymn, "Lord, You Give the Great Commission," as an outline for a discipleship sermon. Suggest that worshipers keep their hymnals open so that you can refer to specific

phrases. The verses are an interesting combination of abstract and very everyday vocabulary. Consider rehearsing the chorus so that children can join in easily as the hymn is sung following the sermon.

Unscramble the letters in each word to find what Amos told people.

"___ ___ ___ ___ ___ ___ ___ ___ ___ ___ ___ ___ ."

( Amos 5: 14 )

Answer: Seek good and not evil.

Write your name in capital letters across the page. Turn each letter of your name into a picture of you being a disciple.

**Example:** My name is CAROLYN. I turned the A into a picture of me drawing this page for you.

# PROPER TWENTY-THREE

## (Sunday between October 9 and 15 inclusive)

### From a Child's Point of View

*Old Testament: Micah 1:2, 2:1-10.* This passage includes (1) Micah's message that God is about to punish the nation for its social and moral sins; and (2) Micah's response to people who do not want to hear such warnings. The summary message is that God holds all groups responsible for their own actions.

Though Micah is warning the Israelite nation, he also speaks to groups of children who sit together on the bus and in the lunch room, form secret clubs and other gangs. Micah 2:1 especially parallels the evil ("mischief," according to The New Jerusalem Bible) plotted by such children's groups.

Children sense the horror of being the object of a taunt song (2:4) more keenly than do adults. If the assonance in the Greek (see marginal note in The New Jerusalem Bible) is explained, older children will feel what it would be like to be taunted in the streets by that little poem.

Children, like Micah's listeners (vss. 6-7), often expect God to treat them with special understanding, overlooking their mean deeds. Micah warns that God expects them to behave kindly—even if they are "just kids."

*Psalm 26* seems more than a little self-righteous to adults. But to children, it can be a picture of a person who has chosen not to go along with the "evil" of groups. As the poet has allied himself with God and spends time at the Temple, so the child praying the psalm chooses to participate in church activities and join other "good" groups rather than be dragged down by groups that are headed for trouble.

*Epistle: II Timothy 2:8-15.* This passage follows a very complex line of thinking that quickly loses the attention of children. But Paul's basic point—that he is willing to be imprisoned in order to do God's work (preaching, in his case)—is attractive, especially to idealistic older children. The picturesque claim (vs. 9) that they can chain Paul, but they cannot chain God's word makes powerful sense to these literal thinkers.

With help, in the hymn (vss. 11-13), older children can begin to understand the call to keep their commitments to Jesus. The first theological affirmation (vs. 11) is one they simply will need to grow into as their thinking matures. But the rest of the hymn can be understood as:

If we do God's work no matter what,
   we shall be partners with God;
If we pretend we do not know God's teachings
  or
   what God wants us to do,
   God will pretend not to know us.
But even when we do not live right,
   God keeps on loving and caring for the world.

*Gospel: Luke 17:11-19.* This story of ten lepers is often told to children to remind them of the importance of saying "Thank you." But the story is not about manners. It is about an appreciative attitude toward life. Nine lepers took their gifts (their cures) and ran. The tenth leper stopped to think about the significance of the gift he had been given and to respond to that gift. He probably responded the same way when someone gave him food, when a sick friend shared space in a dry cave, or when he saw a beautiful sunset. This attitude was a big part of the faith that made him "whole." The story urges us to cultivate such an attitude in our own lives.

All this, of course, is between the lines. Children will need direction to dig out this meaning and apply it to their lives.

## Watch Words

*Faith* is not special knowledge or a magical possession. Micah insists that *faith* is obeying God's laws every day. In the case of the leper, *faith* is being aware of the good gifts that are part of your life.

*Thankful, grateful,* and *appreciative* are adult words about knowing that something is wonderful and good, a gift.

## Let the Children Sing

Sing your gratitude with "Now Thank We All Our God" or "For the Beauty of the Earth."

Ask the children's choir or a children's class to sing "Father, We Thank Thee for the Night." Perhaps the congregation could then sing it with the children as a round.

In response to Micah's message, and in keeping with Paul's commitment, sing "Go Forth for God," or other discipleship hymns mentioned in Proper #22.

## The Liturgical Child

1. Lead in prayer, with several pauses for silent individual prayer. Invite worshipers to thank God for each member of their family, for what they like about their school or job, for something they especially enjoy about their home, for activities they most appreciate at church, and for something wonderful that happened this week.

2. If focusing on gratitude, before you sing "Praise God from Whom All Blessings Flow," point out its meaning and its significance in your order of worship. Be sure to define *blessings* as something other than the prayer we say before meals.

3. Invite all worshipers to make a list of ten good things, people, events, or activities they consider gifts from God. Urge them to put their lists in the offering plate along with their money gifts, as a way to express their gratitude to God.

4. Pray for groups of which we are part. Pray aloud for the nation, community, and congregation in which you all share. Provide silent time for individual prayer—for the class at school or the people at work, for clubs and teams in which they participate, and for their families. Include prayers of thanksgiving, confession, and petition.

## Sermon Resources

1. Describe groups that get "carried away into trouble": the sports fans who start by shouting, "We're Number One!" and end by beating up fans of the other team; or the sixth-grade boys who begin by insisting on special privileges from the younger boys because they are the oldest in the school, and end by playing cruel tricks on the younger kids. Such stories pave the way for talk about group responsibility.

2. Retell some of the events in the story of Pollyanna, a little girl who treats all of life as a gift and has a way of finding the good in everything and everyone. Borrow the book from a public library or rent the video to review the story.

3. The task in preaching about the gratitude of the tenth leper is not to berate worshipers for being ungrateful or insensitive to God's gifts, but to help them look at their lives with appreciation, identify their blessings, and learn disciplines that cultivate gratitude. In pointing out blessings, remember that when children voice thank-you prayers, they often mention their families, special friends (some of whom may be adults), a recent trip or party, unusual but beautiful weather (especially snow), and loved activities such as sports. They resent being told what to feel thankful for (e.g., most children, at certain times, are not at all thankful for their family).

Write or draw 1 person, thing, or activity
that you like a lot in each box below.

|  |  |  |
|---|---|---|
|  |  |  |
|  |  |  |

Write a prayer telling God about
1 of the things you like.

_____

_____

_____

_____

_____

_____

Make up a poem about another thing
you like.

what you like _____

2 words to describe it _____  _____

3 "ing" words about it _____  _____  _____

THANK YOU, GOD.

# PROPER TWENTY-FOUR

## (Sunday between October 16 and 22 inclusive)

### From a Child's Point of View

Today's texts deals with understanding and living with oppression in the world of a loving, just God.

*Old Testament: Habakkuk 1:1-3; 2:1-4.* This passage deals with fairness on the national/global level. Older children appreciate Habakkuk's question when it is presented in personal terms (e.g., a Central American farmer caught in the cross-fire between warring guerrilla bands; a child starving in a country whose leaders live in luxury). They quickly agree with Habakkuk that it is not fair, and they wonder why a loving God allows such things to happen.

God's answer—that in the long haul, justice will be done—seems a bit like a cop-out to children who live so much in their own present. It helps to hear a trusted adult speak with appreciation of this view and cite examples. But it will be some years before children really accept this view.

They can, however, apply God's "sign" to their present. Basically, it says that no matter what seems to get the best results at the moment, it is always better to live by God's ways.

*Psalm 119:137-144.* This is a psalm to sing while waiting for God's justice to be realized. Its vocabulary is a major obstacle to a straightforward message—*judgments, testimonies, precepts, righteousness, commands, laws,* and *faithfulness* are used interchangeably. If it is suggested that all these words describe God's ways, children can begin to understand some of the praise statements. The Good News Bible translation is particularly helpful.

*Epistle: II Timothy 3:14—4:5.* This contains more of Paul's encouragement for Timothy. Verse 3:14-17 suggests that studying the Bible is the way to know about God and what God wants us to do. This is not a new idea for children, but one they need to hear emphasized repeatedly.

In 4:1-5, Paul encourages Timothy to do the work of preaching and teaching to which he has been called. He is specifically warned against putting off doing what is difficult. Like Timothy, children often try to put off discipleship until they are older or until it is easier. They need to be reminded that discipleship is never easy. Paul was put in prison for preaching. We do not know what problems Timothy met, but they were problems he wanted to avoid. Like Paul and Timothy, children can expect problems as they do God's work at school and among their friends. Like Paul and Timothy, children are to be strong and patient.

*Gospel: Luke 18:1-8.* This passage is also about persistence. Jesus uses a story about a villainous judge to make a point. Children are easily confused by this story, unless they are bluntly told that Jesus is saying that even a bad judge will give in to the persistence of an unwanted pest (the woman), so we can expect our loving and fair God to respond to our persistent prayers. They also need to be told bluntly that Jesus was *not* saying that God is like the bad judge, who only responds when someone becomes a pest.

Read with the other texts for the day, this text offers one more instruction on what to do while we wait for God's justice: Pray for God's will to be done on earth.

## Watch Words

Be careful about generalizations such as *the wicked*, *the evil*, and *oppression*. Speak instead about the specific oppressors and evil practices that children recognize.

Note the vocabulary warnings in the commentary on Psalm 119. Call the Bible *the Bible* rather than Scriptures, Holy Book, or other names, unless you introduce the names as you use them.

## Let the Children Sing

The hymns of discipleship mentioned during the last weeks continue to be good choices. "We Shall Overcome" or "They'll Know We Are Christians by Our Love" are especially appropriate and are singable by children.

"Wonderful Words of Life" celebrates the importance of the Bible for direction and has a chorus that children can sing and may know from church school.

## The Liturgical Child

1. Ask an artist in the congregation, or a youth class, to prepare a banner bearing a version of Habakkuk 2:4. Display the banner near the worship center in the sanctuary. The banner should be like the easy-to-read sign that God instructed Habakkuk to make.

2. Invite worshipers to listen to Habakkuk's message "in the shoes" of a homeless person; of a family stuck in a refugee camp; of a Central American peasant who lives with constant war. Introduce 1:1-3 and 2:1 as Habakkuk's question, read it, then interrupt to indicate that 2:2-4 is God's answer, and read those verses.

3. Since Psalm 119 is an acrostic, and each of today's verses is a separate statement praising God's ways, have the text read by a team of readers, each reader reading one verse. The team could be composed of members of a children's class, or church members of a variety of ages. The whole team stands across the front of the church, in the order of their verses, then read in turn from their Bibles or recite their verses from memory.

4. Paraphrase II Timothy 4:1-2, 5, to charge the congregation before the benediction.

5. Point out the Lord's Prayer petition, "Thy kingdom come, thy will be done on earth as it is in heaven," for explanation. Then pray the Lord's Prayer or a litany prayer for God's justice. (To each prayer below, the congregation responds, "Thy Kingdom come, thy will be done on earth as it is in heaven.")

> Lord, it is easy to pray "Thy will be done," but it is hard to do. So much around us seems to go against your will. We need your direction and courage and power. (Response)
> You created the world filled with food, but we see pictures of hungry children every day on TV. Help us find ways to share. (Response)
> God, we all need a home. But so many people do not have one. Work with us to find houses for all who live in our area. Guide those who work to resettle refugees. (Response)
> Lord, guide us as a nation. Give us the wisdom to elect fair leaders. Direct those leaders to laws and policies that are just. Help us treat other countries and people lovingly. (Describe current situations in the world and in your community that cry out for God's justice.) (Response)
> God, make us doers of your justice. Help us play fair at school and at work. Teach us not to make enemies, but to make friends. Give us the courage to stand up for your ways among our friends. And remind us of that way when we are tempted to "forget." (Response)
> We pray in Jesus' name. Amen.

## Sermon Resources

1. Today's texts offer three disciplines to follow while waiting for God's justice: pray (Luke); study the Bible (II Tim. 3); and do God's work in spite of hardships (II Tim. and Hab.). These practical activities are disciplines children can hear about and pursue. (Perhaps they are the three points of a very practical sermon.)

Copy the titles of the hymns for worship today in the spaces below. ( *Hint: Find them in your bulletin or on a board up front.* )

Draw a (circle) around each hymn you already know.

Choose one verse of one hymn to write below in your own words.

Choose another verse of the hymn to illustrate. ( *To illustrate a verse means to draw a picture about it.* )

After you have sung all of the hymns, draw a ☆ beside the title of the hymn that you liked best.

# PROPER TWENTY-FIVE

## (Sunday between October 23 and 29 inclusive)

### From a Child's Point of View

*Old Testament: Zephaniah 3:1-9.* This passage first describes Jerusalem as a city of people who have refused to listen to God's criticisms and warnings; then it quotes God's message about coming destruction; and finally it speaks of redemption. If children are told before the reading that the city of Jerusalem is spoken of as a woman in this passage, they will be able to make sense of verses 1-3.

As a whole, and with adult direction, the passage can speak to children about the importance of learning from criticism and listening to warnings. Just as Jerusalem refused to learn from God's criticisms, many children refuse to hear warnings about their behavior. When people (individuals or groups) ignore such warnings, they usually get into trouble. Because they ignored God's warnings, the people of Jerusalem were conquered and taken prisoner so that they would learn to live as God's people. When they ignore warnings, children get into trouble at school or with the police. If they experiment with matches, cigarettes, or drugs (even though they have been warned against them), children are often physically hurt.

*Psalm 3.* This psalm is easy for children to follow, if it is introduced as the prayer of King David while he was running from an army that was trying to overthrow him. Verses 3-6 speak clearly of David's trust that God will shield (or protect) him. This trust enables him to sleep and not be so frightened. Children are invited to share David's trust, knowing that God will protect them.

*Epistle: II Timothy 4:6-8, 16-18.* These are the observations of Paul, who, realizing that he soon will be executed, is looking back over his ministry. He expresses satisfaction that he has done his best, forgives those who did not stand up for him when he was arrested, and credits God for the power to use his long imprisonment as an opportunity to tell the good news to the Gentiles. It is hard for children, at the beginning of their lives, to appreciate Paul's statements, but they can see, as an example, his forgiveness of those who failed him. Adults would like them to comprehend the satisfaction of having done their best, but few children will appreciate that until they have more personal experience with having done both their best and less than their best.

*Gospel: Luke 18:9-14.* This passage describes the prayers of a proud Pharisee and a repentant tax collector. Children respond quickly to Jesus' caricatures and grasp his point that God is not impressed by show-offs, but by people who are honest—even about their faults. Young children accept the terms *Pharisee* and *tax collector* as labels for the two men, without asking about the significance of the words. The understanding of older children is enriched by definitions of these labels.

Children can link the Pharisee in this parable with the self-satisfied people of Jerusalem in Zephaniah, to further explore the humble openness to self-evaluation, repentance (changing our ways), and growth that are to characterize God's people.

### Watch Words

Instead of *prophecy*, in this case, speak of *warning* and *criticism from God*.

Avoid *repentance*. Speak instead about the people of Jerusalem, the tax collector, and us, as we change our ways to bring them in line with God's teachings.

Paul's *race* and *crown-of-righteousness* images are difficult to translate and do not communicate to children what Paul wants to say. So use them for the adults and speak to children through other passages and images.

## Let the Children Sing

"Jesus Loves Me, This I Know" is a song the tax collector and Paul might have sung. Sing it with the same reliance on God they had.

"Have Thine Own Way, Lord" is a song of submission to God's will for our lives. Children will benefit especially from singing it if you featured a potter earlier this year.

"Take Time to Be Holy" is a hymn older children can begin to sing with growing understanding. Though some of the ideas are abstract, the words and phrases are short and describe familiar activities.

## The Liturgical Child

1. Invite someone to take the part of David as he prayed before going to sleep in his hideout. Go all out with a costumed David, reciting the psalm from memory. Or simply set the context, then give it your best dramatic reading from the lectern. (Read several translations in preparing this reading. The original Jerusalem Bible gives a sharp sense of the beleaguered king expressing his trust in God at the end of a rough day.)

2. Ask the adult choir to present "The Pharisee and the Publican," by Heinrich Schutz. The work features two male solos which capture wonderfully the character of the two worshipers in the story. (Do point out that *publican* is another word for tax collector.)

3. Take the parts of both the Pharisee and the tax collector as you read the Luke text. For the Pharisee, stand to one side of the lectern with haughty posture, and read the words with a rather loud, pretentious tone. For the tax collector, stand to the other side and speak with genuine sorrow, in a calm voice.

4. Prayer of confession and petition:

God of the universe, forgive us when we are so sure we are right that we stop listening to the ideas of others. Remind us that we do not know everything.

Lord, forgive us when we are too impressed with our ideas and with what we can do. Keep us from becoming braggy.

Loving Father and Mother, forgive us when we want something so much that we ignore warnings that we may want the wrong thing. Help us control our "wants."

God of the Bible, forgive us when we think stories about your love are meant for us, and demands for change are meant for other people. Be with us as we read the Bible, and help us hear what you are saying to us. Amen.

## Sermon Resources

For children, these texts urge that we not become so sure of ourselves that we ignore new ideas and warnings. Most children know they do not know everything now, but dream of a day when they will. One starting point for this sermon is to share the secret truth that adults seldom tell children—and that truth is that even grown-ups do not know everything. The best scientists tell us that the more they learn about their field of study, the more questions they have. The best musicians insist that they are always learning more about the music they can draw from their instruments. The best presidents do not know what to do in every situation, but are always searching for new solutions to the country's problems. So to be mature, or grown up, is not to know everything, but to be always looking for new ideas and possibilities.

The people in Jerusalem forgot this truth. They thought they knew everything. They did not want to hear God's criticisms of the way they were living. The Pharisee ignored this truth. He thought he knew everything there was to know about God and how to live. When we pretend to others that we know everything, or when we tell ourselves that we know better than our parents or anyone else or what we read in the Bible, we are forgetting this truth and probably soon will be in trouble.

Trace a path as you follow each person under, over, and around to find Jesus' message to each of them.

1.

2.

1. _____

2. _____

Answers 1. Everyone who humbles himself will be made great. 2. Everyone who makes himself great will be humbled.

Listen to the sermon and pray today's prayers. Then write Jesus' message in your own words.

# PROPER TWENTY-SIX

*(Sunday between October 30 and November 5 inclusive)*

Note: Consider substituting the All Saints lections for those of Proper 26, especially if Sunday falls near Halloween. Also, remember that Reformation Day can be celebrated on the last Sunday in October. It is a good time to tell Reformation stories and focus on Martin Luther's basic belief that God loves us in spite of our sinfulness.

## From a Child's Point of View

*Old Testament: Haggai 2:1-9.* This is a specific message for a specific time. Haggai encourages the people and their leaders to be courageous, to work hard, and not to be afraid as they rebuild the Jerusalem Temple after the Exile. Haggai promises that God will be with the people as they rebuild the Temple and that the Temple will be a rich and important center. It is a somewhat interesting but remote story for children, although the point of the text can be stretched to encourage children today to be courageous, work hard, and be fearless in doing God's work, whatever that may be for them.

*Psalm 65:1-8.* This psalm praises God, who forgives us for sins that overwhelm us (vs. 3*b*), chooses us to be the people of the Temple (vs. 4), does mighty historical deeds on our behalf (vs. 5*a*), and controls nature (vss. 6-7). However, none of the praises are offered in language children can understand and follow easily. One of the best uses of the psalm is to lift specific lines from it for explanation and use in worship.

*Epistle: II Thessalonians 1:5-12.* This letter was written by and for people whose understanding of the universe, geographically and historically, was different from ours. Unless you believe in the physical reality of heaven and hell, complete with fire and brimstone, the vivid descriptions in this passage are hard to explain to literal-minded children. Behind the word pictures is the stated promise that nothing can separate us from God's love and that what is suffered in the line of discipleship will pass. But this too is hard to explain to children. So it is probably best to read verses 6-10, but focus on verses 11 and 12.

Verses 11 and 12, especially as presented in the Good News Bible, offer two significant encouragements to children:

1. Verse 11 expresses the hope that each of us will live up to the calling (or potential) with which God created us. Underlying that hope is the belief that God has a good plan for each person. Children dream of doing something wonderful and good during their lives. Paul, in this text, tells them that he hopes those dreams will come true. He also hopes that they will be worthy of their dreams and God's plan for their lives.

2. Verse 12 encourages readers to live so well that people will say both, "If this person is a disciple of Jesus, then Jesus must be wonderful," and "You can see the loving power of Jesus in this person."

Children will need help to dig both these encouragements out of Paul's words.

*Gospel: Luke 19:1-10.* This story of Zacchaeus is most likely familiar to the children. They relate quickly to the short fellow who is elbowed to the back of the crowd, is resourceful enough to climb a tree in order to see Jesus, and then is singled out by Jesus for special attention. The story gives them hope that Jesus notices and cares for them,

184

particularly if they feel overlooked or shoved to the side.

Younger children will overlook the fact that Zacchaeus was a tax-collecting cheat. Jesus' notice of the short guy is plenty to satisfy their needs. Older children, when they notice this part of the story, will appreciate the fact that not only was Zacchaeus short (an awful fate for a ten-to-twelve-year-old boy in our sports-minded culture), but he was also unpopular—and deserved to be, because he cheated! Zacchaeus was "pond scum" (substitute the ultimate put-down currently used by children in your congregation)! With this richer understanding of Zacchaeus, the story does two things. First, it assures children that Jesus loves and will forgive them—even when they have acted like pond scum. Second, it challenges them to treat the Zacchaeuses they meet with the same forgiving love that Jesus lavished upon the original.

## Watch Words

*Zion, Temple,* and other words related to Jewish nationalistic hopes are difficult to introduce into children's vocabulary.

Avoid the *salvation* that came to Zacchaeus' house. Talk about the friendship and forgiveness Jesus offered, and about Zacchaeus' response.

## Let the Children Sing

Praise God's greatness as the psalmist did, by singing "For the Beauty of the Earth" or "How Great Thou Art."

"I Sing a Song of the Saints of God" is one way to respond to Paul's challenges in II Thessalonians.

## The Liturgical Child

1. Even if you do not celebrate All Saints Day, pray about Halloween. Praise the God who is so powerful that we need not fear any other force in the universe. Pray for fun and safety while celebrating. And pray for the wisdom to remain our loving selves while wearing masks and costumes.

2. Ask the children's choir or a children's class to sing a song about Zacchaeus as an anthem for the worship service. (Most children's groups have a much-loved Zacchaeus song in their repertory.)

3. Point out the phrase "Forgive us our debts (or trespasses), as we forgive our debtors (or those who trespass against us)" in the Lord's Prayer. Briefly describe what it meant for Zacchaeus to pray that phrase, and encourage worshipers to pray it in that spirit.

4. Base the charge that precedes the benediction on II Thessalonians 1:11-12:

May God make you worthy of the life to which you are called. May God give you the power to do the good deeds you want to do. May Jesus look good because of what you do. And may you look good because of what God does through you. Amen.

## Sermon Resources

1. If you are celebrating Reformation Sunday, tell the story of Martin Luther, who learned the same lesson Zacchaeus learned. Both learned that God/Jesus loved them in spite of their sinfulness.

2. Introduce the Zacchaeus Game. Every player takes the role of Jesus, watching for people who are lonely, "up a tree," or just plain having a bad day. When such a "Zacchaeus" is found, the player does something nice for that person. Sometimes the player does not ever know whether the kindness makes a difference. But sometimes the player can see the person respond—almost as readily as Zacchaeus responded to Jesus' request to be his dinner guest.

To motivate children to play, tell about a kind deed someone did for you when you were feeling as closed out as Zacchaeus. Describe the change, however small, that it made in you. Encourage young players to draw pictures of what happens as they play the game during the week, to share with you next Sunday.

Listen when Luke 19: 1-10 is read.
Draw a picture of what happened in
that story. Draw faces that show what
people were feeling.

Most of us dream about doing
something important, something
that would make life better for
people. Draw or write about what
you want to do.

Tell God about your dream. Ask
God to help you make your dream
come true.

# PROPER TWENTY-SEVEN

*(Sunday between November 6 and 12 inclusive)*

## From a Child's Point of View

*Old Testament: Zechariah 7:1-10.* This story is about a carefully planned question that really was not what it appeared to be. Children are quite familiar with and have experienced such scheming questions. They will need to hear the story retold with some background details to recognize the question for what it is and to catch God's response. When they understand what happened, they will enjoy hearing adults being "called on" one of their scheming questions and will be reminded that such questions usually are recognized for what they are.

From God's response, they learn two things:

First, that God is less interested in how many churchy things we do and more interested in whether we love God. Just as a child is not fooled by a neighbor child who comes over to play because her mother sent her, God is not fooled when we come to church because our parents made us come. God, like us, wants real friends.

Second, God is not fooled when we talk about love at church, and then treat people unkindly and unfairly during the week. God wants what we say at church to match what we do.

*Psalm 9:11-20.* This is part of a lament urging God to rescue the oppressed (especially the poor) and to judge the oppressors. Because it is an acrostic, the line of thinking is not direct, but jumps around. Because the language and poetic images are so abstract, children will not follow the whole reading, but will catch phrases within it. Verse 18 is probably the easiest for them and contains the promise on which the whole section is based. With some adult help on verses 19-20,

older children can appreciate the fact that not only individuals but whole nations are expected to obey God.

*Epistle: II Thessalonians 2:13–3:5.* This passage grows out of Paul's love for and friendship with the Christians at Thessalonica. Children gain most from the passage when they stand with the Thessalonians to hear Paul's encouragement and the request for prayer support. Read that way, verses 2:13-15 remind children that God loves them and has put them in a place where they could hear the stories about God and Jesus. In response, they are to remember the stories and obey Jesus' teachings. If they do, God will be with them, helping them.

Children can respond to Paul's prayer request (3:1-2) by praying for their church and for people who are doing God's work.

*Gospel: Luke 20:27-38.* This is the story of another tricky question: "Whose wife will a woman who has been married and widowed seven times be, when all eight of those people get to heaven?" Children do not need to hear about leviratic practices or the Sadducee's motives to understand this question. They will need help with Jesus' answer in verses 34-36. But once it has been explained, the answer is one they readily accept. No one knows what life beyond death is like. That is one of God's secrets. What we do know is that God will still be loving. Therefore, we can expect only that life will be good. That answer puts the question in a familiar class of questions for which there are no answers—only mysteries.

The Sadducee's question is, of course, also a trap question. But to recognize that and to deal with Jesus' point about the God of the living (vss. 37-38) requires in-depth knowledge about the Sadducees and their logic. Explore this with the grown-ups.

## Watch Words

Children usually associate *resurrection* with Jesus and Easter. So for clarity, speak of *life after death* rather than *in the resurrection*.

If you speak about the *Sadducees* at any length, point out that they were *sad, you see* because they did not believe in life after death. This will not help children understand the significance of this passage; it simply helps them recognize a name they will hear again.

## Let the Children Sing

"We Are the Church" describes a church that follows the advice of Zechariah and Paul. This Avery and Marsh song is used in many church schools and appears in some new hymnals. If you cannot use it as a congregational hymn, ask a children's choir or class to sing it as an anthem.

Sing "Lord, You Give the Great Commission," especially if you worked on learning it as a congregation earlier this fall. This hymn also follows the prophecy and Epistle theme.

Sing about life after death with "Come, Christians, Join to Sing" (encourage nonreaders to join in on the Alleluias) and "Near to the Heart of God" (a description of life before and after death).

## The Liturgical Child

1. If you focus on the Gospel reading, display new-life symbols and banners in the worship center. Suggest that flowering bulbs (Easter lilies, if possible) be the flowers of the day. Then refer to them during the sermon.

2. Preserve the acrostic format of Psalm 9 by having it read by a series of readers, each reader reading two verses. Because the acrostic is not pure in this section, it is best not to use letter posters (as suggested for other acrostics). Using different readers will, however, help worshipers pay attention to the changing messages.

3. In response to Paul's request, pray for people doing God's work through the church. Pray for church school teachers, missionaries (by name if possible), the choirs, the staff of the church, church officers (pray about specific work those officers are currently doing), and church leaders beyond your congregation (perhaps the director of the church summer camp your children attend). Include mission projects in which children are participating.

4. Introduce II Thessalonians 2:13–3:5 as part of a letter Paul wrote to friends to encourage them. Then invite worshipers to hear the same Scripture as if it were being written to them.

Adapt the text for use as a Charge and Benediction:

Remember that God loves you. God chose you to hear the good news and to live among God's people. Do not forget what you have learned. Live by it. And may our Lord Jesus Christ, and God the Father, and the Holy Spirit give you the courage and strength to say kind words and do loving deeds today and every day. Amen.

## Sermon Resources

1. Organize the sermon around the different kinds of questions in the texts: genuine requests for information or help (Paul's request that the Thessalonians pray for him); unanswerable questions we all ask (Why can some people sing well and others cannot? What will happen to me after I die?); questions that are not really questions, but statements of what I want to ask (I don't have to clean up my room, do I? We don't need to keep that Temple fast anymore, do we?).

2. Devote the sermon to exploring ideas about life after death (heaven). Identify some ways we describe heaven: winged angels, harps, golden streets, an entry gate manned by Saint Peter, and so on. Invite people to flip through hymns about heaven or eternal life in the hymnal. Review key ideas and word pictures in several hymns. Then work through the Gospel text in order to get to the fact that we really do not know much about what happens after we die. What we do know is that God, who loves us and cares for us on earth, will keep loving and caring for us after we die. We have God's promise and Jesus' promise about that. The cocoon that becomes a butterfly and the egg that hatches into a bird help children appreciate the change that happens to us at death.

No one knows exactly what heaven is like. That is God's secret. But Christians have always drawn pictures and written poems and hymns about what heaven might be like.

Draw or write what you think heaven is like.

Draw a picture of a person in your church who does God's work.

Write a prayer for this person and for his or her work.

# PROPER TWENTY-EIGHT

## (Sunday between November 13 and 19 inclusive)

### From a Child's Point of View

*Old Testament: Malachi 4:1-6 (3:19-24 in the Hebrew Bible).* These are the very last verses of the Old Testament. That, by itself, attracts the curiosity of children. While the passage does form a kind of bridge to the New Testament, it is a slippery one for children. Verses 1-3 speak of a burning oven into which the evil people will be thrown. The evil people are described as stripped branches. A "sun of righteousness with healing wings" appears. The righteous people, compared to calves released from confining stalls, are invited to stamp on the ashes of the evil. Literal-minded children are overwhelmed with nonintegrated pictures. Unless they are helped to interpret this as a promise that God's love will one day conquer the world completely, they probably will tune out, deciding that the Bible is really hard to understand.

Verse 4 is easier. In some ways, it is a summary of God's message to the people in the Old Testament. It calls on people to keep God's laws as they have been presented by Moses.

Verses 5 and 6 point to the New Testament by urging people to watch for Elijah. This makes sense if the children are reminded that people compared John the Baptist to Elijah.

*Psalm 82.* This psalm is a literary vision that is confusing to children. The poet sets the scene in an assembly of the gods and depicts God judging the other gods for their unjust governing of the earth. Adults can assume the mind-set of the psalmist's readers to hear the poet's praise of God's power and justice. Children cannot. They tend to ask why other gods are mentioned here, when there is only one God.

In verses 3-4, children may hear God's commands to all people, especially to the leaders.

*Epistle: II Thessalonians 3:6-13.* This is a very practical teaching about life in the church. Everyone, of every age, is to be a contributing member. For children, who are unable to earn their own money, the message is that they are to take part in the work at home and at church and in the community. They are to do their part of the chores, and they are to watch for other things that need to be done and do them. That is one of the responsibilities of being a member of God's family. Understanding this passage is not nearly as difficult as disciplining ourselves (no matter what our age) to do the work.

*Gospel: Luke 21:5-19.* This is Jesus' answer to the question, "When will 'the end' come?" In recent years there has been an increase in people predicting the "end of time" or the "second coming." As the year 2000 approaches, there probably will be more. Children need to be prepared for these well-publicized announcements, and this passage is good preparation. Jesus says plainly that no one knows when God will act. Anyone who sets the date is to be ignored.

Jesus also forewarns his disciples (and us) that there will be times when being a Christian will get us into trouble. In those situations, we are to be strong, knowing that God is with us and will help us. Persecution, whether it be teasing or imprisonment, is part of being a follower of Jesus in a selfish world.

## Watch Words

Make it clear that *work* is doing what needs to be done, rather than having a job that brings in money.

Remember that children take apocalyptic language literally, unless you help them do otherwise. If you frequently use terms such as *second coming, day of the Lord,* or *end of time* in this service, be sure to tell children what the term(s) mean to you in your tradition.

## Let the Children Sing

Sing "Rejoice, the Lord Is King" to celebrate God's lordship over all history. The repeated chorus makes it child-accessible. (Yes, boys will grin as they sing of every bosom swelling with pure, seraphic joy.)

Sing "Take My Life and Let It Be Consecrated" to commit your whole bodies to doing God's work.

## The Liturgical Child

1. Adapt the litany prayer below to fit the work done in your congregation; congregational response to each prayer: "Lord, help each of us see our share of the work and do it":

There's so much to do, Lord, just to keep our building clean! There are dishes to wash after every supper, and sidewalks to sweep, and grass to mow and rake, and garbage to empty. (Response)

And who will keep the furnace working, fold the bulletins each week, buy candles for the sanctuary, and remember to order the church school books? (Response)

And then there are the demanding jobs, God. We need church school teachers who will spend time preparing and leading lessons every week. We need people who will see needs in the community and lead us out to meet them. We need people to make sure our money is spent wisely to do your work. (Response)

We need people who will spend a snowy day delivering Meals-on-Wheels, or walk all ten miles of the CROP Walk, or be a Bible school helper. (Name mission projects in which your children work.) (Response)

And God, we need alert people who quietly do the little things. We need people who will drive an older member to the doctor's office, baby-sitters who refuse to charge for church meetings, children who are leaders among younger children on the lawn after church. (Response)

Lord, there's so much to be done. It will take all of us working together to get the work done. Be with us as we work. Help us work wisely and efficiently. And let us know your peace and happiness in all we do; for we work and pray in your name. Amen.

2. Base a prayer of confession on Psalm 82:4-5. Before each phrase of the psalm pray, "Lord, you call us to . . . ," following it with a phrase that describes why we do not do as called (e.g., "Lord, you call us to give justice to the weak and to orphans, but we are so busy taking care of ourselves that we have no time or energy to look out for others.").

## Sermon Resources

1. If you talk about the importance of work, describe the jobs children can do at home, at church, and in the community. Be specific. If you cannot identify some jobs that are more than busywork, put the congregation to work identifying and instituting some.

2. Tell stories about people who have predicted the end of time. One recent example is the man who announced that the world would end on September 12, 1988, based on the prophecies in the book of Daniel. Many people started to attend prayer meetings every day. Some sold their homes and gave the money away in preparation for the last day. When the world did not end, the man announced that he had made a mistake in his figuring, and set a new date.

Turn each letter of WORK into a picture of you working at home or church.

This is me washing a window on church clean-up day.

# WORK

Write a prayer about your work.

God, there are some jobs I really like. Thank you for_____

_____.

But I need to confess to you that _____

_____.

Help me to work on _____

_____.

Amen.

# PROPER TWENTY-NINE CHRIST THE KING

## (Sunday between November 20 and 26 inclusive)

### From a Child's Point of View

*Old Testament: II Samuel 5:1-5.* This passage is read on Christ the King Sunday to remind worshipers of the Davidic reign. For children, it is a rather dry account of how David became king. There is little except the familiar name of David to draw their attention and no clear message for them.

*Psalm 95.* This psalm focuses on two ways to treat a king: (1) We praise a king, and (2) we obey a king. The first seven verses are an opportunity to praise God, the King of the universe. Its short phrases are filled with familiar images of God and God's rule. Children can be full participants in this praise with little help.

Verses 7b-11 require some background. First, it needs to be explained that these verses are a warning delivered by the priest (minister) to the worshiping congregation. The warning is that God is not only to be praised but also to be obeyed. That warning is as appropriate for children today as it was for the people in that day. If God is our King, we are to obey God every day. (Children can follow these verses if told that at Meribah and Massah, the people had not obeyed God. They do not need to hear the story of that disobedience.)

*Gospel: John 12:9-19.* This is an account of Palm Sunday, when Jesus was welcomed as king with the messianic shout, "Hosanna!" (Children recognize "Hosanna!" as a shout meant only for Jesus.) For children, the most interesting and powerful part of this story is Jesus' decision to make his entrance on a donkey. Every child knows that kings ride big, beautiful, spirited horses. By riding a common donkey, Jesus proclaims himself to be a humble king—not one who will make war and expect a fancy palace.

*Epistle: Colossians 1:11-20.* This passage is a description of Christ, the cosmic ruler. Verses 15-20 are a hymn rich in poetic images that are totally foreign to children. One approach is to invite the children not to try to understand, but to feel the majesty of Christ in these fancy words. (If you do this, provide a majestic reading in which the poetic words and phrases are given their full dramatic impact.) A second approach is to encourage children to listen hard for short phrases they understand. Most will recognize several of the short phrases describing Christ.

Verses 11-14 come *before* the poem in Colossians, but may make more sense to children *after* they have heard and reflected on the poem. These verses focus attention not on Christ the King, but on us, Christ's subjects. It is a wish (or prayer) that we, who are fortunate to be the subjects of such a king, be given the power to serve our king well and faithfully. In many ways it parallels the warning about obedience with which Psalm 95 concludes.

### Watch Words

*Christ* is another name for *Jesus*. Often we use *Jesus* when telling stories about Jesus' life on earth, and *Christ* when we talk about Christ as the lord of the whole universe. (This might be a good time to clear up the common childhood misconception that Christ is Jesus' last name.)

Speak of Christ as *King* today, rather than as the *Messiah*.

Legitimate concerns are being raised by feminists and liberation theologians about using the language of *king*ship to describe Christ. These issues can be well explored with both adults and children. But to most children today, kings exist in imaginative stories. In these tales, kings are just as likely to be good and caring as they are to be autocratic and mean to their subjects. Princes are even more likely to be good. Therefore, children enjoy the language and culture of kingship so much that it is worth occasionally speaking of *Christ the King*, his *rule* or *reign*, and his *power*, *glory*, and *majesty*. Call on people to obey as *loyal* subjects.

## Let the Children Sing

There are many great hymns that praise Christ the King: "Rejoice, the Lord Is King," "When Morning Gilds the Skies," "From All That Dwell Below the Skies," and "Come, Christians, Join to Sing." These have repeated choruses or phrases that make them easy for nonreaders. "Let All the World in Every Corner Sing" is a less familiar hymn, but one with simple language for middle-elementary readers.

Recall Palm Sunday with "All Glory, Laud, and Honor."

## The Liturgical Child

1. Explain that Psalm 95 is set in a worshiping congregation and includes the praises of the congregation and a warning by the worship leader. Alert worshipers to the significance of Massah and Meribah. Then invite the people to read verses 1-7a praising God the King. Consider making it a responsive reading, with two sides of the congregation reading short praises back and forth. A worship leader than takes the priest's role to read verses 7b-11.

2. Read the Colossian hymn (vss. 15-20) twice. First, read it from the translation of your choice. Invite worshipers to feel the richness of the big words that praise Christ the King. Then have a group of children read the following sentences,

which put the praises into simple language. Each phrase is read by one child; three or more children may take turns.

> When we see Christ, we are seeing God also.
> Through Christ, God created everything in heaven and on earth.
> Through Christ, God created everything visible and invisible.
> Before anything else was created, Christ was here.
> Christ holds all the world in his hands.
> The church is Christ's Body, and Christ is the head of this Body.
> Christ was the first to rise from the dead.
> Christ is first in every way.
> Christ was God, living among us as a person.
> Through Christ, we all can be God's friends.
> Christ brought peace to the whole universe by his death on the cross.

3. The Lord's Prayer is a prayer of the loyal subjects of a loving king. Point out the "king" phrases: "Thy will be done on earth as it is in heaven" and "Thine is the kingdom and the power and the glory forever." To emphasize the relationship of God's kingship to each of the prayer requests, pray the prayer responsively or in unison, repeating "Thine is the kingdom, and the power, and the glory" after each phrase.

4. Paraphrase Colossians 1:11-14 for the Charge and Benediction:

> Go forth with all the power of Christ the King to serve loyally and patiently wherever you are. Give thanks to God, who has called you to be among the King's people, has sent Christ to save you, and has forgiven you. And remember, Christ the King will be with you forever. You have his promise. Amen.

## Sermon Resources

Display two crowns on the pulpit or in the worship center—one a kingly crown (perhaps a wise man's crown is among the Christmas pageant costumes); the other, a crown of thorns. Compare the kings who would wear each crown. Then describe what would be required of followers of the king who wears a crown of thorns.

Create a poem about the kind of king Christ is.  Listen to our songs and prayers for words to use in your poem.

Christ, the King

2 words that
describe Christ  _____  _____

2 "ing" words
that discribe Christ  _____  _____

Christ, my king

Listen carefully when John 12: 9-19 is read.  Draw a picture of what happened in that story.

# ALL SAINTS

## (November 1 [or] First Sunday in November)

### From a Child's Point of View

*Old Testament: Daniel 7:1-3, 15-18.* This is the beginning and end of a less-known story about Daniel, one of God's saints. Because it is less familiar, the whole story (1:1-18) probably should be read.

In the story, Daniel and three of his friends take a risk in order to show their loyalty to God by keeping Jewish dietary laws while they were captives in a foreign court. The unstated implication of the story is that because of this loyalty, they became wise, capable, respected members of the king's court. Children will hear this message quickly.

Children need to know only that one way Jews showed their loyalty to God was by not eating certain foods. Older children will be interested in some of the details of kosher cooking. But the focus is not on eating. It is on loyalty to God. Children today seldom show their loyalty by what they eat. But they can show their loyalty to God in their refusal to drink alcoholic beverages, smoke cigarettes, or experiment with drugs, all of which destroy the bodies God gave them. They can also follow God's rules about loving behavior, even when it is risky.

*Psalm 149.* This psalm is a call to God's people to celebrate their identity. Verses 1-5 call worshipers to use musical instruments and dance in praising God. Verses 6-9 describe a war-like sword dance that was part of worship. The implication of these last verses is that God wants the people to conquer and enslave other nations. Because such religious nationalism was reinterpreted by Jesus, it might

be wise to omit these verses. They tend to confuse children.

*Epistle: Ephesians 1:11-23.* This passage shows Paul at his most complicated. Children will not be able to keep up with the abstract language and compound/complex sentences. Read this for the grown-ups.

There are several ideas within the passage which speak to children: (1) Saints are people chosen by God; (2) God's Spirit (the Holy Spirit) gives us the ability to learn about God; (3) Christ is the ruler of the universe; (4) the church is made up of saints and belongs to Christ.

*Gospel: Luke 6:20-36.* Here are two sections of the Sermon on the Plain. First is a list of "blessings" and "woes." Especially to children hearing them for the first time, they sound backward. It is important to tell children that they also sounded backward to Jesus' listeners, and to adults today. Jesus said them that way to get everyone's attention—and it worked! With this background, children will be ready to explore what Jesus meant.

Jesus is not saying that it is better to be poor and miserable than rich and happy. He is saying that if you are a sharing saint, you probably will share so much of what comes your way that you will never be rich; that if you are a caring saint, you will be too aware of people who need help to be happy all the time; and that if you are a committed saint, you will take some stands that will make you unpopular. To children, this means that saints are to find pleasure in sharing instead of "hogging stuff," in finding ways to make other people happier, and in working for God's justice.

The second section, about loving enemies, is

"hard" for people of all ages. The difficulty for children is that it speaks in very concrete language about their everyday dealings with enemies. Most children have personal experience with name-calling (cursing), slapping, stealing from each other, and the problems that come with lending belongings. This section gives specific instructions for the way to treat an impossible sibling today and those who make your life miserable at school tomorrow. The two keys to this text are verses 32-35 and 31. Verses 32-35 insist that being kind to friends is no big deal. (Jesus is not interested in manners or getting along, but in active peacemaking.) Most children find this rather amazing, challenging, and strangely logical and attractive. Verse 31 is the Golden Rule. Most children have learned it in a more general setting. Hearing it here as a rule particularly for dealing with enemies can give it new power.

## Watch Words

Define *saint* as a person who does God's will. Include all members of your congregation as potential *saints*.

Children who see *enemies* as bad often deny that they have any enemies. They need help to identify those who treat them and are treated by them as *enemies* before they can be serious about following Jesus' directions.

## Let the Children Sing

"I Sing a Song of the Saints of God" (first choice), "For All the Saints" (the Alleluias can be sung by all), and "We Are the Church" are the best All Saints hymns for children.

If your celebration includes the Lord's Supper, sing "Take Our Bread," a good Communion hymn which, through frequent use, can be learned by elementary readers.

## The Liturgical Child

1. Display pictures or other reminders of the saints of your congregation in your worship center. If you have banners from church anniversaries, hang them.
2. Invite children to come to worship dressed as one of the saints. (Those who come without costumes can be recognized as saints "in real life.") Children may lead the choirs in the processional or may be invited to stand briefly at the front to identify the saints they are to the congregation. An older children's class may be asked to undertake special duties, such as collecting the offering in their costumes.
3. Introduce the reading of Daniel by naming the four heroes of the story and encouraging worshipers to listen for the risk they took with their food.
4. Turn Psalm 149:1-5 into a responsive poem by asking the congregation to respond to each phrase read by the worship leader, saying, "Praise the Lord!" Practice saying it together, as if you mean it, a few times before reading the psalm.
5. Point out and explain the phrase "Praise him above, ye heavenly hosts" in the Doxology. Identify the "heavenly host" as saints of the church who have died. State the meaning of the phrase in the context of the song.
6. Pray for saints of the past and present. Include a few saints children will recognize. Give individual worshipers time to pray for saints who have been and are important as examples to show us how to live.

## Sermon Resources

1. Outline a job description for a saint in your community. Name qualifications, personal qualities, abilities/skills required, and rewards offered. Use some examples from children's experience to illustrate your points. Work to create a job description that could be claimed by a worshiper of any age.
2. Tell stories about saints. Include stories about one or two well-known saints (Daniel, Martin Luther King, Jr., Mother Teresa, or others you recognize) and some stories about less-known saints, who could be anyone in your church. Include at least one child saint at work in a local setting—making peace on the bus, participating in mission projects of the church, or caring for people.
3. If you celebrate the Lord's Supper, highlight words and phrases used in your ritual to describe the gathering around the Table of the communion of saints past, present, future, from all lands. Put the phrases into children's words. If appropriate, elaborate on the phrases during the liturgy to name specific saints of your congregation.

197

Today is

# ALL SAINTS' DAY.

Listen carefully as you worship. Then draw a picture of one saint in action.

SAINT _____

Now picture yourself as a saint. Draw yourself being a saint at home or school.

SAINT _____
( my name )

*All Saints' Day /* © *1991 by Abingdon Press.*

# THANKSGIVING

## From a Child's Point of View

*Old Testament: Deuteronomy 26:1-11.* This passage describes the liturgy for offering the first fruits. Thanks is offered both for the harvest and for God's action during the Exodus and in the conquering of the Promised Land. Because of its structure and its assumption of extensive knowledge of the Exodus saga, it is a hard passage for children to follow.

On Thanksgiving, this text calls worshipers of all ages to identify God's gifts to them and God's action in their world. Most church children know that they are to be thankful for their food. But we cannot assume that nonagricultural children, for whom food is constantly available in supermarkets at an affordable price, will genuinely see food as a gift, rather than as an expected part of life. They benefit from hearing stories of food production described in terms of God's activity.

Verses 5-11 describe with gratitude God's activity in the life of the Jewish nation. Worshipers are called to identify with gratitude God's activity in the life of the church today. (Remember that the church, not a nation, is today's equivalent of the Jewish nation in this passage. This is not a call to credit God for national successes.)

*Psalm 100.* This psalm, with its short praises, is one children can appreciate easily. They do need to be told before the reading that this is a song for God's people, the church, and that the phrase "enter his gates with thanksgiving and his courts with praise" is an invitation to come to the Temple/sanctuary to worship God with others.

*Epistle: Philippians 4:4-9.* In this letter, Paul encourages us to develop a happy, thankful attitude. Paul states that one key to this attitude is to avoid being overly concerned about what is going on at the moment. That is a hard lesson, which most of us learn only after years of experience. Children, who live so much in the present, have trouble keeping the moment in perspective. So the value of this message is in introducing a truth with which children will struggle for years.

Verses 8 and 9 contain more directions for a happy life. Paul says that the kinds of activities and interests with which we fill our lives determine our happiness. Children need to hear that the activities they choose will determine how happy they are. Paul's list is abstract. Children need to paraphrase it with examples of activities that lead to happiness.

*Gospel: John 6:25-35.* This passage requires symbolic thinking that is beyond children's mental maturity. So John's discussion of the bread of heaven will mean little to them. But they can grasp John's point that, as important as food is, God's gift of Jesus is even more important. Food can keep us physically alive, but without God's love and forgiveness, that life is not too great. This point will need to be presented and discussed by the preacher.

## Watch Words

Vocabulary presents few problems on Thanksgiving, *unless* worship leaders wax abstract and poetic to explore these fairly concrete themes.

## Let the Children Sing

"Now Thank We All Our God" and "For the Beauty of the Earth" are probably the best Thanksgiving hymns for children.

"Come, Ye Thankful People, Come" and "We Gather Together to Ask the Lord's Blessing" are standard Thanksgiving fare. Unfortunately, they are filled with obsolete language. Schoolteachers used to help children dig out the messages behind the words. That happens less and less today. So either be sure church school teachers or choir directors are working with the children on these hymns, or select other more understandable hymns for children.

"All People That on Earth Do Dwell" is challenging reading for children. But with adult direction, older children appreciate its base in Psalm 100.

"We Plow the Fields and Scatter," while less familiar, is filled with simple food images for harvest worship.

## The Liturgical Child

1. If you focus on God's gift of food, plan for a cornucopia instead of flowers in the worship center. Also consider banking around the worship center the food staples that have been collected for distribution in your community. The sight of Communion elements surrounded by food is powerful for worshipers of all ages.

2. See the First Sunday of Lent for an idea about presenting the Deuteronomy passage dramatically.

3. Read or sing Psalm 100 as a litany. Choose a responsive version of the psalm from your hymnal. Read responsively between either pastor and people, or two halves of the congregation. Provide leaders who will maintain the upbeat tone and pace of the praises. Or invite the congregation to sing "Rejoice, give thanks and sing" (the chorus of "Rejoice, Ye Pure in Heart") after the worship leader reads each phrase of the psalm.

4. "Give us this day our daily bread" can be the congregational Response to a litany about food:

We praise you, God, for all the foods you have spread before us. We thank you for (name foods that are favorites in your community). (Response)

We praise you, God, for seeds that take food from the soil and water from the rain, to grow into corn and apple trees and lettuce. We thank you for the growing seasons, the spring rains, followed by summer sun and fall harvests. (Response)

We ask you to watch over farmers who plant and care for crops, and scientists who work to improve our crops. Teach us to work within your plan to produce food for the whole world. (Response)

Lord, guide and direct those who haul food from farms to hungry people, those who operate grocery stores, and political leaders who decide how much food goes to which people. Help them to be fair. (Response)

And last, God, we pray for people who are hungry. Whether they are hungry because of famines or floods or wars or poverty or unfair governments, be with them. Support them, and help us find ways to share our food with them. (Response)

We pray in Jesus name. Amen.

## Sermon Resources

1. Tell the story of the food supplied for a traditional Thanksgiving dinner, highlighting God's role in each phase of production and distribution.

2. Describe a variety of mealtime blessings. Point out some prayed by children. Describe family mealtime-blessing practices and silent blessings for meals at work and at school. Encourage families to try a mealtime blessing, if they do not use one, or to experiment with some new possibilities, if they already have blessing customs.

3. To explore Paul's message in Philippians, tell stories from your past about things that seemed dreadfully important, and over which you worried and made yourself miserable, but which turned out to be not so important (e.g., winning a championship, or receiving a certain gift on your birthday).

There is no Worship Worksheet for this service. Events of the service should hold the attention of children.

# SCRIPTURE INDEX

This index is provided especially for those who do not use the lectionary every week. The page numbers are those on which the commentary for each text appears. Read all the suggestions for the Sunday a text is featured to find the related worship suggestions.

# TABLE OF LITURGICAL DATES 1991–1995

## Year C, 1991–1992

| | | | |
|---|---|---|---|
| Dec. 1 | 1st Sunday of Advent | May 17 | 5th Sunday of Easter |
| Dec. 8 | 2nd Sunday of Advent | May 24 | 6th Sunday of Easter |
| Dec. 15 | 3rd Sunday of Advent | May 28 | Ascension Day |
| Dec. 22 | 4th Sunday of Advent | | (Note: May 31 may be observed |
| Dec. 24/25 | Christmas Eve/Day | | as Ascension Sunday.) |
| Dec. 29 | 1st Sunday After Christmas | May 31 | 7th Sunday of Easter |
| Jan. 1 | New Year's Eve/Day | June 7 | Day of Pentecost |
| Jan. 5 | 2nd Sunday After Christmas | June 14 | Trinity Sunday |
| Jan. 6 | Epiphany | June 21 | 2nd Sunday After Pentecost |
| | (Note: January 5 may be observed | June 28 | 3rd Sunday After Pentecost |
| | as Epiphany Sunday.) | July 5 | 4th Sunday After Pentecost |
| Jan. 12 | Baptism of the Lord | July 12 | 5th Sunday After Pentecost |
| Jan. 19 | 2nd Sunday After Epiphany | July 19 | 6th Sunday After Pentecost |
| Jan. 26 | 3rd Sunday After Epiphany | July 26 | 7th Sunday After Pentecost |
| Feb. 2 | 4th Sunday After Epiphany | Aug. 2 | 8th Sunday After Pentecost |
| Feb. 9 | 5th Sunday After Epiphany | Aug. 9 | 9th Sunday After Pentecost |
| Feb. 16 | 6th Sunday After Epiphany | Aug. 16 | 10th Sunday After Pentecost |
| Feb. 23 | 7th Sunday After Epiphany | Aug. 23 | 11th Sunday After Pentecost |
| March 1 | Transfiguration | Aug. 30 | 12th Sunday After Pentecost |
| March 4 | Ash Wednesday | Sept. 6 | 13th Sunday After Pentecost |
| March 8 | 1st Sunday of Lent | Sept. 13 | 14th Sunday After Pentecost |
| March 15 | 2nd Sunday of Lent | Sept. 20 | 15th Sunday After Pentecost |
| March 22 | 3rd Sunday of Lent | Sept. 27 | 16th Sunday After Pentecost |
| March 29 | 4th Sunday of Lent | Oct. 4 | 17th Sunday After Pentecost |
| April 5 | 5th Sunday of Lent | Oct. 11 | 18th Sunday After Pentecost |
| April 12 | Passion/Palm Sunday | Oct. 18 | 19th Sunday After Pentecost |
| April 16 | Holy Thursday | Oct. 25 | 20th Sunday After Penetecost |
| April 17 | Good Friday | Nov. 1 | All Saints |
| April 19 | Easter | Nov. 8 | 22nd Sunday After Pentecost |
| April 26 | 2nd Sunday of Easter | Nov. 15 | 23rd Sunday After Pentecost |
| May 3 | 3rd Sunday of Easter | Nov. 22 | Christ the King |
| May 10 | 4th Sunday of Easter | Nov. 26 | Thanksgiving |

# Year A, 1992–1993

| | |
|---|---|
| Nov. 29 | 1st Sunday of Advent |
| Dec. 6 | 2nd Sunday of Advent |
| Dec. 13 | 3rd Sunday of Advent |
| Dec. 20 | 4th Sunday of Advent |
| Dec. 24/25 | Christmas Eve/Day |
| Dec. 27 | 1st Sunday after Christmas |
| Jan. 1 | New Year's Eve/Day |
| Jan. 3 | 2nd Sunday after Christmas |
| Jan. 6 | Epiphany |
| | (Note: January 3 may be observed as Epiphany Sunday.) |
| Jan. 10 | Baptism of the Lord |
| Jan. 17 | 2nd Sunday After Epiphany |
| Jan. 24 | 3rd Sunday After Epiphany |
| Jan. 31 | 4th Sunday After Epiphany |
| Feb. 7 | 5th Sunday After Eiphany |
| Feb. 14 | 6th Sunday After Epiphany |
| Feb. 21 | Transfiguration |
| Feb. 24 | Ash Wednesday |
| Feb. 28 | 1st Sunday of Lent |
| March 7 | 2nd Sunday of Lent |
| March 14 | 3rd Sunday of Lent |
| March 21 | 4th Sunday of Lent |
| March 28 | 5th Sunday of Lent |
| April 4 | Passion/Palm Sunday |
| April 8 | Holy Thursday |
| April 9 | Good Friday |
| April 11 | Easter |
| April 18 | 2nd Sunday of Easter |
| April 25 | 3rd Sunday of Easter |
| May 2 | 4th Sunday of Easter |
| May 9 | 5th Sunday of Easter |
| May 16 | 6th Sunday of Easter |
| May 20 | Ascension Day |
| | (Note: May 23 may be observed as Ascension Sunday.) |
| May 23 | 7th Sunday of Easter |
| May 30 | Day of Pentecost |
| June 6 | Trinity Sunday |
| June 13 | 2nd Sunday After Pentecost |
| June 20 | 3rd Sunday After Pentecost |
| June 27 | 4th Sunday After Pentecost |
| July 4 | 5th Sunday After Pentecost |
| July 11 | 6th Sunday After Pentecost |
| July 18 | 7th Sunday After Pentecost |
| July 25 | 8th Sunday After Pentecost |
| Aug. 1 | 9th Sunday After Pentecost |
| Aug. 8 | 10th Sunday After Pentecost |
| Aug. 15 | 11th Sunday After Pentecost |
| Aug. 22 | 12th Sunday After Pentecost |
| Aug. 29 | 13th Sunday After Pentecost |
| Sept. 5 | 14th Sunday After Pentecost |
| Sept. 12 | 15th Sunday After Pentecost |
| Sept. 19 | 16th Sunday After Pentecost |
| Sept. 26 | 17th Sunday After Pentecost |
| Oct. 3 | 18th Sunday After Pentecost |
| Oct. 10 | 19th Sunday After Pentecost |
| Oct. 17 | 20th Sunday After Pentecost |
| Oct. 24 | 21st Sunday After Pentecost |
| Oct. 31 | 22nd Sunday After Pentecost |
| Nov. 1 | All Saints |
| | (Note: November 7 may be observed as All Saints' Sunday.) |
| Nov. 7 | 23rd Sunday After Pentecost |
| Nov. 14 | 24th Sunday After Pentecost |
| Nov. 21 | Christ the King |
| Nov. 25 | Thanksgiving |

# Year B, 1993–1994

| | | | |
|---|---|---|---|
| Nov. 28 | 1st Sunday of Advent | May 15 | 7th Sunday of Easter |
| Dec. 5 | 2nd Sunday of Advent | May 22 | Day of Pentecost |
| Dec. 12 | 3rd Sunday of Advent | May 29 | Trinity Sunday |
| Dec. 19 | 4th Sunday of Advent | June 5 | 2nd Sunday After Pentecost |
| Dec. 24/25 | Christmas Eve/Day | June 12 | 3rd Sunday After Pentecost |
| Dec. 26 | 1st Sunday After Christmas | June 19 | 4th Sunday After Pentecost |
| Jan. 1 | New Year's Eve/Day | June 26 | 5th Sunday After Pentecost |
| Jan. 2 | 2nd Sunday After Christmas | July 3 | 6th Sunday After Pentecost |
| Jan. 6 | Epiphany | July 10 | 7th Sunday After Pentecost |
| | (Note: January 2 may be observed as Epiphany Sunday.) | July 17 | 8th Sunday After Pentecost |
| | | July 24 | 9th Sunday After Pentecost |
| Jan. 9 | Baptism of the Lord | July 31 | 10th Sunday After Pentecost |
| Jan. 16 | 2nd Sunday After Epiphany | Aug. 7 | 11th Sunday After Pentecost |
| Jan. 23 | 3rd Sunday After Epiphany | Aug. 14 | 12th Sunday After Pentecost |
| Jan. 30 | 4th Sunday After Epiphany | Aug. 21 | 13th Sunday After Pentecost |
| Feb. 6 | 5th Sunday After Epiphany | Aug. 28 | 14th Sunday After Pentecost |
| Feb. 13 | Transfiguration | Sept. 4 | 15th Sunday After Pentecost |
| Feb. 16 | Ash Wednesday | Sept. 11 | 16th Sunday After Pentecost |
| Feb. 20 | 1st Sunday of Advent | Sept. 18 | 17th Sunday After Pentecost |
| Feb. 27 | 2nd Sunday of Advent | Sept. 25 | 18th Sunday After Pentecost |
| March 6 | 3rd Sunday of Advent | Oct. 2 | 19th Sunday After Pentecost |
| March 13 | 4th Sunday of Advent | Oct. 9 | 20th Sunday After Pentecost |
| March 20 | 5th Sunday of Advent | Oct. 16 | 21st Sunday After Pentecost |
| March 27 | Passion/Palm Sunday | Oct. 23 | 22nd Sunday After Pentecost |
| March 31 | Holy Thursday | Oct. 30 | 23rd Sunday After Pentecost |
| April 1 | Good Friday | Nov. 1 | All Saints |
| April 3 | Easter | | (Note: November 6 may be observed as All Saints' Sunday.) |
| April 10 | 2nd Sunday of Easter | | |
| April 17 | 3rd Sunday of Easter | Nov. 6 | 24th Sunday After Pentecost |
| April 24 | 4th Sunday of Easter | Nov. 13 | 25th Sunday After Pentecost |
| May 1 | 5th Sunday of Easter | Nov. 20 | Christ the King |
| May 8 | 6th Sunday of Easter | Nov. 24 | Thanksgiving |
| May 12 | Ascension Day | | |
| | (Note: May 15 may be observed as Ascension Sunday.) | | |

# Year C, 1994–1995

| | | | |
|---|---|---|---|
| Nov. 27 | 1st Sunday of Advent | May 25 | Ascension Day |
| Dec. 4 | 2nd Sunday of Advent | | (Note: May 28 may be observed |
| Dec. 11 | 3rd Sunday of Advent | | as Ascension Sunday.) |
| Dec. 18 | 4th Sunday of Adent | May 28 | 7th Sunday of Easter |
| Dec. 24/25 | Christmas Eve/Day | June 4 | Day of Pentecost |
| Jan. 1 | New Year's Eve/Day | June 11 | Trinity Sunday |
| | 1st Sunday After Christmas | June 18 | 2nd Sunday After Pentecost |
| Jan. 6 | Epiphany | June 25 | 3rd Sunday After Pentecost |
| | (Note: January 1 may be observed | July 2 | 4th Sunday After Pentecost |
| | as Epiphany Sunday.) | July 9 | 5th Sunday After Pentecost |
| Jan. 8 | Baptism of the Lord | July 16 | 6th Sunday After Pentecost |
| Jan. 15 | 2nd Sunday After Epiphany | July 23 | 7th Sunday After Pentecost |
| Jan. 22 | 3rd Sunday After Epiphany | July 30 | 8th Sunday After Pentecost |
| Jan. 29 | 4th Sunday After Epiphany | Aug. 6 | 9th Sunday After Pentecost |
| Feb. 5 | 5th Sunday After Epiphany | Aug. 13 | 10th Sunday After Pentecost |
| Feb. 12 | 6th Sunday After Epiphany | Aug. 20 | 11th Sunday After Pentecost |
| Feb. 19 | 7th Sunday After Eiphany | Aug. 27 | 12th Sunday After Pentecost |
| Feb. 26 | Transfiguration | Sept. 3 | 13th Sunday After Pentecost |
| March 1 | Ash Wednesday | Sept. 10 | 14th Sunday After Pentecost |
| March 5 | 1st Sunday of Lent | Sept. 17 | 15th Sunday After Pentecost |
| March 12 | 2nd Sunday of Lent | Sept. 24 | 16th Sunday After Pentecost |
| March 19 | 3rd Sunday of Lent | Oct. 1 | 17th Sunday After Pentecost |
| March 26 | 4th Sunday of Lent | Oct. 8 | 18th Sunday After Pentecost |
| April 2 | 5th Sunday of Lent | Oct. 15 | 19th Sunday After Pentecost |
| April 9 | Passion/Palm Sunday | Oct. 22 | 20th Sunday After Pentecost |
| April 13 | Holy Thursday | Oct. 29 | 21st Sunday After Pentecost |
| April 14 | Good Friday | Nov. 1 | All Saints |
| April 16 | Easter | | (Note: Nov. 5 may be observed |
| April 23 | 2nd Sunday of Easter | | as All Saints' Sunday.) |
| April 30 | 3rd Sunday of Easter | Nov. 5 | 22nd Sunday After Pentecost |
| May 7 | 4th Sunday of Easter | Nov. 12 | 23rd Sunday After Pentecost |
| May 14 | 5th Sunday of Easter | Nov. 19 | Christ the King |
| May 21 | 6th Sunday of Easter | Nov. 23 | Thanksgiving |